Praise for
Heartbreak Kennel

"Cary Unkelbach's deep love and respect for living creatures, nurtured by her parents, Evie and Kurt Unkelbach from whom I bought my first Labrador in 1964, flows onto the pages of this beautifully crafted book. She's told a true story, as suspenseful as any mystery, as emotional as a romance novel, and as intense as her sense of justice. You'll find that you can't wait to find out what happens next as she seamlessly weaves the bizarre, troubling tale of a Labrador breeder with the amusing, heartwarming story of Max. The surprise ending will shock you and you'll realize you know what to look for when you buy a puppy, what can go wrong even when someone is well intentioned, and what dogs crave more than anything else. You'll want Cary to be your lawyer, want her to help you buy and train your puppy, and want her to be your friend because you trust her. Any book that makes you feel so many things is a 'must read'."

— Julie Sturman, of *Julie Brown's Directory to Labrador Retriever Pedigrees 1971-2010* and AKC Breeder of Merit

"*Heartbreak Kennel* is a compelling read both for dog enthusiasts and for those interested in courtroom drama. Cary's extensive experience as a prosecutor and civil trial attorney is reflected in her writing style and presentation of this meticulously researched and engrossing true story."

— Thomas J. Curry, District Court Judge (Retired), 18th Judicial District, Colorado

"Alternating between the true crime story of Dodie Cariaso and the adventures of Max, one of the dogs she bred, *Heartbreak Kennel* is a riveting exploration of the best and worst practices of dog breeding and canine ownership. It's a captivating, eye-opening look at how a dog breeder turns passion into obsession."

— Monica Kern, University of Kentucky psychology professor (retired), Ph.D., psychology, Harvard University

"Loved *Heartbreak Kennel!* Kept me up most of the night because I couldn't put down this fast-paced book that reads like a novel! It's a fascinating story about a college-educated, successful businesswoman, turned breeder, who succumbs to the lure of the dark side of dog breeding. *Heartbreak Kennel* can only heighten awareness about the dangers of buying dogs from seemingly trustworthy breeders. The stories about Max made me smile and laugh and serve as heart-warming reminders of the importance of responsible dog ownership. If everyone read this book before they adopt or buy their next canine, I might be able to retire from the world of dog rescue!"

— Polly Kruse, Safe Harbor Lab Rescue board member and Labrador owner

"*Heartbreak Kennel* delivers a buyer beware message through an intriguing story about a rogue Labrador breeder and entertaining tales of one of her canines that was adopted by the author. This compelling read emphasizes the importance of verifying information conveyed by so-called 'reputable breeders.' It also poignantly reminds new and veteran canine owners of the consequences of irresponsible dog breeding and ownership."

— Susan Oviatt-Harris, AKC obedience and tracking judge

"*Heartbreak Kennel* is a must read for anyone thinking of buying a dog from a breeder. This gripping story of a Colorado breeder teaches questions to ask and homework to do to avoid costly mistakes and heartbreak."

— Mary Downs, Safe Harbor Lab Rescue board member
and Labrador owner

Heartbreak Kennel

The True Story of Max and His Breeder

Cary Unkelbach

Walden Resources Press

Heartbreak Kennel: The True Story of Max and His Breeder
by Cary Unkelbach

Copyright © 2020 Cary Unkelbach

Published by

Walden Resources Press

For more information about the author, visit www.caryunkelbach.com

ISBN: 978-1-7349222-0-2 (paperback)
ISBN: 978-1-7349222-1-9 (e-book)
Library of Congress Number: 2020906856

Book design: Nick Zelinger, NZGraphics.com
Editing: Jennifer Top, Bruce Goldberg
Cover photo: Max pictured on summit of Mt. Yale
Author and back cover photos: Dave Olmstead

PET004000 PETS / Dogs / General
BIO000000 BIOGRAPHY & AUTOBIOGRAPHY / General
TRU000000 TRUE CRIME / General

First Edition
Printed in the United States of America

For my husband Dave Olmstead

Contents

CHAPTER 1

Heartbreak

She heard human voices for the first time in more than two days. Her rail-thin body crowded nine infant chocolate puppies, all soaking wet from a sea of excrement inside an airline crate positioned within a horse trailer. Other dogs barked nearby. The unfamiliar voices drew closer to the Labrador mother.

Fifty miles to the south, Vikki Weeks picked up the telephone in the Denver home that she shared with her husband.

"Hi, it's me. I'm in Missouri," came the familiar voice of her sister-in-law Dodie Cariaso.

"Why are you in Missouri?"

"I couldn't take it anymore so I left. I fed and watered them and left. I left a note for Carl [Cushatt] to call the Humane Society. I can't deal with it. The dogs are tying me down. I'm Jesse McClure now. I'm gone," Dodie said.

"Well—"

"Just wanted to call and let you know that I was fine," the cheerful voice said. "Goodbye."

Vikki relayed the conversation to her husband James Wilson. The couple realized Dodie intended to stay in Missouri. They knew that James's son had helped move her Labrador retrievers to a new location but didn't know where or how many dogs she had. The canines would be in crates. Meteorologists predicted temperatures in the high eighties for that Saturday.

They needed to find the Labradors to feed and water them. After that, they weren't sure what they'd do.

James called his son to learn the dogs' whereabouts and arranged to meet him. They'd drive together to the canines' location in northern Colorado.[1]

———

Rigo Neira looked forward to watching a movie inside an air-conditioned theater to find relief from the heat on that Saturday, July 3, 2004. His cell phone rang at about 12:30 p.m.

He listened to a coworker from the Larimer County Humane Society explain that a man called around 8:50 a.m. to report his new tenant had "skipped" and left behind about twenty Labradors. The man said he'd try to find homes for the dogs and bring the remainder to the Humane Society in Fort Collins. After checking on the animals again, he called back with a revised estimate of the number of dogs: sixty to eighty.

As the Humane Society's director of animal protection and field services, Neira knew about the sad fact of abandoned dogs. And no wonder: each year about 3.3 million dogs land in shelters. A fifth of these are strays that reunite with their owners. But for the remainder—more than 2.6 million dogs—it's either adoption or, for many, death.[2]

Neira recognized that the Labradors' location needed to be preserved as a crime scene because they'd probably been abandoned. That meant the dogs couldn't be removed from the property until his staff documented their health and living conditions.

He instructed his coworker Dave Janny to call back the man and tell him that Humane Society workers would come to his property to coordinate the animals' treatment and care, and to instruct him not to give away any more canines. He'd meet Janny at the shelter where other employees would assemble to form a response team.

Less than two and a half hours later, Neira, accompanied by Janny and shelter behaviorist Tim Kloer, pulled into Carl Cushatt's driveway. Carl's ranch home stretched behind tall evergreen trees that lined the north side of the county road in rural southern Larimer County. A few other houses on the north side of the paved road sat amid mostly treeless, flat grassland.

The trio met Carl, an over-the-road truck driver in his early sixties. As they walked around the west side of the house, they spotted a light-yellow Labrador male and three small Labrador puppies running around the fenced-in backyard. Carl identified the Labradors as some of the abandoned canines.

The men strode north toward fields and barnlike structures. A stench of feces permeated the air. They stared at rows of medium-sized airline dog crates adjacent to a semitrailer. Three temporary chain-link-fenced runs, each about twelve feet by four feet, and a three-sided fenced area lay behind the rows of crates. Inside the runs, a few crates housed adults and puppies. Other crates had doors open so canines could walk in and out of them.

Several adult male Labradors barked aggressively and curled back their lips. Kloer watched as they jumped on the fencing and stared "hard" at the workers. Other dogs panted, appearing friendly but thirsty. A skeletal-thin chocolate female and her tiny puppies wandered around one of the runs.

Unattached fence panels rested against one end of the semitrailer. Towels, scissors, baling wire, and a few dog bowls lay on an upright, white folding table near the semitrailer's other end. Two bags of dog food sat nearby; only one was opened.

Neira took charge. He listened to Carl recount what led up to his call to the Humane Society.

Carl said he'd left on Thursday morning, July 1, for Dodge City, Kansas. His new tenant, Cate [Dodie] Cariaso, called him the next day on his drive back to Colorado.

"Are you in Kansas?" she asked. "Have you heard from any neighbors?"

"What's going on?"

Dodie said she was calling from his property and needed to hang up because she was on "someone's phone." She'd talk to him upon his return.

Carl wondered about the call. He checked his phone's caller ID and didn't recognize the 785 area code. The truck driver had a bad feeling that evening when he arrived home and didn't see his new tenant. The next morning, he looked for her and discovered the Labradors. He called the 785 number to contact her but reached the Holiday Inn in Abilene, Kansas, about 150 miles from the Missouri border.

When Carl checked again on the dogs, he spotted the white table near one end of the semitrailer. A small piece of white paper, with a note written in green ink, caught his eye. It was dated "Fri AM."

"Dear Carl—I am so sorry, but due to all the problems with the neighbors . . . I just can't stay. The dogs were all fed & watered yesterday! Please call the Longmont or Larimer Cty. Humane So. to come get all my beautiful Labradors . . . I will love all of them forever!! Thank You For Your Kindness! Cate."[3]

Carl telephoned the Larimer County Humane Society and spoke to Janny. Next, he gave away twelve weaned puppies to friends, family, and neighbors.

Hours later, the truck driver signed a release relinquishing all the dogs to the Humane Society. Response team members took over. Besides the trio who first met Carl, team members included Joe Olsen, the Humane Society's CEO and president, and Dr. Miranda Spindel, the shelter's veterinarian. The Humane Society's director of operations, who was also a veterinarian, and her veterinarian husband volunteered.

One team member photographed the scene as first encountered to document the dogs' living conditions and their physical appearance. Weaned puppies were crammed together in crates, as were mothers and their puppies. The adult males and most of the non-nursing females were housed in individual crates too short for the animals to sit without hitting their heads. Feces plastered most of the walls and floors of crates, which were too small for mothers to lie comfortably while their puppies nursed. One couldn't lie down at all. None had food or water.

Many of the dogs lay down once the initial excitement of the rescuers' arrival wore off. They panted as the sun's intensity increased.

Workers opened crate doors. Puppies walked out. Adults froze in place, unresponsive to coaxing. Some growled. Others pulled back, thrashing and fighting when workers tried to leash or hold them. Workers dragged them from crates with a catch pole, a six-foot steel pole with a plastic-coated loop.

Some watered the animals; others cleaned crates. They discovered puppies with ulcerations on their stomachs and back legs; some were soaked wet from sitting in their urine and feces. Puppies' untrimmed toenails dug into their mothers, whose ribs protruded as if the animals lived in a concentration camp. Their fur had fallen out or was caked with feces and urine. Excrement and urine also covered the weaned puppies.

Several of the Labradors, adults and puppies alike, exhibited untreated, infected puncture and bite wounds. Others had minor scars.

Workers opened the nearby horse trailer that was hitched to a van and discovered the chocolate mother and her seven- to ten-day-old puppies in a crate with a bowl of feces-soiled water. She tucked her tail between her legs. Her ribs protruded through excrement-soaked fur.

In all, Dodie had left behind ninety-seven canines: ninety-six Labradors, including twelve puppies that Carl had given away, and Ebony, her springer spaniel. Carl claimed ownership of Ebony when asked about the dog as she ran loose. He knew that Ebony was Dodie's "personal pet" and slept with her in the van. She'd join Smoky, his shih tzu.

Rescuers counted eighty-four Labradors on-site. Fifty-five were puppies: ten weaned pups and the remainder from nine litters, ranging in age from about seven to ten days to four to five weeks.

Of the twenty-four adult females, one looked pregnant, and two others appeared extremely emaciated and probably had recently whelped puppies. Females and puppies represented the three Labrador colors: black, chocolate, and yellow. Three yellow and two chocolate males were among the abandoned adult dogs.

With input from some of the other workers, Neira and Dr. Spindel determined which Labradors were unfit for adoption because they were "dying, injured, sick and/or behaviorally unfit."[4] They didn't believe the Humane Society had the resources to heal or care for these animals.

Dr. Spindel put down more than half of the eighty-four Labradors: thirty-four puppies and twenty adults. They included five of the nine litters and their mothers.

The chocolate mother and five of her nine puppies that workers found inside the horse trailer survived. Dr. Spindel rated the mother's body condition a two on a scale of one to ten, with a ten being fat and one totally emaciated.

James and his son arrived. They saw chaos: the dogs, trailers, a crowd of onlookers, Humane Society workers, police, and members of the press. James hadn't expected to find anyone with his sister's Labradors. He'd come to feed and water them.

The two men blended into the crowd and sat on the tailgate of a pickup truck. James realized that the authorities were probably looking for his twin sister but didn't want to disclose that she was in Missouri. He observed the harried-looking young female veterinarian examining the dogs and vaccinating some puppies. Some of the Labradors looked frightened and darted out of crates as they tried to avoid the workers. The dogs were hungry and thirsty, James noted, and the conditions, in the hot summer sun, were horrible. He watched the workers feed, water, and photograph the dogs.

After a while, James stood up to stretch his legs and wandered around a trailer to an area not visible to onlookers. He stopped short. A pile of body bags lay before him. He'd had no idea that any of his sister's dogs had been euthanized. He turned and walked back to the pickup. Then he and his son quietly left.

My husband Dave and I listened to a story about dozens of abandoned dogs on that night's television news. I recognized the name of the suspect—Dodie Cariaso.

Horrified, I knelt down and hugged our three Labradors: Molly, daughter Brew, and granddaughter Taz. We all still missed Max, our beloved adopted Labrador that had passed over the Rainbow Bridge the year prior. His breeder's name?

Dodie Cariaso.

How could this woman, who committed these atrocities, have bred such a terrific dog as Max? I'd grown up in a family who raised and showed Labradors and couldn't fathom the horrific abuse inflicted on this gentle breed. As a dog lover, I wanted to know so much more than what the media reported. Who was this woman?

Several years later, those nagging questions and Max's memory led me on my years-long odyssey to find answers. I expected to uncover an uneducated woman who sold puppies from her backwoods home. Instead, I discovered a witty, successful businesswoman who bred dogs and sold puppies to the public. This college-educated woman instilled trust and loyalty in many puppy buyers, portraying herself as a reputable dog breeder while outwitting the authorities for years. How could her loyal friends and family have no clue about her deception?

Chameleons like Dodie may be why an estimated 825,000 purebred dogs, many bought from breeders for hundreds if not thousands of dollars, land in shelters each year.[5] Unexpected behavioral or health issues caused by these disreputable breeders undoubtedly prompt many owners to discard their canines.

How and why do some breeders abuse canines? Media stories don't focus on that question, only on the atrocities. Now I had the chance to try to find an answer. I'd use my investigative skills as a former prosecutor and reporter to call on contacts in Colorado's legal and Labrador retriever communities to piece together the puzzle of Dodie, a woman whom I could have easily met but never did.

My years-long investigation reveals what led Dodie, whose own life ended tragically and bizarrely, to transition from dog lover to abuser. Her story imparts a warning—pet buyers beware—and represents a microcosm of the larger world of animal abuse and disreputable breeders who may come across as an upstanding neighbor, friend, or even relative. It teaches how to recognize the often-overlooked signs of animal neglect and ways to intervene to avoid heartbreak and tragedy for man's best friend.

Max was very fortunate that his first owner whisked him away from Dodie's kennel at just five-plus weeks. Otherwise, he might have suffered years of neglect at his breeder's hands. Instead, his often comical, upbeat journey contrasted sharply with those of many of Dodie's dogs and millions of other canines—mixed breeds and purebreds alike—that land in shelters through no fault of their own. Like many responsible dog owners, we'd given Max what canines need: jobs that he mostly loved, such as hiking companion or puppy sitter, because they gave him a purpose. He, in turn, gave us unconditional love and affection.

The total number of dogs that are neglected and/or abandoned each year in this country is unknown. Most animal abuse probably goes unreported. Until 2016, a national database of crimes against animals didn't even exist. That's when the Federal Bureau of Investigation (FBI) first listed animal cruelty in its own serious crime category. More than a third of law enforcement agencies across the country now submit incident reports, containing specific details of crimes against animals and information about the accused perpetrators, to the FBI for inclusion in this category.[6]

Fortunately, most of the 50 percent of American households that own at least one of the estimated 90 million dogs in this country don't abuse their canines.[7] Instead, they spend mightily on their pets, an estimated $75 billion a year.[8] But those are the lucky animals.

For the unlucky ones, lessons gleaned from the inextricably intertwined stories of Max and Dodie may save some from abusers and uncaring owners. Reputable breeders and responsible owners are crucial to any effort to decrease this nation's canine shelter population of 3.3 million.

Chapter 2

Suburban Girl

The couple smiled broadly as they walked arm-in-arm out of a Roman Catholic church on August 20, 1970. Dodie wore a full-length white wedding dress and veil. Her bleached blonde hair was pulled back from her pretty face and gracefully flowed down below her shoulders. She held a bride's bouquet in one hand and clasped her groom's arm with the other. Fred Cariaso's eyes, almost hidden by his straight bangs, sparkled. His wavy medium-length black hair and mustache were neatly trimmed for the occasion.

The twenty-three-year-old newlyweds ran down the church steps amid a shower of rice. The waiting car carried them to a two-story white Dutch Colonial house that sat on an expansive, tree-shaded double lot in nearby Glen Ellyn, just west of Chicago. That's where Jane and Robert Wilson raised Dodie and her two brothers, James and Doug.

About 150 of Dodie's closest friends and relatives gathered for the reception in the backyard next to a curvy in-ground pool. Members of Fred's small family and a few friends from his hometown of Cheyenne, Wyoming, comprised the groom's guest contingent.

Fred, dressed in his black tuxedo, looked serious as he helped his beaming bride cut the traditional wedding cake. He'd just married the love of his life but felt uncomfortable at the reception. Decades later, he recalled that he thought the party "was really a pretentious kind of affair, more of a social gathering as opposed to a celebration."[1] It reminded him of Dustin Hoffman in *The Graduate*. "Plastics, my boy. Plastics."

He shifted his slim five-foot-eight frame: he couldn't wait to escape to the rented honeymoon cabin in South Dakota. His in-laws had paid for the accommodations, and his parents had given them a new blue Camaro. Was Fred's uneasiness a result of the couple's different backgrounds?

In November 1968, Fred met Dodie in a bar where he worked part-time. They discovered their mutual interests: a love of the outdoors and skiing. Both were Roman Catholics and sophomores at the University of Colorado. Fred majored in architecture and Dodie in art. He felt physically attracted to her and liked that she sketched and dabbled in pottery.

They came from dissimilar backgrounds. Fred had grown up in Cheyenne with parents of modest means. His father had attained his American citizenship years after he ran away as a teenager from the Philippines and attended high school in this country. Next Fred's father joined the US military, and upon his discharge from the service, he worked as a hotel manager in Cheyenne while his mother waited tables at a local restaurant. He'd taught Fred to hunt and fish and instilled in him the belief that one could succeed in America through hard work.

In stark contrast, Dodie had been raised in an affluent family in the suburbs of Chicago. On March 23, 1949, in an Oak Park hospital, Robert and Jane Wilson had welcomed their premature twins, Cathy, short for Catherine, and James. Toddler James couldn't pronounce Cathy, so he called his twin Dodie. A year-plus later, brother Doug joined the family.

They lived in a plain brick house in Glen Ellyn, an upwardly mobile bedroom community of Chicago, and then moved to a more spacious home outside of which Fred and Dodie's wedding reception would be held. Raised as Catholics, the children attended a nearby local school. Jane had converted to Catholicism before she married Robert, a devout Catholic. The family wore their Sunday best to mass each week.

Dodie's mother Jane fell in love with skiing while she studied pre-med at Colorado College in Colorado Springs. After graduation, she joined her family's successful business, F. H. Smith Manufacturing Co., in Chicago, and earned her private pilot's license so she could fly her Taildragger plane. Dodie's father Robert had dropped out of college to support his mother and family in Toledo, Ohio, after his dad died during the Depression.

Dodie's family bought with cash, not credit, except for their home. Her father ran his own business from their house, selling furniture and equipment to churches and governments. This outgoing salesman made good money, and his wife contributed by primarily working bookkeeper and office jobs. The family owned two cars, including an occasional new one, and a television—the first on their block in the 1950s.

They vacationed in Michigan's Upper Peninsula, Wisconsin, and Minnesota, where they fished, swam, or walked and slept in a homemade camper. They also enjoyed annual ski vacations in Winter Park, Colorado. The children as young teenagers attended a private summer camp for six weeks in northern Minnesota. There, Dodie played sports, rode horses, and took arts and crafts classes.

Years earlier, Dodie had fallen in love with horses when her parents paid for horseback lessons for their children. Unlike her siblings, Dodie spent as much time as possible at the stables. She rode English-style and learned dressage and to jump. Although she wanted her own thoroughbred, she settled for competing with other people's horses at shows. The Wilsons supported these horseback activities with part of a $250,000 bequest to Dodie's mom from a favorite aunt. That money also paid for the in-ground pool at their home.

As older teenagers, Dodie and her brothers accompanied their mother on summer-long cross-country trips to visit national parks and other scenic areas in the United States and Canada. They slept in the family's yellow and black Pontiac Catalina station wagon or in the homes of friends or relatives along the way. Their dad remained in Glen Ellyn to run his business.

Life changed for Dodie when she entered high school. Her parents decided their children would attend a public school, Glenbard West, because they believed it offered a better education than the parochial equivalent. Dodie didn't adjust easily to the 2,000-student high school and cried nearly every day during her freshman year. James recalled decades later that his often-moody twin felt rejected and resented the in-crowd when she didn't make the cheerleading squad. She gravitated toward individual activities and to animal lovers and artists.

Then hormones took over. Boys became more important than horses to Dodie as a high school junior. She shopped, attended concerts and movies, and frequented teenage haunts, occasionally driving her parents' cars. Dodie also practiced with an all-female guitar band. Somehow she managed to earn A's and B's, although she studied little.

As a high school senior, she wrote about a dream life in her journal: "I love painting and sketching & making things, but I never have any time. Skiing & riding & guitar are my 3 real loves. If I had my choice, I'd live in the mts., with a beautiful thoroughbred hunter, a Dalmatian like our nutty Akelar, and sketch & paint all summer & ski & go to school in the winter. What a dream world I have built up around myself."[2] Was this daydream world just a passing teenage fantasy?

"Some people say I'm pretty but 'it's too bad she is so heavy.' Because of my weight problems, I'm not popular at Glenbard." She weighed 157 pounds and stood five foot six.

"At times I'm very boring. I'm a very cynical and sarcastic person, mainly I suppose, because of my weight. At times I hate people and only love horses because I find that people don't like me. I always think people are talking behind my back and therefore am very self-conscious. It's terrible and at times ruins any fun I might have been having."

Dodie journaled about relationships with family members, including her brothers, who noticed that she often cried and/or lashed out at their sweet, good-natured father to get her way. She thought her dad was "young at heart and spirit" and "the most sincere and honest person I know in this whole world. He never lies nor ever cheats." Dodie tangled more with her mother, who, like her daughter, could be blunt. But Jane possessed social graces and belonged to the local garden and bridge clubs. While Dodie called her twin James "a good friend," she accused younger brother Doug of making high school difficult for her because "he was so popular."

Fred dated very little before he met Dodie, who managed to often juggle at least two boyfriends during her high school years. She agonized over which steady boyfriend she preferred: one came from a family of money and one didn't. "It's wrong, but I feel that we are better matched coming from similar financial backgrounds & societies & therefore get along better. But then when I'm with Bob I feel that just understanding counts (Yet I don't understand Bob at all!)."[3]

Dating history and family backgrounds weren't the only differences between the newlyweds. As long as Fred paid half of his out-of-state college tuition, his father paid the other half. Dodie's parents paid for their offspring's tuition and required only that the siblings contribute $200 each toward college expenses. Even so, Dodie needed part-time work and hired on at a local dry cleaner. She summed up her first day in her journal: "Everyone looked at me so queerly . . . like I didn't belong there." So, she located a better-paying job at a factory in its machine shop and packaging department. Although she complained about lacking spending money when she made bank deposits with her earnings, she managed to water ski and attend movies and concerts.

Dodie started her higher education about a hundred miles away from Fred at her mother's alma mater—Colorado College, a small, private liberal arts college in Colorado Springs. She focused on boys instead of academics and excelled in art but struggled with other subjects. Once again, Dodie felt rejected by fellow students.

She wrote almost daily in her journal. Her entries captured extreme mood swings: "Today was another very bad day" to "today has to be the best day I've had since I got here." She felt dejected when she didn't have dates, elated when she did. When several sororities failed to ask her to pledge, she wondered, "What's so wrong with me that no one likes me? I guess I have a dud of a personality or something." She rebounded the next day after she accepted a date.

The following fall, Dodie transferred to the University of Colorado in Boulder. That's when she assumed Dodie as her first name, perhaps symbolic of a fresh start.

After they met that fall, Dodie saw Fred daily until she returned to Glen Ellyn for the Christmas holidays. There she dated a local boyfriend and broke up with another beau. She returned early to college to be with Fred.

During his courtship, Fred met Dodie for lunch on weekends at Lake Eldora, where she taught downhill skiing to children and prided herself in having regular customers. "It was a job she really loved . . . I could see a lot of happiness hanging out on the ski slopes," he recalled decades later.[4] He fell head over heels in love.

Dodie viewed Fred as an extremely intelligent and ambitious man. "No one could ever give me a better life and no two people get along as well as we do. I want to live the rest of my life with him," she confided to her journal. Fred proposed about a week later. Dodie accepted and wanted "to marry him soon because I love him so much. I just can't wait! We are just so very perfect for each other!"

Years later, Fred thought that Dodie might have believed that his family had more money than they did because they lived comfortably, gave to the poor, and paid half of Fred's out-of-state college tuition. She may have wished that Fred was from Jackson Hole, a wealthy town south of the Tetons. That's the hometown she'd assigned to Fred in her journal, although she'd truthfully told her family that he hailed from Cheyenne.

Fred presented an expensive marquee diamond ring to her on Valentine's Day. "I just love it and love Fred more every day," Dodie journaled. Fred thought their marriage would last forever.

The whirlwind, expensive courtship continued. The couple ate out and attended concerts: Fred enjoyed classical music and Dodie preferred folk. They played guitars together and skied at different resorts in Colorado and Utah with discounted passes that Dodie obtained through her Lake Eldora job. In the summer, they backpacked to high alpine lakes so Fred could fish. Dodie enjoyed camping but not her heavy backpack. Fred was her mountain man.

They learned each other's dreams. Dodie's now included marriage to Fred without children and a career as a thoroughbred horse breeder.

Fred loved Victorian architecture and studied to become an architect. He labored as a tradesman so he could both work with his hands in the field and sketch plans in an office. Fred was willing to put children on hold; adoption might be a good option later.

Dodie was 1,000 percent supportive of his dreams and ambitions, Fred thought. Life couldn't be better with his artist fiancée.

About six months into their marriage, Fred's love-stricken eyes cleared as the couple tried to live on a student's budget. They'd moved from their Boulder apartment into a one-bedroom cabin in the small mountain community of Nederland, about fifteen miles southwest of Boulder and just east of Lake Eldora. They lived rent-free in exchange for Fred's work to remodel the cabin, which was situated on three acres and had a stream running through it. Their landlord, one of Fred's professors, paid for the remodeling materials.

The couple argued about money. Fred paid with cash only, searched for bargains, and applied his carpentry skills to fix old tables and chairs. Dodie fancied antiques and wanted to buy on credit when they shopped for furniture.

Fred worked construction jobs that paid good money, $10 to $15 an hour, to cover the couple's basic living expenses and part of his college tuition. He expected to provide for his new bride, and she expected that of him. That's why she didn't have a checking account but he did.

The couple's life revolved around work, part-time college, and an occasional night out. Dodie sought a more active social life and thought Fred put her second to his work. Fred had little time to socialize; he studied to make straight A's and worked to pay their bills. Dodie didn't care much about studying and received C's. Her parents continued to pay for her tuition.

Fred recalled later that she seemed happiest when he bought a pricy present for her, or they dressed up to eat at an expensive restaurant. She loved to order market-price entrees even though Fred protested the expense.

Dodie spoke regularly on the telephone with her mother. The two women argued when Dodie asked for money, but her mother often relented and sent funds anyway.

One of these conversations was etched into Fred's mind. Proud that he had bagged his first elk, he knew the couple would eat well that winter.

"Fred can't afford to buy beef, so we are going to have poor man's beef this winter," Dodie told her mother.[5]

His happiness evaporated. He wondered why he hadn't noticed Dodie's mood swings from sweet and happy to bitter and sad. Had he really been so blinded by love? He worked on renovating their cabin over the Christmas holidays, and his wife flew home to be with her family in Glen Ellyn.

Dodie taught skiing that winter at Lake Eldora. She liked to be fashionable and bought new skis and ski clothes with her earnings. When Fred questioned her spending, Dodie pointed out that her job gave discounts.

"You couldn't tell her anything, including me," Fred recalled decades later. She didn't know how to say that she was sorry. She'd say that he "would get over it." But he knew that "some things we just don't get over."[6]

Dodie socialized with her fellow Lake Eldora ski instructors even when she wasn't teaching and told Fred that one of the male ski instructors encouraged her to run off with him to start a ski school on the East Coast. But she stayed with Fred.

Although the couple didn't entertain at their cabin, Dodie's younger brother Doug occasionally drove up from Denver where he attended college to join them to ski at Lake Eldora or hike in nearby Rocky Mountain National Park.

However, Dodie welcomed only guests whom she invited. When their landlord stopped by to help with cabin renovations, Fred tried to guide Dodie out of their guest's earshot before her anger disintegrated into tears over what she apparently thought was an invasion of her privacy.

"Get away from me. Don't touch me," Dodie said when Fred tried to calm her.

She'd storm out of the cabin and drive off in the Camaro or escape on Witchy Blue, a half-thoroughbred, half-saddlebred horse that they'd bought for $600. Fred ended up watering and feeding the gray mare after he refused to give money to his wife to compete in horse shows.

The couple weathered their first year of marriage. Fred's steady work converted the cabin into a 1,500-square-foot home, complete with a fireplace, dining room, family room, and a second bedroom.

In 1971, Los Angeles music producer James Guercio purchased the more than 4,000-acre Caribou Ranch near Nederland on the road to the ghost town of Caribou. The following year, he started to convert an old barn into a music recording studio. Guercio, well known as the producer for the rock band Chicago, attracted other star artists, including rock guitarist Joe Walsh and music producer and technical engineer Bill Szymczyk, who finished their *Barnstorm* album in 1972 at the new studio. Other rock 'n' roll stars flocked to the ranch.

Dodie hired on as a trail ride wrangler and a waitress during the summer at the ranch. She duded herself up when she led trail rides, a job that she considered professional.

Fred remodeled some of the ranch's cabins. He'd see his wife, smiling and happy, from a distance. She loved to rub elbows with the rich and famous rock 'n' roll stars, but her smile faded as soon as she approached him. Then she'd try to ignore him; she didn't want others to know that her husband was the man in the torn T-shirt with cement in his hair.

"How nice you look," she'd greet him later at home. Her sarcasm stung. She threatened to throw out his dirty and tattered work clothes.

He objected. The clothes served their purpose. His wife didn't understand. She wanted new; old could be discarded.

They argued.

She claimed that she was a *Mayflower* descendant. Some of her mother's ancestors emigrated from England, but none came over on the *Mayflower*.

"So, does that make you better than me because my dad came from the Philippines, and my mother was born next to an Indian reservation in New Mexico?" Fred asked.

Dodie didn't respond. But Fred knew she considered her family as upper class; the middle class was beneath her.

She "had a tongue on her sometimes. Sometimes she would say things and often times that's mightier than the sword," he recalled later.

Fred noticed that his wife found it difficult to be happy and looked at the glass as half empty. He bought a potter's wheel for her after they married, and she loved making pottery. But she'd complain that she should have charged more after one of her beautifully crafted wares sold on consignment. She received many compliments on her pottery, which helped "feed her need for attention." Dodie always wanted to be "the star of the show," Fred recounted years later.

The couple's schedule didn't draw them closer together. Fred often stayed at their mountain cabin to get a good night's sleep so he could rise early the next morning to work a construction job. Dodie frequently fired her pottery in the university's kiln at night before she'd go dancing with friends.

Fred maintained marital accord by buying something new for Dodie when he bought something new for himself; hence the second horse, Shadow Beau, a retired thoroughbred racehorse, purchased for the sizable sum of $850. Fred had no idea why his wife wanted two horses.

Shadow Beau proved an expensive peace offering. He gorged himself in a grain bin and developed laminitis, an inflammation of the hooves. Dodie cried and thought he'd never jump again. He recovered, only to cut himself on wire. His total vet bill of more than $1,000 exceeded the couple's budget. That meant monthly payments. Fred cautioned Dodie that they didn't have the facilities for two horses and that he didn't want to spend money on this "type of thing. We have other things to do." But Dodie professed her love for the horses and assured him that things would change. She never jumped Shadow Beau again after he healed.

Then there were the dogs: first Liebchen, a husky mix, inherited when they moved into the cabin. A neighbor's German shepherd found her irresistible, so they kept one puppy from the litter and named him Faux Pas.

Next came Amy, a black, part Labrador retriever puppy. She lived a very short life. The couple spent $600 on veterinarian bills trying to save her after a neighbor shot her when she chased his chickens. About a month later, Fred came home from work and learned that Dodie, perhaps during one of her mood swings, had taken Liebchen to the vet to be put down. She still held Liebchen responsible for Amy's death because he had taught the puppy to chase fowl.

Dodie then purchased an eight-week-old black Labrador puppy and brought her home to a surprised husband. She registered puppy Kelly with the American Kennel Club (AKC). Later she bred Kelly to a mostly Labrador and kept Saber, one of the chocolate pups, but sold the others for $25 each.

Faux Pas and Kelly ran freely on the couple's property until a local resident's traps, intended to catch roaming dogs, snared and fatally injured them. Suddenly, Saber, the mostly Labrador, became the couple's only dog.

Veterinarian bills weren't the only drain on the couple's finances. Dodie fancied not only new clothes with labels but also new horse bridles and saddles as well as an upgraded stereo system. Fred reluctantly agreed to purchase the stereo system on credit. Less was more to him. To his wife, there was no success without excess.

He noticed another difference between them when his parents took two, months-long trips to the Philippines, Japan, Hong Kong, New Zealand, and Australia. He encouraged his parents to spend their hard-earned money on themselves; Dodie complained that they were spending his inheritance. He thought she felt entitled to the money and wondered if she believed his parents should have used their vacation funds to help the couple buy a horse farm.

Fred realized that they could never have enough money to satisfy his wife. She'd always want more.

———

During the winter of 1972–73, the couple talked about their plans for after graduation. Dodie envisioned Fred as an architect in an office in San Francisco, Chicago, or another large city. He aspired to work on residential projects in the field and didn't have any interest in commercial buildings.

Dodie longed to buy a thoroughbred horse farm and breed horses. Fred said they couldn't afford to do so.

He wanted to live in Alaska as soon as he graduated. Alaska "was too wild" and not a good place to breed horses, Dodie retorted. And, they should have bought a house instead of living in their rent-free cabin, she said.

That June, the couple bought a two-story 1892 Victorian house in Cheyenne. Dodie's parents contributed $1,000 toward the $16,500 purchase price. Fred thought that the house might be their ticket to the country once he restored it. Dodie disagreed. She dreamed of living on an acreage in a suburban area where she could breed horses and still enjoy the amenities of city life.

And she thought Cheyenne was a place without culture and "all the people are ugly."

Fred disagreed. He'd grown up there.

"Look around you, Fred. We need to get out of this place."

"You are out of your mind."

Fred slept in a tent in the backyard of their new house. He gutted the home's first story to renovate it into their living quarters. Dodie remained in Colorado and lived in their cabin. She sometimes visited him on weekends but complained about the house purchase and camping arrangements.

The couple drifted further apart. Fred, still a part-time college student, wanted to build his career as an architect, keep expenses to a minimum, and avoid debt. Dodie yearned for him to be an instantly successful architect and desired to immediately buy a horse farm. Fred refused to take a "huge risk" and enter the horse breeding business. He couldn't reach his dreams and goals if he did.

One Friday night that summer, Fred drove to Nederland to surprise Dodie for a weekend visit. He walked into their cabin only to discover her interest in a much older and prominent architect. He left and knew his marriage was over.

The couple filed a joint divorce petition in August to terminate their nearly four-year marriage. Neither hired a lawyer.

They divided up their property: Dodie would own Witchy Blue, the part-thoroughbred horse; the Camaro; and their household furnishings. Fred would take the motorcycle, his tools, and Saber, their mostly Labrador. He'd own the Cheyenne house and be responsible for all related expenses as well as all joint debts incurred before they filed for divorce. The Cheyenne home's $170 monthly mortgage payment was their only known debt.

Dodie immediately repainted the Camaro yellow and installed mag wheels. Fred knew that she liked "sparkle and flash" and wanted "to turn your head when you saw it." He felt irritated that she spent money on the car instead of necessary living expenses. She sold their thoroughbred Shadow Beau and used her own money to buy a part-thoroughbred.

On August 18, 1973, Dodie graduated from the University of Colorado with a bachelor's degree in fine arts. She moved in with the older architect.

Nearly three months later, a judge found that Dodie's marriage was "irretrievably broken"[7] and granted the divorce during a hearing attended only by Fred. The judge didn't award maintenance to either Dodie or Fred.

Dodie moved out of the architect's home and rented a small apartment in a house in Boulder. She put her thoroughbred horse farm dream on hold; she had to earn a living now.

CHAPTER 3

Christmas Present

"Oh, no! What in the world . . ." I shook my head and stared at the white foam that littered the family room.

"What's wrong?" Dave asked.

Foam was everywhere—on the floor, on a chair, on part of the secondhand couch. One partially eaten couch cushion lay at our feet.

Molly, our blockheaded twenty-month-old Labrador retriever, stood in the background and wagged her thick otter tail. She'd been quite busy while Dave, my stepson, and I went out for our 1994 Christmas Eve dinner. We'd left behind our black beauty, who loved to sleep and eat more than anything else, to guard our house in Franktown. Her surprise Christmas present didn't amuse us.

Days later I still smarted from Molly's destruction, which created the daunting chore of locating an upholsterer. I finally found one just north of Castle Rock and stopped in at our vet's office on my way home from dropping off the couch cushion. As I picked up some supplies, I told the vet's assistant about Molly's special holiday gift.

Her eyes lit up. "Does Molly need a friend?" She knew that we'd lost my yellow Labrador, Whiskey, to old age the previous June.

"Well, maybe she does. She is probably bored and still misses Whiskey."

"One of our clients is looking for the right home for his good-looking yellow Labrador retriever. The dog is really nice, and his owner paid a lot for him, $300," she said. Their client traveled more and more for his job. The three-year-old Labrador named Max needed more attention.

I assured her that I'd talk to my husband and would call if we had any interest. But I questioned the wisdom of adopting a three-year-old dog. The concept was foreign to me. For more than forty years, my parents raised and showed Labradors on the East Coast. To my knowledge, they'd never adopted a dog. They'd always evaluated their canines' potential mates and relatives' conformation, temperament, health, and other general information before deciding on a breeding. I knew I wouldn't have this wealth of information if we adopted a dog.

For the next several days, Dave and I discussed at length whether another dog should join our family. Molly would be two years old in a few months. We planned to breed her and keep a puppy. My elderly mother, who'd given us Molly, lived in Connecticut with four Labradors. Nearly three years prior, she'd had a heart valve replaced.

Dave and I agreed that we needed to be prepared to give a home to my mom's Labs should something happen to her. Six dogs seemed like a lot of canines. We just didn't know if my mother would outlive all of her dogs as she had my father.

I resorted to my best problem-solving skills. That's why I drew chart after chart to illustrate how many dogs we might have for how many years depending on the health of my mother and her dogs and if we adopted Max. I wanted to make sure that we were ready to care for him forever in case we fell in love with him.

Finally, after countless charts and days of discussions that extended over our New Year's holiday in the small central Colorado mountain community of Buena Vista, we decided that I'd call our vet's assistant to get the telephone number of Max's owner, John Ulrich. After all, we concluded, it wouldn't hurt to meet the dog.

I identified myself and the purpose of my call when John answered the phone.

"I have been dreading this call," he said quietly.

I didn't know what to say. Dave and I had debated for days as to whether to check out Max. Now his owner said he'd dreaded the call.

John said that he'd looked for a family to adopt Max since the previous summer and had rejected several. He didn't believe that he could give Max the life that he wanted for him because he traveled too much. When the vet's assistant told him about us, he feared we'd call. Our home just might be right for Max.

I was convinced that John didn't want to give up Max.

We talked some more, and John agreed for me to meet Max at his house. Dave couldn't accompany me because of a business commitment but wanted to visit if I thought Max looked like a good match for us.

John agreed.

I located John's two-story home in a subdivision on Castle Rock's west side. John greeted me at the front door, and we walked back to the kitchen-dining area. A sliding glass door led outside to a wooden deck. That's when I first saw Max, a medium-yellow-colored Lab, with darker yellow ears and deep brown eyes, outlined in black as if he wore mascara. He sprung up and down on his somewhat long legs with boundless, puppy-like energy.

John, who was a portly man, and I walked out onto the deck. We closed the door behind us and greeted the wild jumping dog. Max furiously wagged his tail and appeared overjoyed at interacting with people. He was beyond outgoing. When he settled a bit, I noticed his smaller head and dark tan nose, where the once black color had faded. Had the discoloration occurred when he dug holes? I wondered. John led me down the deck stairs to Max's fenced-in yard. I knew Max was well loved when I saw the heated dog house. The small, narrow yard contrasted starkly with our five-acre property, which had a half-acre, fenced-in area for Molly. But there weren't any signs of digging. Good.

I quickly learned that John didn't allow Max into his house except on the coldest of nights, when the Lab slept in a dog crate. His theory was that Max couldn't be a hunting dog if he lived in the house. Being housedogs had never affected my parents' Labs' performances in field trials, I recalled, but kept those thoughts to myself.

John encouraged me to take Max for a walk. I declined because I thought the yellow jumping jack would take me for a walk, which would only further aggravate my bum shoulder and neck.

We left Max on the deck and went inside to sit at John's kitchen table, where he had gathered his dog's paperwork.

I reviewed Max's pedigree and recognized only the Simerdown kennel prefix. Simerdown had been around for years, and its owner, Linda Vaughn, was a well-respected Denver-area Labrador breeder who showed her dogs in the conformation ring.

"I've never heard of Dodie Cariaso, Max's breeder, and don't know the dogs named on the pedigree," I said.

John urged me to call Dodie for more information about Max's lineage.

"That won't be necessary." Max's looks weren't going to make him Molly's future mate or the next show champion. But he appeared orthopedically sound and might perform well in obedience trials. Years later I wondered if I'd called Dodie to learn more about his upbringing and lineage, as my parents would have recommended, whether that conversation would have changed my mind about whether to adopt Max.

John appeared eager for me to take his dog. I told him that Dave must meet and like Max, and Molly and Max needed to get along. He agreed.

Would he sign over Max's ownership to us on the AKC registration certificate? If he did, I could show Max in AKC obedience trials. John consented to the transfer.

I watched Max as he bounced up and down just outside the closed sliding-glass door. Then he stood. His deep brown eyes bored into me.

"Please, please like me," his eyes pleaded.

I know, boy, you want more attention, I thought.

I thanked John for his time but didn't commit to taking Max. I assured him that Dave would call to set up a time to meet his dog.

On my drive home, I couldn't rid myself of Max's soulful eyes. And, Max wasn't such a bad-looking Lab.

Dave took Max for a walk on the following weekend. He was duly impressed when the dog didn't pull him; in fact, Max heeled better than Molly, whom I was training for her first obedience trial. I knew that Dave had fallen for Max when he returned home.

John had concurred that the final step in the adoption process was for Max to meet Molly at our home. We also believed John wanted to make sure our home was suitable for his dog.

Max and John arrived on a sunny Saturday morning in January 1995. Max seemed as wild as ever. He met Molly in our fenced-in backyard and never looked back. They ran and played; they'd both found their new best friend. John watched as he sat on the stairs of our wooden deck. He called Max and waved his ball cap. The goofy Lab ignored this apparent cap-waving ritual and kept playing with Molly.

John looked sad as he walked out of our backyard. His boy hadn't even said goodbye. But he seemed satisfied that Max had a good new home and signed over his AKC registration to us. We shook hands and promised to stay in touch. John's eyes glistened as he wished us all well. I glanced at Max's registration and realized our new ward was four, not three, years old. Way too late to revisit my charts.

We let the two new best friends play for most of the morning in the backyard because we needed to bathe Max before he came into our home. His yellow coat was filled with dirt and grime from the gravel run at John's.

After lunch, Dave and I gathered up the dog bath supplies, hooked up the hose, and attached a leash to Max's collar. The fifty-degree day was as pleasant as there was in mid-January in Colorado. Max stood nicely as we washed and dried him. It certainly wasn't his favorite event, but we all survived. Molly, his moral support, was nowhere to be seen. We spared her a bath.

Based on our discussions with John, Dave and I knew that Max wasn't a housedog and only slept inside on the coldest of nights, and then only in a crate. The unspoken words were that Max wasn't housebroken.

Our home had a couple of antiques sprinkled among our second-hand furniture. Dave's proud possessions were his stereo equipment that included two, four-foot-high Infinity speakers strategically positioned a couple of feet from one wall in the living room. The entire house was carpeted except for the kitchen's linoleum floor. Whiskey, now deceased, and Molly as well as the cats, Pest and Dillie, agreed that the linoleum was sacred and never to be soiled. They believed that the carpet was an excellent place to leave a present or two when sick.

We walked Max on a leash into the house and led him around his new quarters. He seemed relaxed so we unhooked his leash. Free at last, Max ran straight into the living room and lifted his leg.

"No!" Dave and I shouted in unison.

Max's aim missed Dave's prized speakers. I took our adoptee outside.

Although he had joined our animals' conspiracy against the carpet's well-being, he only had an accident or two over the next few days but never again near the speakers. Undoubtedly the near miss contributed to Dave's affirmation that Killkenny's Maximilian would never see the inside of an animal shelter: he was our forever dog.

CHAPTER 4

Prolific Potter

Pottery became Dodie's meal ticket—at first. She needed access to a kiln, so she joined the Brimstone Potters, a pottery cooperative, housed within an industrial park building on the outskirts of Boulder. The cooperative not only provided space for budding and experienced potters to craft and fire their wares in kilns but also hosted semiannual art sales.

Outwardly, Dodie moved on from her divorce, although she retained her married name and focused on creating pottery. But inwardly, she harbored anger and appeared much more reclusive than before her divorce, her younger brother Doug recalled later.[1]

Doug felt the sting of her wrath when he proudly told his parents that he and his future bride Kathleen had purchased a house in Denver to renovate and resell for a profit.

Dodie listened.

"You think you are so smart," she shouted, sounding angry and appearing envious.

A year or two later, Dodie bought her own home near the center of the small town of Berthoud, located halfway between Boulder and Fort Collins, two larger communities north of Denver. She obtained loans from the seller to pay $27,500 for a two-story house on a lot too small to keep horses. Just a year-plus later in 1978, she paid off these loans when she and her parents took out a twenty-five-year, $28,250 bank mortgage on the property. At the same time, her parents loaned her $6,000.

Dodie hired Rueben Zoller, a handyman, to convert her home's garage into a pottery studio. Friends helped build a kiln once she received town approval after an extensive permitting process.

She no longer needed to use the Brimstone Potters' kilns, so she hunted for a better location to market her wares and learned that the Trimble Court Artisans provided retail space for its members. Trimble Court was established in 1971 when several Colorado State University (CSU) art students approached Mary Trimble, one of their liberal arts professors, about forming an artist group. Trimble, a descendant of a pioneer family in the Poudre Valley, wanted to give back to the community, so she charged the all-female artist group only a dollar a year to rent three rooms in the Trimble Court Alley in downtown Fort Collins.

Dodie applied for membership. A jury committee, comprised of several Trimble Court artisans, evaluated her work's quality and sales potential. The committee quickly approved her application to join the thirty-plus-member cooperative.

To come anywhere close to meeting her spending habits, Dodie needed to sell large quantities of pottery. Dressed in blue jean overalls with her hair pulled back into a ponytail, she labored for hours at a potter's wheel in her home studio. She promoted her creations as "Funky and Functional Stoneware and Porcelain" and called her business Symposium in Mud.

Her creations ranged from dishware to pie pans to hanging flower baskets. For festive occasions, she crafted punch bowls and cups. She shaped mounds of clay into small and large standing vases, bases for kerosene lamps, and picture frames. Many of her pieces were large, and many had etched designs. For glaze colors, she applied earth tones, mostly browns and some blues.

Dodie's artistic flair spilled over to her dress. Fellow potters noticed that she dressed up and accented her attire with a hat and gold shoes when she arranged her pottery display at the Trimble

Court store. She commanded twice the space of any other potter and set out between fifty and eighty pottery pieces on her L-shaped display made out of seven-foot rough wooden shelves.

Artists generally kept 60 percent of their sales, and Trimble Court retained 40 percent, although some had fifty-fifty arrangements. Each member worked a set number of hours per month in the cooperative's store unless they paid others to work for them. Dodie declined to work in the store; she didn't enjoy dealing with customers and thought she'd make more money by using the time to craft additional pottery.

Dodie believed that she should be paid more when she placed her wares on consignment in galleries in Jackson Hole, just outside Grand Teton National Park; Cody, near Yellowstone National Park; and even Cheyenne, a community that she despised. She also sold pottery in the resort towns of Aspen, Vail, Telluride, and Breckenridge and closer to home in Estes Park, Boulder, and Denver. During the summer months, she retailed her pottery at art and craft fairs throughout Colorado.

The hardworking potter carved out time to date a college-educated man and visit her siblings. She drove to Eagle on Colorado's western slope to ski or hike and stay with James and his wife. Doug and Kathleen enjoyed their visits with Dodie at her Berthoud home and liked her boyfriend, as did James. She celebrated the holidays with her brothers and their spouses as well as her parents, who had moved to the Denver area from Glen Ellyn. Kathleen noticed a gentler side to Dodie: her sister-in-law showed more love and appreciation to her father.

Dodie's pottery business did well but failed to support her lifestyle. She bought on credit to furnish her home and took out loans, paying each off before obtaining a slightly larger loan amount. She boarded Witchy Blue but yearned to buy a house on property where she could keep her part-thoroughbred mare and raise horses.

In early 1981, Dodie discovered a 3.75-acre property, nestled in an agricultural area and surrounded by open fields just southeast of Loveland and northeast of Berthoud. She inspected the 1900 white farmhouse and its outbuildings. The 1,764-square-foot home contained three bedrooms and one bath. She stood on this plains property and stared at the snowcapped mountain peaks to the west. Her teenage dream to live in the mountains, close to skiing, on property where she could have horses, almost could be realized. The two-story house cried out for maintenance, the property needed landscaping, and the outbuildings required repairs. She also needed a pottery studio.

Dodie chose to incur more debt to buy her "dream" farm. With her parents' assistance, she made a $15,000 down payment to close on the $75,000 property on April 15, 1981. At the time, she still owned her Berthoud house, which had a mortgage and secured a $10,000 loan.

Renovations started quickly. James installed skylights in the farmhouse's roof and drywalled part of the home. He fenced in an area around the house and built a corral for Witchy Blue.

Once again, Dodie hired handyman Rueben Zoller, this time to turn an old calving barn into a pottery studio, complete with a space for retail sales. He insulated and drywalled the interior walls and wired the building for electricity.

That summer, Dodie met Nancy Zoller, the handyman's daughter-in-law, who also was a potter. The two women quickly became friends. Upon Dodie's encouragement, Nancy joined Trimble Court.

Nancy enjoyed Dodie because she was fun, bold, opinionated, and "most of the time" made good sense. "She would listen and then tell her story."[2] Dodie talked about rocky relationships and her family, who she said had "kind of ostracized" her. She admired that Dodie could afford her farm and pay $7 an hour for handyman work on a potter's income.

The farm's renovations came with a cost. Dodie paid off the $10,000 loan apparently by taking out a $17,000 loan, also secured by her Berthoud house.

Although she liked to spend, Dodie worked hard and efficiently to produce large quantities of pottery. The laborious process wasn't quick or unique but gave her time each day for errands or other chores.

First, Dodie threw clay on her potter's wheel to make a series of vessels, such as mugs, bowls, vases, or other shapes. Next, she allowed the vessels to dry before she trimmed the shapes and added any distinctive designs before she fired them in a kiln.

After the kiln slowly cooled over a day, Dodie removed and glazed the pieces. Once dry, she stacked the glazed pieces into her kiln, a process that often took a couple of hours, and then fired her wares for about fourteen to eighteen hours. The kiln cooled for at least a day before she removed the pottery. A good-sized kiln, of about three feet by three feet by three feet, could accommodate 100 to 150 different-sized pieces at a time. It took at least two to three weeks to make that many pieces.

When Dodie believed that she was in a stylistic rut, she experimented with new forms and designs as well as decorative and glaze techniques. She attended a graduate ceramics class taught by Herb Schumacher, a nationally known potter, and studied pottery at the Anderson Ranch Art Center near Snowmass with Cynthia Bringle, another well-known potter. [3]

She fashioned different, more decorative designs to form an ornate Victorian style. Sometimes she incised a free-flowing flower design into the pottery to create a second new style. She worked with blue and gray glazes with the occasional copper red. Dodie had her own style and stamp. Clay was therapeutic and helped to center her. [4]

Dodie sculpted an ornate southwestern look as her third new style.

Life was good for Dodie. She lived on a farm where she could raise horses. Her pottery sold well, and her debt decreased when her Berthoud house sold for $63,000 in April 1982.

She met a new beau. Described by some as a cowboy who wore tight jeans and a cowboy hat, he enjoyed woodworking and restoring antiques when not working in the oil fields. He didn't ski but seemed good with animals. She married him in November 1982 in a Baptist church in a small northern Colorado community. About twenty friends and family members, including Dodie's brothers and mother, gathered afterward for a luncheon reception at her farm. Her dad had died the previous summer.

Dodie's family questioned the "need for this guy in her life" but could only wait to see if the marriage and her happiness lasted.

CHAPTER 5

Killkenny Kennels

odie's paternal ancestors immigrated to the United States from County Cork in southeastern Ireland during the potato famine of the 1850s. But it was County Kilkenny, just to the north, where thoroughbred horse farms were scattered amid lush rolling hills, that provided the name for Dodie's next venture: breeding Labrador retrievers. She still wanted to raise thoroughbred horses, but purebred dogs were less expensive to rear.

She purchased her foundation Killkenny dog, Samba, a black Labrador puppy with kind, medium brown eyes framed by large ears, and a moderately long muzzle, in 1978 from a quality breeder, Diana Richardson of Boulder.[1] Richardson competed with her dogs in the conformation ring and at obedience trials, and she worked them in the field. Her Williston Labradors' ancestors came from well-known English, Scottish, and American East Coast bloodlines. She advertised in the nationwide *Breeders Directory to Labrador Retriever Pedigrees*[2] that she had puppies usually twice a year for show, field, and home and listed health clearances for her featured dogs.

Samba's dam (mother) was a conformation champion and had earned a working certificate.[3] Her hips were certified as normal by the Orthopedic Foundation of Animals (OFA), a nonprofit organization founded in 1966 to manage and combat canine hip dysplasia by evaluating radiographs of canine hips, providing genetic counseling, and managing data. Dodie registered her puppy as Satin Samba of Williston with the AKC.

At the time, reputable breeders such as Richardson evaluated their Labradors for only two genetic disorders: hip dysplasia and hereditary eye diseases.[4] They didn't breed dogs with hip dysplasia, a polygenic (multiple-gene) disorder,[5] because they didn't want to produce puppies with the crippling malady. Breeders asked veterinarians to send their dogs' hip x-rays to OFA to be evaluated by several randomly selected, board-certified radiologists. These independent radiologist contractors separately evaluated each hip radiograph before they collectively determined if the dog had normal hip conformation. If they agreed that there was no evidence of hip dysplasia, the hips received an OFA normal rating. The foundation entered results of all its examinations, including dysplastic findings, into its database for research purposes.

By 1978, OFA required dogs to be at least twenty-four months old for evaluations, other than for preliminary findings. It rated dysplastic hips as mild, moderate, or severe. Dogs with a "questionable" hip status, neither conclusively normal nor dysplastic, received a border-line rating. Over the years, OFA refined its normal classification for nondysplastic hips to excellent, good, or fair ratings.

Reputable breeders understood that there weren't (and to this day still aren't) any genetic or mechanical tests to determine if a dog carried the polygenic traits of hip dysplasia.[6] Although they didn't breed dysplastic dogs, they understood that they could breed two dogs with normal hip conformation and still produce some dysplastic pups. When this happened, they knew that both parents were carriers of polygenic traits of hip dysplasia.[7] These polygenic traits could be passed on for generations without detection until either two carriers were bred to each other or a carrier was bred to a dysplastic dog. Knowledgeable breeders recognized that there was no guarantee that puppies would be dysplasia-free. They also understood that the odds dramatically improved for producing dysplasia-free puppies if the parents' hip x-rays showed normal hip conformation and known carriers weren't bred to one another.

Less than five years before Dodie bought Samba, the Canine Eye Registration Foundation (CERF) was formed in response to concerns of hereditary eye diseases such as hereditary cataracts and progressive retinal atrophy (PRA), which leads to total blindness. There weren't genetic tests to detect PRA, which is inherited as an autosomal recessive trait,[8] at that time. CERF maintained a registry of all dogs that were examined by members of the American College of Veterinary Ophthalmologists.[9] It issued certificates, valid only for a year, to dogs clear of eye diseases. Reputable breeders had their breeding stock's eyes examined annually because they knew that if two PRA carriers, or one with PRA and the other a PRA carrier, were bred to each other, at least some of the puppies would go blind. Before Richardson bred Samba's dam, she tested the dog's eyes, which were found to be disease-free.

Dodie didn't follow these accepted practices. She bred Samba before the dog received an OFA hip clearance and apparently failed to have the canine's eyes certified as clear of any diseases.[10] OFA certified Samba's hips as normal when she was forty months old, well after her first litter. Dodie's practice of breeding her younger females, without OFA hip clearances, to stud dogs, usually with hip clearances, continued for years.

She didn't breed Samba again because the dog was spayed after contracting pyometra, an infection of the uterus. Instead, she bred Samba's chocolate daughter, who never received an OFA hip rating.[11] She used Killkenny as her kennel name for the first time when she registered a chocolate puppy from that litter with the AKC.

Dr. Millissa Culver, a 1971 CSU Veterinary School graduate and Dodie's veterinarian, emphasized the importance of OFA hip certification before a dog was bred. She viewed her client as an average dog breeder who obtained OFA hip certifications and tried to do everything "just right." Dodie bred for fun and to supplement her income "a little bit," Dr. Culver recalled years later.[12]

Many reputable veterinarians and breeders believed that female dogs should be bred, at the very most, no more than every other heat cycle. In fact, many breeders often bred a female only once or twice during her lifetime because their primary goal was to improve the breed, not to make money.

Dr. Culver advised otherwise. Her philosophy was that since a female can only whelp so many litters because her uterus is damaged every heat cycle, healthy females can be bred until reproduction problems occur, usually at about age six for Labradors. She recommended that they then be retired, spayed, and, if possible, placed in new homes.

Dodie bred Samba's chocolate granddaughter to a yellow stud dog. She kept a favorite, a dark fox-red colored yellow, with a brown nose and brown eye rims, from that December 1983 litter and registered the pup as Killkenny's Charmin' Find. Charmin' would become Max's grandmother.

Marney McCleary, who bred a few Labrador litters and owned stud dogs with both field and conformation backgrounds, befriended Dodie. The two women shared an interest in Labradors and Irish heritage. They talked in person and on the phone about dogs and pedigrees. McCleary perceived her new friend as an extremely bright, opinionated, and outspoken person with a know-it-all attitude about Labradors.[13] Dodie didn't seek her advice about stud dogs.

McCleary liked the very attractive, well-kept woman with long strawberry blonde hair. As she toured Dodie's immaculate farmhouse with its Victorian style, she spotted a beautiful green velvet couch and beaded lamp shades. She noticed a few Labradors had run of the house and that there were two litters, raised in separate bedrooms. The property looked clean.

I just wish my house looked like this now, McCleary thought. She and her husband were remodeling their home.

McCleary invited Dodie to attend events hosted by the Labrador Retriever Club of Greater Denver (Lab Club). Years before, Labrador enthusiasts Susan Biddulph, Karen Case, and Donna Stacey discussed the need for a local specialty, a show just for Labradors, as an alternative to traveling a minimum of 450 miles to another club's specialty. They banded together with a few other supporters, including McCleary, to form the Lab Club in January 1978. Most members showed their Labradors in the conformation ring, but some were interested in field and obedience work. They shared a goal to improve Labradors by breeding the best possible dogs while learning and having fun. Members declared the club was formed "to promote good will, friendship, support and knowledge among those involved with Labradors" in the Denver area.[14]

The new club immediately published *The Retriever Believer,* a monthly newsletter that provided information about show events, winners in the show ring, health, and training. Members could advertise their litters in its "Litter Box." Club membership gradually grew as word spread. By 1981, the club's roster listed twenty to twenty-five members.

McCleary quickly learned that Dodie wasn't interested in the club or its activities. Dodie, who always declined invitations to Lab Club events, had other interests: showing horses and selling pottery in galleries and shops as well as at her farm studio.

Dodie's periodic pottery sales at her studio attracted more than customers. The Colorado Department of Transportation apparently received a complaint about the amount of traffic generated by her business. Weld County insisted that she seek a special use permit to sell pottery out of her studio or face a zoning violation because her property was zoned residential.

In her March 1985 permit application, Dodie reported that she supported herself with her full-time pottery business, sold mostly through galleries and gift stores, and delivered all of her orders. She didn't have any employees. Located 250 feet off the main road, her studio generated little traffic, and her closest neighbors lived a quarter mile away. She disclosed that she showed horses but failed to mention that she raised dogs.

When Dodie appeared at the Weld County Planning Commission's public hearing on her permit application, no one spoke for or against it. The Planning Commission unanimously recommended that the Board of County Commissioners approve Dodie's application. Dodie attended the county commissioners' July 10, 1985 public hearing, but again no member of the public commented. Commissioners approved her permit but required that she widen her driveway's entrance. The permit meant Dodie could legally sell pottery from her studio.

Dodie continued to peddle her wares at various art and craft fairs during the Memorial Day to Labor Day season, primarily in Colorado.

At an art fair in Boulder, Dodie introduced herself to stained-glass artist Barbara Marcus. The single women immediately became friends. Dodie's second marriage of less than three years had ended in divorce in August 1985 after a volatile separation, which included temporary restraining orders lodged against both parties.

Barbara admired Dodie's home, full of Victorian-style antiques with lace doilies on the arms of sofas and chairs. As they walked up the stairs to the second floor, Dodie pointed to family pictures on the wall and said her mother, aunt, and grandmother graduated from universities at a time when most women didn't attend college.

The artist looked at Dodie, who was in her mid-thirties, and saw not only a strong and independent, beautiful woman but also a "Colorado pioneer woman from a refined and academic family."[15] She found herself duly impressed by the witty and outgoing woman.

Barbara placed some of her stained-glass art on consignment in Dodie's studio and joined Trimble Court upon her friend's encouragement. The two women sometimes traveled together to sell their wares at art and craft shows.

In the 1980s, talented potters earned an estimated $10,000 to $12,000 in a good year. Mugs sold for less than $10, a good-sized mixing bowl for $35, and a lamp base or a decent-sized vase for $40. When Barbara traveled with Dodie to art and craft fairs in Nebraska, $3,000 minus expenses for Dodie rated a good show.

Dodie led Trimble Court potters in gradually raising prices and wholesaling wares. Fellow potters questioned how she could make money by wholesaling at half the retail price but also recognized that she walked away with a check after a delivery. They also understood that she had to make more and more pottery to be ready for another wholesale delivery.

About the same time that Dodie ramped up her pottery production, she decided to breed more Labradors and looked to buy show-quality females to add to her Killkenny line. She contacted Lee Burdick, a Lab Club member who lived in western Colorado, to learn more about a two-year-old flashy "perpetual motion" yellow female listed for sale in *The Retriever Believer*. Dodie said she worked with "handicapped children" at a ski resort and wanted a Labrador.

Burdick explained the importance of eye and hip clearances as well as diet and necessary shots before she sold Burbury Crystal for $300 in February 1986. She allowed Dodie to pay in installments and would transfer Crystal's AKC ownership registration only after she received full payment. She mentioned Linda Vaughn when Dodie inquired about a Labrador breeder with quality stud dogs.[16]

Three months later, Dodie called Burdick to report that Crystal had whelped six puppies sired by a yellow show dog owned by Vaughn. A shocked Burdick hadn't received final payment for Crystal and still owned her in the AKC's eyes. Dodie paid the last installment a few weeks later.

Vaughn recalled that Dodie said she'd bred a few litters, and she seemed as "nice and good a person as anyone."[17] Dodie had produced Crystal's hip and eye clearance documents, which she'd received from Burdick. Vaughn didn't observe anything out of the ordinary when she visited the litter at Dodie's. Instead, she noticed nice-looking paint horses.

Fred also didn't see anything amiss during a short visit at his ex-wife's farm that October. He and his hunting companion stopped in after spotting a pottery sale sign and gave some deer and antelope meat to a "dolled up" Dodie. Fred looked over her pottery, and the former couple chatted about what they were doing. He noted that the house appeared orderly and clean and only saw five or six dogs.

Dodie gave him the impression that she was seeing someone, so Fred left after about ten minutes because he didn't want to complicate any relationship. She thanked him for the meat and invited him to drop by again. He watched as she put on her "saleswoman face" to greet the public and then drove off.

Weeks later, Dodie had an opportunity to observe quality Labradors at the Lab Club's first conformation and obedience trial specialty. The show was held in Longmont, just seventeen miles south of her farm. The club flew in noted Labrador breeder Margie Cairns, who started her Blaircourt kennels in Scotland decades before with her husband, Grant. The club chose Mrs. Cairns, because of her hallmark status as a foundation Labrador breeder, to judge the main conformation competition. She attracted the entries of 139 Labradors, including Vaughn's yellow, Ch. Simerdown's Bennigan, CD, AWC, the sire of Crystal's first litter.[18] Winnie Limbourne, a well-respected California Labrador breeder, judged sweepstakes. New Mexican Nancy Pollack, known for her upbeat and understanding personality, attracted twenty-three obedience entries. Owners from both coasts entered their Labradors, although most of the entries came from the Colorado-New Mexico area.

Dodie didn't compete at the show but may have attended to look for potential stud dogs. She bred for a mellow temperament and a "show dog look," Dr. Culver later recalled.

About two months after the show, Dodie bred Charmin' to Vaughn's Bennigan. That litter produced Max's dam. By then, Dodie had decided to breed only Labradors. She'd bred a couple of litters of Chesapeake Bay retrievers and springer spaniels but had decided against breeding those breeds again because of dwarfism in one Chesapeake litter and the required coat care of springers. But Dodie kept a springer as a house pet and preferred that breed to Labradors, Dr. Culver recollected.

———

She looks really pretty, McCleary thought, as she looked at the black female sired by her former show dog.

Dodie owned the young female but didn't like her looks.

"Let her mature," McCleary said.

Dodie again complained about the dog's looks when McCleary returned to Dodie's farm to scrutinize the canine a second time.

"There are no guarantees" (with breeding), McCleary said. "If you don't like her, place her." She looked around and saw way too many dogs. They seemed "frantic," as if they didn't get enough attention, and not as well cared for as when she first met Dodie.

McCleary harbored concerns that Dodie didn't think hip clearances were important. She believed that Dodie insisted on breeding to studs with hip clearances but knew that not all of her friend's brood females had those same clearances. Dodie used good breeders, McCleary thought, by breeding to their quality and often conformation champion or field trial titled stud dogs but refused to do anything with her canines, much less spend time and money to earn titles. And, once Dodie exhausted one breeder's goodwill, she moved on to another breeder. McCleary decided to distance herself.

Dodie's dog numbers grew.

In 1988, Weld County discovered that Dodie's canine population far exceeded the number permitted by its zoning. Dodie had a choice: apply to amend her studio's home business special use permit to include her kennel or downsize the number of her canines. She fumed, irritated that someone could tell her what she could have on her property. But she acquiesced and applied for a permit amendment to allow her to keep a maximum of sixteen dogs.

In her amendment application, she disclosed that she owned eleven adult dogs and one puppy less than six months old but had "no intention of ever owning more than 16 dogs at one time." She raised three to four litters a year as a hobby, not a business, and had bred "quality AKC Labs for show or field" for the past ten years. And, she didn't board any dogs.

Dodie also described her facility: three separate kennel yards enclosed with six-foot fences and a few dog runs. She cleaned daily and sprayed the facilities with disinfectant and deodorizing chemicals every five months. Her dogs were all current on their vaccinations, and puppies were born in her house in a room designed for "their special needs." She monitored her dogs' behavior because she worked at home.

She promised that all of her "excessive barker" adult dogs would be debarked by April 15th. Debarking[19] means a veterinarian surgically cuts a dog's vocal cords to reduce a bark to a hoarse or rasping sound. She pledged that all future canines would be debarked at six months of age if they barked excessively and vowed to stay in close touch with her neighbors about noise control.

A Weld County Animal Control officer inspected Dodie's kennel facilities as part of the application process. She observed that the dogs had large yards to exercise in and dog houses for shelter. The canines were in "excellent condition." Water containers, attached to a fence to prevent spillage, were clean. "Ms. Cariaso apparently does a limited amount of breeding and simply has the dogs as a hobby."

The officer didn't perceive that barking was a problem because some dogs had been debarked, and all were quiet during her visit. "This facility is a well-kept kennel, and the dogs are well cared for."

In early May 1988, Weld County planning commissioners conducted a public hearing on Dodie's permit amendment application. They considered two opposition letters. Two neighbors spoke. One, who owned seventy-five adjoining acres, opposed the "commercial dog kennel" without any explanation. Another cited traffic concerns, depreciation of property values, noise of barking dogs, and smell if the kennel wasn't kept clean as reasons for his opposition.

Another neighbor, Stanlyn Johnston, who occasionally cared for the animals when Dodie traveled to art and craft shows, supported the application and wrote that the dogs were kept in clean conditions.

Dr. Culver penned that Dodie produced "good quality, healthy puppies," and her dogs "always appear clean, happy, well fed, and well cared for when she brings them to the hospital." She'd found the dogs well housed with adequate space and shelter at Dodie's kennel.

Planning commissioners recommended approval of Dodie's application to county commissioners, who focused on noise concerns at their June 1, 1988 public hearing. Dodie assured the commissioners that her seven outside dogs had been debarked. Dr. Culver explained that debarking didn't eliminate but reduced the noise of a barking dog and commented favorably about her client's facilities. A puppy buyer and another individual spoke in favor of the permit. Dodie submitted letters of support from three neighbors.

Three different neighbors opposed the permit amendment. They objected to the dogs' barking and expressed concern about the possible devaluation of their properties.

Commissioners approved the permit amendment (kennel permit) with conditions. Only debarked dogs were allowed outside between 10 p.m. and 7 a.m., and animal wastes needed to be disposed of "in such a manner so as not to cause a public nuisance." Dodie also needed to widen her driveway's entrance, the identical but unenforced condition required by her studio permit.

The kennel permit limited Dodie to sixteen dogs but failed to define dogs, resulting in uncertainty as to whether the total number included puppies. The permit automatically expired if Dodie sold or leased her property. It authorized access to her farm by personnel from the county health and county planning services departments as well as the Berthoud Fire Department at any reasonable time to ensure compliance with the permit and "all applicable Weld County Regulations." County commissioners could revoke the permit if she failed to comply with any of its conditions.

But Dodie knew that county animal control officers would inspect her kennel only if they received a complaint, or if one of her dogs escaped and killed a neighbor's calf. That's what the animal control officer had said when she inspected Dodie's facilities during the permit amendment application process.

That understanding allowed Dodie to increase her Labrador population without the county's knowledge as long as the dogs didn't bark excessively and stayed on her property. She could make additional money by selling more puppies, and if she used her own stud dogs, she'd eliminate stud fees. And her stud dogs might generate income if they were bred to other people's canines. That's why she searched for quality male pups from breeders and looked among her own litters for future stud dogs.

In late November 1988, Dodie bred Crystal to Vaughn's Ch. Simerdown's Montgomery WC. From that litter, she kept a blocky-headed, fairly light-yellow male and registered him as Killkenny's McIvory O'Keef. She returned one final time to Vaughn in 1989 to breed to a chocolate show dog but kept a female from that litter instead of a prospective stud dog.

That same year, she located a blocky-headed black male pup with a field and show background. She registered him as Killkenny's Thunderson Rage and called him Thunder. He developed into a longer-legged, lean Lab with a good disposition. Dodie didn't like him.

"You hang on to this dog and you will make more money with this dog than any other dog that you own," Dr. Culver said. She thought he looked like "the Lab of fifty years ago."

"You're crazy," Dodie wanted to sell him.

"People are going to buy a dog like the one they had when they were kids, and when they see these 'European' show dogs, they'll think that's not what we had. But then when they look at Thunder, they are going to buy a dog from you." And they did. Dodie kept the big black.

In early 1990, Dodie bought a chocolate puppy, a future stud dog, from founding Lab Club members Gladys and Gerald Burke, who bred chocolates primarily for pets and occasionally competed in obedience.[20]

Dodie bred the chocolate male as well as her two other stud dogs, McIvory and Thunder, before OFA certified their hips. By breeding her stock to one another, she could forgo health clearances as she pleased and decide at what age to breed. Thunder sired a litter at the tender age of eleven months.

Four of Dodie's dams whelped litters within a month in the late fall of 1990. Thunder sired three of the litters; one produced Max on November 9, 1990.

Most breeders would have had help to care for so many litters, but Dodie managed alone. By now, Dodie's dog numbers undoubtedly exceeded her county kennel permit's limit of sixteen. Weld County hadn't visited her kennel, so the permit violation went undetected.

CHAPTER 6

The King of the Litter

"I picked Max because he was in charge of the litter; he was the king of that litter," John Ulrich recalled years later.[1]

Where the small, light-yellow puppy went, so went his four litter-mates. If one got out of line, he placed his paw on that sibling. This puppy's dark brown eyes, accented by black rims and his black nose, underscored the determined expression on his nearly white face. His ears and fur along his topline were a shade darker than the rest of his coat. John watched the puppies play in an outbuilding and then outside in a barnyard behind Dodie's farmhouse.

He had bred, owned, and trained vizslas, short-haired sporting dogs, for hunting mostly upland game birds in Indiana. Now he lived in Colorado and wanted to buy his first Labrador to hunt ducks. He planned to leave empty-handed if he questioned the puppies' conditions or saw any signs of a puppy mill operation, defined by the courts as a large-scale commercial dog breeding facility where "the health of the dogs is disregarded" to maintain a low overhead and maximize profits.[2]

But the pups and their pen looked clean; the farmhouse appeared kempt. He noticed only a few other Labradors besides the five puppies.

John asked to see the puppies' sire and dam because he knew as a former dog breeder that the parents often were the key to looks and temperament. He wanted a hunting dog with a good temperament and conformation. And, he wanted an AKC registered pup.

He didn't harbor any concerns about the conditions of the parents or the puppies, so he bought Max for $300.

Dodie gave him a copy of a "Displasia [sic] Agreement," Max's pedigree, an AKC registration form, and Photostat copies of pictures of Max's parents. John understood that the Labrador breed had hip dysplasia issues and a stubborn temperament but didn't know about the breed's other genetic problems.

The agreement explained that "a good deal of responsibility in preventing canine hip dysplasia lies [with] the puppy's new owner. Recent studies indicate as much as 60% of all dysplasia cases are environmentally, not hereditarily caused." It emphasized the importance of keeping the puppy in proper weight, avoiding jogging or running, or allowing jumping down from high places.

Dodie agreed to replace Max with another puppy if OFA found his hips to be dysplastic based on x-rays taken between twenty-four and twenty-seven months and written proof that a reputable veterinarian had neutered him. But John couldn't return him.

The agreement was good for three years from the date of sale. It lacked any reference to eye issues, such as PRA. On the bottom of the agreement, Dodie wrote Max's breed, sex, color, date of birth, and AKC litter number. Dodie and John both signed the December 20, 1990 agreement.

The proud new owner then drove home with his nearly six-week-old puppy even though most breeders wouldn't have sent puppies to new homes at such a tender age.

John registered "the king of the litter" as Killkenny's Maximilian with the AKC. The king's proud owner learned that his spirited, healthy bundle of fur liked to chew. Max ate a hole through a wall in a downstairs room where he stayed while John was at work.

Several months later, Max moved outdoors to a run with a heated dog house because John thought his new ward should live outside to become a good hunting dog in the winter. Max's coat would grow thick and his nose wouldn't be affected by the many smells inside a home.

John realized that his six-month-old puppy was a hardhead, so he hired a trainer in nearby Elizabeth to teach some obedience to Max. The exuberant pup stayed with the trainer three days before John picked him up. John and Max returned to the trainer twice a week for the next three months. The trainer first worked Max before John took over under the trainer's supervision. The pup learned to sit, down, stay, and come within a couple of weeks.

Max's proud owner also tried to train him to retrieve to hand. After John threw a dummy, his boy would gallop out, stop just long enough to pick it up, and then run back toward John but sit just out of his master's reach. When John stepped forward, Max backed up far enough so his master couldn't grab the dummy. "It was a game to him." The game continued in the water. Max retrieved the dummy but didn't quite deliver it to land or John's hand.

He noticed a wanderlust look in Max's eyes when he gave a command. He realized that he was taking away a level of freedom and choice from his boy. Once released, Max galloped around with such pure exhilaration and glee that John knew his dog just wanted to be free.

After a promotion, John, a bachelor, traveled more extensively on business and had much less time for Max. He considered finding Max a new home because he knew his dog was happiest when he ran in fields. By mid-1994, he didn't know what was worse: knowing Max was penned up so much of the time or thinking about giving him up.

Three months later, John told an old hunting friend and his Castle Rock vet that he wanted to find someone to adopt Max. He knew he wouldn't allow his boy to join the ranks of millions of shelter dogs.

Instead he sought a home where Max could retrieve and swim or run free. John interviewed a couple of families, but they weren't a good fit for the king.

CHAPTER 7

Equine Love Affair

A chance meeting with a horse breeder edged Dodie closer to a third venture: raising horses. That happened in 1984 when Carol Mayberry, who bred Arabian as well as part-Arabian pinto horses, stopped by Dodie's studio after she noticed a pottery-for-sale sign. The two women quickly discovered their shared interest in the arts and horses. Carol, who owned about seventeen horses, rode Western and exhibited her young registered equines in halter classes. Dodie owned Witchy Blue, the part-thoroughbred, and Meriah, a powerfully built registered quarter horse.[1]

The two women also had dogs in common. Carol competed with several of her Pembroke Welsh corgis in the conformation ring and bred an occasional litter as a hobby. Dodie, who supplemented her potter's income with puppy sales, considered herself an expert dog breeder.

Dodie took a particular interest in her new friend's black and white pintos when she toured the thirty-five-acre ranch where Carol lived with her parents. She quizzed Carol about the horse breeding business after she learned that her new friend made money by breeding three or four mares a year and selling foals and yearlings. Carol shared what she knew. During their next visit, Dodie announced that she just started breeding paints and handed Carol a "Passion for Paints" business card. Dodie thought Arabians were "too hot-headed and flighty" and preferred a taller, lankier breed for jumping. And, she apparently believed that she could make money raising and selling horses.

To the general public, pinto and paint horses appear the same. Both have spots or splotches of color. They originated in Europe, coming to America in 1519 when Spanish explorer Hernando Cortez sailed to the New World with horses, including one described as a pinto with "white stockings" on his forefeet. Three centuries later, herds of spotted horses roamed the western plains. The Comanche Indians reportedly favored these painted or spotted horses.

The main distinction between pintos and paints is lineage. A registered pinto must have specific coloring but can be most any breed. However, the American Paint Horse Association (APHA) only registers paints produced by parents registered with APHA, the American Quarter Horse Association, or the Jockey Club (thoroughbreds). They also must have a "definite natural paint marking," including fairly specific patterns on their heads and legs as well as a certain amount of white. Colors of paint horses vary and include black with white as well as chestnut, dark bay, buckskin, or palomino, all with white.

Dodie felt drawn to paints because of her long-standing affinity for thoroughbreds. She still dreamed of breeding thoroughbreds but settled for the less expensive paints. Paints generally commanded a higher price than pintos because of their required lineage. Her foundation paint horse stock descended from the sorrel-colored Meriah and two other APHA mares.

But Dodie didn't just breed horses; she enjoyed riding. On occasion, she and Stanlyn Johnston, who lived with her husband just west of a hog farm bordering Dodie's property, rode their horses around the neighborhood. Brought up in the rodeo world, Stanlyn never had met anyone like Dodie. She noticed that Dodie dressed up for their neighborhood rides and readied her horse just so. Nothing was simple for Dodie. But then, Stanlyn remembered, Dodie was raised around horse show people.

Stanlyn learned more about her new friend during chats over tea in Dodie's home. She sensed Dodie hadn't wanted a divorce from her first husband, Fred. But Dodie seemed very happy, very much into her pottery and dogs, and "knew where she was going."[2]

However, Dodie expressed her disgust with "how backward the Loveland people were" after the community failed to turn out for a gathering, complete with wine, to watch a woodcarver cut a face into a large old tree in her front yard. Her friend was ahead of her time, Stanlyn thought, and wanted more "culture," museums, art shops, and the like. But that wasn't Loveland in the '80s. A Loveland native, Stanlyn saw the town as pretty much comprised of retirees.

Dodie bred for black and white registered paint foals that could sell for $1,000 or more. Solid-colored foals commanded $200 to $800 and could be registered only as breeding stock. The sales price of paint foals depended on not only color but also lineage and the breeder.

Local black and white paints' stud fees ranged from $250 to $400, less than some other breeds, primarily because of the difficulty in producing colored foals. Dodie planned to sell some foals and keep others to raise and train as jumpers before she sold them at higher prices.

To maintain her horses in style, she'd constructed a ten-stall, nice-looking stable complete with a tack room by 1987. That same spring, she bred three paint mares to a black and white stallion. The breedings produced only solid-colored foals the following year. Repeat breedings in 1988 also failed to produce the treasured black and white foals.

———

Just as Stanlyn sensed, Dodie missed Fred. En route to Nebraska in the summer of 1988 to sell pottery, she drove miles out of her way to drop in on him in downtown Cheyenne as he renovated the historic Victorian Nagle mansion.

Fred noticed Dodie's white lacey top and short skirt. She'd pulled her bleached blonde hair back into a ponytail and a few curls framed her face. Although a bit heavy, she looked in good physical shape and took pride in her appearance. He hadn't seen or spoken to her for nearly two years since he'd dropped by her farm.

Dodie looked at Fred's black Labrador.

"Your dog's conformation isn't very good," she said. Fred knew she bred Labradors and sensed that she was trying to ascertain if he wanted another dog. He didn't.

Dodie mentioned arthritis in one of her hands and showed him the pottery that she had brought. Fred complimented her wares.

Over lunch, Dodie asked about Fred's father, who had died earlier that year, and mentioned that her father had passed away.

"I'm sorry to hear that," Fred said.

"Well, I really didn't know my dad really well anyway."

Her comment struck him. When did she lose her connection with her dad, or was her statement just a defense mechanism to deal with her father's death? he wondered. He knew that she thought her father was overly religious and believed that she would have respected him more had he stood up to her mother, who ran the show.

Dodie mentioned a previous violent relationship that ended poorly and asked how Fred was doing. He replied that he was happily involved with a neighbor. Dodie choked up and launched into reasons why their marriage failed.

Although fiercely independent, Dodie seemed to want a man in her life. After Carol Mayberry married in 1988, she sensed that Dodie's attitude toward her changed.

Carol didn't have to worry about "this or that" now that she was married and had someone to take care of her, Dodie said. The two women managed to remain friends and often discussed dogs.

Dodie bragged about her Labradors. She labeled corgis, Carol's chosen breed, a joke, and asked why Carol didn't buy a Labrador, a very popular breed. Labradors ranked as the second most popular AKC breed in 1988, surpassed only by the cocker spaniel.

Carol noticed dogs in every nook and cranny of the backyard during her final visit to Dodie's farm. The Labrador population had grown dramatically, and the canines' conditions weren't as clean as previously. Over the years, she'd occasionally cared for Dodie's animals when her friend traveled to art and craft shows. She didn't know if the current amount of feces represented a daily or accumulated amount but believed that Dodie was working "her tail off." As she surveyed the farm, she saw many more horses than on previous visits. Dodie had gone into breeding horses "in too big a way"; she had "too many, too soon" for one person to handle. Their friendship continued over the phone and when Dodie stopped by Carol's home.

As Carol distanced herself from her longtime friend, and Stanlyn and her husband moved to Oklahoma, Dodie befriended a second neighbor, Lisa Dickens. She occasionally invited Lisa for an early morning breakfast of scones and champagne at her home. Dodie's property reminded Lisa of quaint old New England homes, surrounded by overgrown trees, bushes, and wildflowers. Lisa perceived her neighbor as a very strong-willed and opinionated woman who loved to debate.[3] At times, they rode their horses together around the neighborhood.

Dodie asked Lisa to feed her animals when she infrequently traveled to craft fairs. Dodie paid Lisa in cash, or cash and some of her pottery. Lisa accepted Dodie's gift of Tilly, a young, light-yellow Labrador, built like a tank, that her friend didn't want to add to her "breeding program." But Lisa returned Tilly after the Labrador and her other canines became a pack. Dodie sold Tilly for $50 to a family with children.

Thoroughbred horses remained Dodie's true passion. In 1991, she bought a seven-year-old retired racehorse and called him London Fog. He'd been sold in 1988 for $7,500. Dodie told Dr. Culver that she'd been able to buy the gelding because most people couldn't ride him. She quickly taught the 16.2 hand thoroughbred to jump.

That fall she entered London Fog in the Arapahoe Hunt horse show, hunter trials and pace event in Larkspur. The following year, she again entered him, as well as Meriah, her quarter horse mare, in the event.

Dodie dressed up for these events. She wore a red hunting cap and gloves, a red top with a yellow scarf, black breeches, and English black leather boots, plus spurs. But her dress and horses failed to make her accepted by the hunt and horse show groups.

"They're just money people; I'm just a country girl," she lamented to her twin James.

He recognized that his sister wanted to be a "privileged, unique country person" who bred horses without earning that status. She felt entitled, but he didn't know why. He also thought their mother felt entitled and "always had sort of a resentment of people that had big, big money." Maybe that had worn off on Dodie, he wondered years later. Unlike Dodie, their mother hadn't dwelt on those feelings.

James noticed his sister became more reclusive and more content to just deal with animals that gave her unconditional love. She never seemed satisfied and always wanted to buy a horse better than the one she'd just purchased. Some Sundays she'd pack a lunch and drive to the mountains to take pictures of houses for sale as she searched for a better home and life.

CHAPTER 8

Juggling Act

To maintain her lifestyle and fund her obsession with horses, Dodie juggled her time and finances among three businesses: puppies, equines, and pottery. Although she cut back on selling pottery at art and craft shows and increased her equine population, she fortuitously expanded her puppy business in sync with the rise of the popularity of the family-friendly Labrador retriever. Labradors became the AKC's most popular breed in 1991.

At the same time, she started to make misrepresentations about her dogs, perhaps innocently at first, but later apparently to bolster their worth.

And, her spending habits continued: buying what she wanted, sometimes purchasing with credit and not always paying bills.

In 1990 she treated herself to some fun toys, all purchased on credit: a 19-inch TV, a VCR, a mid range-priced stereo, golf clubs, a bike, ski equipment, upscale Gibson guitars, and camera equipment. Just two years later, she'd racked up more than $1,000 in court judgments by failing to pay bills.

Then came more bad news: Trimble Court's directors threatened to close the store where Dodie retailed much of her pottery. They'd discovered its bank accounts empty and some members' artwork, including Dodie's, missing from the shop. The cooperative owed these members payment for their stolen goods.

Several members offered to work extra hours and forgive any payment for the missing wares to keep the shop open. Dodie, who paid others to work her store hours, caught several members by surprise when she walked into the shop one morning, turned on the lights, and operated the cash register. After Trimble Court reorganized and became incorporated, Dodie opted to become a member of its board of directors.

The cooperative's potters respected Dodie's work; some thought she might have been Trimble Court's best-selling potter in the '80s and '90s. Dodie worked very hard, made large quantities of pottery, and displayed as many as eighty pieces at a time in the shop.

Fellow potters noticed a change in Dodie's appearance and demeanor from her early days at Trimble Court. Now she always rushed while she restocked her wares and paid little attention to her appearance. Dressed in jeans and a T-shirt covered with dog hair, she'd carry eighteen boxes of pottery into the cooperative's store from her van where a couple of Labradors patiently waited. She'd arrange the pottery on her display and other artists' shelves. That broke Trimble Court's cardinal rule: Don't touch another artist's display. After she left, some members "de-Dodied" the store and placed her wares back on her shelves even though she'd forbidden anyone to touch her display.[1] At times, she restocked at night when no one else was there.

Some members winced when Dodie strode into the store. They viewed her as abrasive and crabby, a loner and self-made person whom no one really liked. She was interesting but more to be feared. To others, she appeared happy and friendly. She had good business sense but rarely discussed anything personal or spent time cultivating friendships.

As her animal populations grew, Dodie spent even less time with artist friends outside of Trimble Court visits. At the cooperative, she'd talk about her dogs and how she wanted her puppies in good pet, not hunting, homes. She sold to both types of homes.

On one shelf of her pottery display, Dodie placed a photo of herself next to two Labradors as if they were her children. Fellow potter Nancy Zoller believed she loved her canines. Friends since 1981, Nancy and her husband had occasionally dropped in at Dodie's farm but never saw the inside of the farmhouse. Now the two women mostly talked on the phone about whether they should retail, wholesale, or consign their wares. Dodie had made it clear she didn't want visitors.

After she met her future husband, stained-glass artist Barbara Marcus also saw Dodie less frequently. When the friends chatted, Barbara recognized that Dodie enjoyed breeding dogs much more than her pottery business.

"Wow, this is just so much easier than selling pottery," Dodie told Barbara after she sold a puppy for $400 or $500. "She loved her dogs so much, and people gave her money for her doggies; she was in heaven about it."[2]

Dodie developed carpal tunnel caused by years of throwing clay onto the potter's wheel. She took some of her dogs' prescription medicine to ease the pain. However, the malady didn't stop her from boasting to a fellow artist that she made plenty of money and didn't need a man to support her.

Yet she'd spend on a Friday what she anticipated she'd make in Sunday puppy sales generated from her ad in the weekend newspaper, James recalled later. And the anticipated revenue usually didn't cover her expenditures.

Dodie's sales skills kept her afloat—at least for now.

———

Graphic artist Bland Nesbit snapped photographs of the five-week-old yellow puppies and captured Dodie's smile next to the head of an older, almost white pup, an obvious favorite, that she held in her arms.

Three weeks earlier in March 1992, Nesbit had driven from Aspen to look at tiny puppies in a backroom of Dodie's farmhouse after a Denver newspaper ad caught her attention. Fourteen two-week-old Labrador puppies, all yellow except for a larger chocolate, lay on blankets in a wooden whelping box. The pups and Athena, their dam and Max's, looked clean.

Most breeders wouldn't have permitted prospective buyers to visit a two-week-old litter to avoid stressing the dam and puppies, and for other health concerns. Dodie not only sanctioned Nesbit's visit but also allowed her to pick up a favorite pup. She bragged about the quality of her Labradors and boasted that McIvory, the puppies' sire, had excellent hips, even though OFA had certified them only as fair.

"I'm not gay, but I just don't like men," Dodie said in an offhand manner.[3]

The comment struck Nesbit as odd. Dodie seemed to be a loner and a bit different. But Nesbit also thought that she appeared to be a reputable, knowledgeable breeder who correctly handled the puppies, asked appropriate questions, and produced all the usual AKC papers, pedigrees, and hip clearances.

Weeks later, Dodie acted "perfectly nice" and business-like toward Nesbit's husband when the couple played with the clean, healthy, and "appropriately plump" five-week-old puppies.[4]

Nesbit fell for a cute, chunky pup that dangled her rear legs as she sat on a rock. She asked the name of a handsome light-yellow adult male that sat in a similar position. Dodie identified him as McDougal, the brother of McIvory. However, McDougal was really McIvory's son. Had Dodie intentionally misrepresented this relationship and McIvory's hip rating to make her dogs look more attractive, or had she innocently misspoken?

The couple placed a $150 deposit down for Louise, the chosen pup, and returned when she turned forty-nine days old. They paid an additional $200 and flew home with Louise, her pedigree, her parents' OFA hip clearance certificates, and a contract. A year later, Nesbit referred a good friend to Dodie, and that friend referred another friend to the breeder. The Aspenites were pleased with their mellow, friendly Killkenny Labradors. Dodie had solidified an Aspen connection.

———

Dodie recapped 1992 in an upbeat Christmas card. She highlighted hunting on London Fog, "fun" with the Labradors, and trail riding with her paints. She'd experienced the empty-nest syndrome after selling her last colt, so she bred four mares and expected foals in the spring. She characterized the Labradors as the "JOY of my life" with the moms and pups filling her days. Her "pottery biz is hanging in there," but she wished for a better economy. She hoped to expand into a line of colorful art nouveau drawings that she'd wanted to do for a long time. "As the years pass so quickly, I now realize that I better get started or it may never get done. Time management is the key to it all, but there are never enough hours in the day!"

In early 1993, Dodie asked Susan Burke to show a yellow female Labrador that she'd bought from breeder Linda Vaughn, who'd referred her. But Dodie hadn't purchased any canines from Vaughn. When Dodie decided that she couldn't afford Burke's handler fees, she inquired if she could breed her yellow's offspring, Athena, to Burke's Ch. Jess-Mor's Blue Note (Ben-Hur). The black commanded a $400 stud fee and was one of the top ten conformation winning Labradors in the United States at the time, according to Burke.[5]

Based on their discussion, Burke thought Dodie was new to Labradors and had just become interested in breeding and showing dogs. Dodie mentioned that she showed horses but deliberately failed to reveal that she'd bred any canine litters other than the one that produced Athena. By January 1, 1993, she'd bred a minimum of twenty-four Labrador litters since the late '70s as well as at least two litters each of springer spaniels and Chesapeake Bay retrievers.

Dodie paid Ben Hur's stud fee and produced Athena's clearances that Burke required: OFA hip certification, eye exam, and a negative test for brucellosis. Burke never saw any of the puppies whelped on May 1, 1993.

Gerry Hurley and his wife Jennifer did. On their second visit to Dodie's, a six-week-old black puppy from that litter followed Gerry as the young couple walked around and looked at the Labradors.

They'd first visited to consider buying Dodie's main yellow stud dog, McIvory, because Gerry sought an AKC adult Lab so he could join a hunt club. Dodie wanted to sell McIvory because she said the four-year-old dog fought all the time with his son, McDougal. The couple didn't see any fighting. Instead, both canines, in their adjacent, eight-by-four-foot outside pens, sat quietly and just watched them. McDougal, with a very broad head and extremely light-yellow fur, looked taller than his father. McIvory appeared thin but clean from a recent bath and took to Jennifer.

Dodie invited the Hurleys into her farmhouse's mudroom where she opened the lid to an enclosed wooden bench, too small for an adult dog. The couple peered inside and saw tiny puppies.

"Do you think they can get enough oxygen?" asked an alarmed Jennifer, a nurse.[6]

"Oh, yes."

The dogs appeared to live in "pretty clean" conditions, the couple thought as they scrutinized the mudroom and kitchen.

They bought McIvory for $300, a hundred dollars less than the asking price, and after Dodie agreed to have him neutered.

On the way home, Gerry joked about the "puppy farm." They'd seen dozens of Labrador puppies: black, chocolate, and yellow, ranging from white to fox red. Jennifer corrected him; there weren't any puppy farms.

But there were puppy mills. According to the ASPCA, some characteristics of puppy mills include dogs housed in "overcrowded and unsanitary conditions without adequate veterinary care, food, water or socialization." Puppy mill breeders usually don't meet prospective buyers in person but often sell "directly to pet stores, at flea markets or swap meets, and over the internet or through newspaper ads."[7]

———

Gerry fell for the black puppy when the couple returned weeks later to pick up McIvory. Dodie identified the pup's dam Athena incorrectly as McIvory's sister. Had Dodie once again misspoken or purposely misidentified the dam as part of a sales pitch because the Hurleys had fallen for McIvory? The couple negotiated a $450 price for the $600 pup that they named Murphy and agreed to pick him up when he was old enough to leave his littermates.

They drove off with McIvory, assorted pedigrees, and his OFA "fair" hip certificate. On one pedigree, Dodie had upgraded the OFA hip ratings for three dogs, including McIvory. The changes appeared deliberate because she'd only listed a partial number LR-41316 instead of OFA's full registry number, LR-41316F29M, for McIvory. The F indicated a fair rating, 29 referred to McIvory's age in months at the time of the x-rays, and M designated his gender.

McIvory refused to eat and drink at his new home and breathed heavily in the hot weather. The Hurleys' veterinarian discovered the dog's neutering incision was infected and his throat had scar tissue from one, possibly two, debarkings.

Although well-mannered and gentle, McIvory feared men, including Gerry. His new owners learned that he only felt comfortable in his crate, so they purchased a much larger one and set it outside to encourage him to explore their yard. At first, he didn't.

When the couple telephoned for suggestions on handling McIvory, Dodie explained that he feared men because her ex-husband had thrown him down stairs. They didn't know that she'd divorced her second husband three and a half years before McIvory came into this world. Dodie sent a follow-up note encouraging them to play ball or Frisbee. "The more you play with him—the quicker he'll forget his past!"

In early July, the Hurleys picked up puppy Murphy along with his AKC registration form and other documents with the pup's lineage. Dodie had penned in Fld. CH. (field trial champion) after the name of his granddam Charmin' even though the dog hadn't earned that title. Had Dodie added the title because she knew Gerry was interested in hunting?

Murphy's hip guarantee was much more limited than Max's. Dodie no longer guaranteed that the pup's hips would pass OFA certification. Instead, she'd decide if he'd be replaced by a puppy of equal value provided that Dr. Culver x-rayed him and found him "so severely dysplastic as to be lame for life and not able to function as a hunting or otherwise active dog." This guarantee was good for two years from the date of sale; Max's hips were guaranteed to be dysplasia-free for three years. Consistent with Max's contract, Dodie didn't guarantee Murphy for any other genetic disorder, including elbow dysplasia or PRA.

Although Dodie discussed the hip clearances of McIvory and Murphy's parents with the Hurleys, she failed to disclose that Montgomery, McIvory's sire, was a PRA carrier. When his owner, Linda Vaughn, made that discovery in 1990, she immediately notified Dodie and all other owners of females that had been bred to Montgomery of his carrier status. She also sent an article that explained PRA and immediately retired her stud dog.

———

Dodie applied the strategy to her horse business that she'd used during the early days of breeding dogs: occasionally buying quality animals and breeding her stock to animals owned by reputable breeders.

When she met Shirley Gonzales, owner of the Circle S Painted Acres Ranch south of Berthoud, Dodie realized that they shared the goal of selling black and white paints with regular spotting patterns, known as tobianos. At the time, tobianos commanded the highest price among paints.

"You've got cowboy horses," Dodie said.[8]

Shirley surmised that Dodie acted a bit haughty and snobby because her new acquaintance rode English, and she rode Western. She thought English riders believed they were a bit better than Western riders. But Dodie turned friendly and trusting once the two became better acquainted.

Dodie purchased a colt sired by one of Shirley's stallions, Nuestro Peso, for about $2,500 after she learned that he consistently produced black and white offspring. By then she owned at least six mares, several foals, and her prized thoroughbred gelding, London Fog.

Her horse population and related expenses grew. Equine care wasn't cheap. Dodie fed hay to all her horses and grain to London Fog and a couple of mares to keep weight on them. Her equines needed a variety of vaccinations twice a year, pregnant mares more often; shoeing or hoof trim every six to eight weeks; and annual teeth care as well as unexpected veterinarian visits. She incurred other expenses including upkeep on her barn, fences, truck, and horse trailer; new bridles, saddles, and saddle pads; jumps, leg wrappings, brushes, and curries; and stud fees as well as entry fees and attire for horse shows. Given her propensity for fine clothing and tack, her total equine costs before unexpected veterinarian expenses easily could have totaled $30,000 to $40,000 in 1993.[9]

As her equine costs grew, Dodie "pushed the pencil a little closer" on dog-related expenses. Dr. Culver noticed that her client's joy about new puppies dissipated as she bred more; puppies became just puppies. "It's a dollar bill laying there, several hundred dollars' worth of bills laying there." That wasn't unusual, Dr. Culver recalled later, as "it happens to all the dog breeders."

CHAPTER 9

Mr. Personality

D ave and I hadn't considered how much we wouldn't know about
Max when he joined our family in January 1995. We'd never
adopted a puppy, much less a full-grown dog, and hadn't thought
about whether his breeder, Dodie Cariaso, had spent any time social-
izing Max and his littermates before they went to new homes. We
learned from John that our new unhousebroken dependent had some
obedience and field training. He'd given us Max's pedigree, a breeder's
sales contract, vaccination records, and training facility documents.

Max took only a couple of weeks to housebreak. My Sorel boots
fell victim to his jaws but were still wearable. Our furniture remained
intact. Max appeared clueless about toys. Molly quickly introduced
him to the joy of chewing Nylabones.

My parents bred, raised, and showed Labradors in the conformation ring for more than forty years, so I had specific ideas about the
looks of the ideal Labrador. Max didn't fit that image. He was a bit
light on bone; had a straight front shoulder, a longer back, and
narrower head than desired; and ambled when he trotted. His
temperament was tops: happy and loving toward other dogs and
people. We were unconcerned about his hyperactive behavior because
we thought he'd settle down with time. He just wasn't the perfect mate
for Molly, who had a lovely blocky head, a short-coupled body, a thick
coat with a dense undercoat, and an otter tail. She needed a mate
with better front movement, beefier hindquarters, and a personality
like Max's.

Dave deferred to my desire for a better-looking stud for Molly. We
made Max's emasculation appointment quickly because Molly was

due to come into heat in February. Max quickly recovered from his surgery, and Molly came in season soon after.

She didn't show any interest in Max until about ten to twelve days into her heat cycle. Then she fell totally in love, and, much to our surprise, Max fell totally in love with her. Soon they tried their best to have a litter of puppies. To put it succinctly, Molly was the horniest female dog that I had ever seen. After they completed their love ritual, Molly seduced Max over and over again until he neared exhaustion.

Alarmed, I called our vet's office to verify that Molly couldn't get pregnant. Did the vet successfully neuter Max? Yes, nothing could happen, came the reply.

Nothing happened except that Molly and Max had a great time. Molly made Max understand about a week later that she was no longer interested in his advances. The tryst began anew six months later when she came into heat. We knew that Molly would be a willing partner with the approved stud.

Dave and I quickly learned that Max was a people pleaser. His nonthreatening manner and medium yellow color won over non-dog and dog lovers alike. People forgave his indiscretions.

During his first spring with us, I readied Molly to compete for her Companion Dog degree. My friend Patty also wanted her golden retriever, Savannah, Molly's best friend, to earn the same obedience title. One Sunday, Patty invited us to her south Parker home so that we could walk to a match (practice show) at the nearby equestrian grounds. Dave was away on business, so Patty agreed that our new adoptee could stay with her husband and children while we girls competed.

After Molly and Savannah finished their class, we meandered back to Patty's house, enjoying the warm, sunny day. Max greeted us at the front door and jumped up and down as he furiously wagged his tail. Dirk, Patty's husband, smiled. Days later I learned that Max had become very nervous in our absence and eliminated in the house. I apologized profusely. Patty just passed it off as one of those things that dogs sometimes do. Of course, her kind husband had cleaned up Max's indiscretion well before we arrived back at their home.

Six months after he joined our family, Max still refused to lie down when we watched television in the family room after dinner. Molly ignored him and slept in a dog bed. The intensity of Max's after-dinner vigil had lessened, but he still stood with a goofy expression on his face, wagged his tail, and eyed us about a foot from the couch. We chalked up his behavior to being overly happy as a housedog.

One night, Dave studied Max's face as he popped open a can of Coors beer. Max vehemently wagged his tail and edged closer.

"Do you think he likes beer?" Dave asked.

"Maybe," I said. Max licked his chops.

"Well, let's find out."

Dave retrieved a bowl from the kitchen. He poured a small amount of Coors into the bowl and placed it before Max. The contents were gone in seconds! Dave poured a little more beer. Max happily slurped it up and then stared at Dave. His brown eyes pleaded for more. Our adopted dog was an alcoholic or would be if we allowed him as much beer as he wanted. So began the after-dinner ritual of Dave and Max sharing a Coors.

Another household tradition commenced at Christmas. Each Christmas morning, I placed a wrapped can of Coors among the other dog and human gifts under the tree. Molly, a teetotaler, sniffed for food. Max methodically smelled and nudged each package until he pawed one, his can of beer. In consideration of his liver, we allowed him a full can of beer only on Christmas and at a rare party with two-legged drinking partners.

Max's propensity for beer became common knowledge among my husband's business associates. Two of Dave's Kansas City friends, in Colorado for a business convention, drove to our home for a beer party hosted by Max. They appeared skeptical that the yellow Labrador loved beer. Tom was fifty-one and about six foot three, with an emerging beer belly. Pete was a bit shorter and slimmer, and a couple of years older than Tom. Neither had met Molly or Max.

Beer flowed continuously as Tom and Pete enjoyed our view of Pikes Peak. We ate dinner at the picnic table on our deck. Max and Molly lay down a few feet away. Tom periodically bellowed commands to the dogs. He thought they would pay more attention to him if he spoke louder and louder. Simply put, he wasn't a dog person, nor was he used to being around canines. The dogs increasingly ignored his commands and watched him eat dinner. But Max sat up and stared harder when Tom drank beer.

Dave had bought quite the microbrew stash. When dinner ended and the serious drinking began, our guests offered a drop or two of their beer to Max. Then they shared more than a few drops.

I had no idea when the party ended because Molly and I retired hours earlier. I had to work the next day. Max stayed behind to drink and bond with the three human males under the stars away from the city lights. The next morning, Molly, Max, and I awakened to start the new day. Max greeted the morning with his usual exuberance and showed no signs of a hangover.

Another night during that same business convention, Dave invited over his friend Walt and his two sons, ages ten and thirteen, for a cookout. Soon bored with grown-up talk, the two boys ran around our fenced-in backyard. I handed them an old football.

From the deck, Max watched the boys toss the football to each other until he couldn't contain himself. He joined in the fun and tried to snag the football whenever the boys missed a pass. Then the real game began. Max grabbed the ball and ran off as far away as possible. He played keep-away until one of the youngsters caught him and only then reluctantly gave up the ball. He'd pant and wag his tail as he waited for another round of keep-away, which inevitably occurred.

Max also interacted kindly with other dogs. Our Franktown neighbors adopted a cockapoo named Jingles. He looked like a rat with curly fur, yapped at other dogs, had one or two teeth left in his mouth, and thought he was mighty even though he only weighed eight pounds at most. His owner, Dean, a lean six foot four, liked to walk his tiny dog up and down the dirt road past our driveway. One day, Dave and Max looked up from their front yard chores and spied the pair walking down the road. They sauntered down the driveway to greet them.

Jingles galloped down the road toward Max. Our boy had grown tired of the antics of the yapping, growling puff of fur, so he left Dave's side and cantered right through the mighty dog, rolling him over. Jingles looked a bit dazed when he stood up. Max wagged his tail and then trotted past him to greet Dean.

So began the friendship of Max and Jingles. After that, whenever Jingles spied Max, he'd trot hesitantly toward him. Max, in turn, would trot over to sniff him but never again rolled over the little dog. He might have taught Jingles a valuable life lesson: don't mess with the big boys.

Max also gave me the tools to work more effectively as a civil defense attorney. During one employment lawsuit, my co-counsel and I found ourselves at extreme odds with the plaintiff's attorney. We simply couldn't communicate during numerous depositions in the Denver area. The next deposition was scheduled in Billings, Montana, where one of the defendants lived. I flew there the day before the deposition to prepare him while my co-counsel remained in Denver to save on costs.

I felt hostility ooze from my opposing counsel when my client and I stepped into the small deposition room. He was ready to pounce on my client. The morning went as I expected, sparring by both sides.

Long before the Billings deposition, I'd learned never to talk to one's client about anything relating to the case in front of opposing counsel. During the morning break, I chose a benign topic to discuss with my client. We stood within earshot of the court reporter and opposing counsel.

"A storefront sign, 'Max for Senate,' caught my attention as I walked over from my hotel this morning. It gave me clarity as to which candidate I will vote for in Colorado's US Senate race," I joked. "Max, our yellow Labrador, is the perfect candidate!"

At the time, I didn't know that veterinarian Wayne Allard, the Republican candidate who would go on to win the 1996 Senate election, had once employed Dr. Culver, Dodie's vet.

Fortunately, my client knew of my fondness for dogs. The deposition resumed and continued until noon when both sides went their separate ways.

After the noon hour break, opposing counsel walked into the deposition room and handed me a pin, "Max for Senate." He'd picked it up from the candidate's office on his way back from lunch. I smiled and thanked him. We joked together, probably for the first time.

At the deposition's conclusion, my client informed me of his previously scheduled dinner commitment. I realized that I was on my own. I disliked eating by myself, so I invited opposing counsel to dinner, Dutch treat. He also was alone in Billings.

He looked surprised, hesitated, and then accepted. We had a pleasant dinner and discovered that we had mutual friends. The case settled amicably within a couple of months. I thanked Max, our Killkenny dog, for breaking the ice.

CHAPTER 10

Risky Business

Dodie worked hard to become a successful horse breeder but risked damaging her primary source of income—puppy sales— when she rejected some of her canine veterinarian's advice and failed to obtain health clearances for her breeding stock. These and other dicey decisions threatened the revenue needed to support her horse business.

In 1993, Kristen Everhart asked the owners of a handsome yellow Labrador for his breeder's name when she spotted the dog outside the Wheeler Opera House in Aspen. She thought the canine looked a bit different from "American" Labradors because he appeared shorter and stouter. These "type" Labs had fewer health problems, she'd heard.[1] She wanted an AKC puppy to have an idea of what the dog might look like as an adult and thought a canine from good lines had a better chance of good health.

The twenty-five-year-old called Dodie, who immediately interviewed her. Did she and her husband have children? Did they own their own home? Had they had pets, and how long had the animals lived? How much would they exercise their puppy?[2]

Dodie's questions impressed Everhart because she'd learned from her Minnesota grandparents, who had bred and competed with their golden retrievers, what a reputable breeder should ask. Dodie assured her that the puppies' parents had eye and hip clearances and guaranteed the puppies' hips.

Everhart asked about problems with parvo, a highly contagious and often fatal viral disease to puppies. Dodie said she hadn't had any issues and cautioned that a dam with the disease could transmit it to her puppies.

Everhart felt comfortable. The breeder appeared knowledgeable, reputable, and very concerned about where her puppies would live. She also knew that her neighbors raved about the pup that they'd purchased from Dodie, so she mailed a deposit for a yellow female puppy to the breeder.

That summer Dodie battled parvo after a prospective puppy buyer brought the malady onto her property. Puppies became stricken with parvo at about five to six weeks of age because their dams didn't have enough immunity to give them. Vaccines at the time weren't good enough to ward off the disease.

Dr. Culver treated Dodie's and another breeder's parvo-diseased puppies, but many were lost over several months. She tried different treatments, cared for some of the puppies in her hospital, and treated many as outpatients at their respective kennels because of the numbers involved. The veterinarian instructed the breeders to mix some of diarrhea from one of the surviving puppies that didn't get "real sick" with the adult females' food. Once these adults digested this food mixture, their immunity to parvo was boosted. Pregnant dams, in turn, gave "very good immunity" to the puppies when born. Dodie rejected the vet's advice; the solution was too gross.

"Quit breeding for a while. Let's get this thing under control," Dr. Culver said. Don't take your dogs off of your place and "be real careful" if you "breed to outside dogs."

Dodie turned to others for help. She telephoned Carol Mayberry-Sanchez, her horse and corgi friend, and cried as she talked about the parvo outbreak and loss of puppies. She called a Lab Club member to purchase disinfectant for her kennels. Dodie battled the parvo outbreak for about six months and lost forty to sixty puppies, Dr. Culver recalled later.

Dodie ushered Everhart and her husband into her farmhouse when they arrived to choose their new eight-week-old family member. She reviewed the health clearances of the puppies' parents and explained why she thought one of the puppies would be the best fit but left the choice to them.

They walked outside to an area that appeared to be a nursery. Dodie handed a disinfectant spray bottle to the couple. She asked that they spray their hands and shoes before they stepped into the middle portion of the nursery, where three yellow puppies romped on clean cedar shavings. She undoubtedly took these precautions to kill parvo or other germs.

The couple played with the puppies and saw the black dam. When they asked to meet the litter's sire, Dodie brought McDougal into the general area but didn't allow him near the puppies.

Everhart fell in love with the pup that Dodie had recommended. The puppy had a bit of lighter fur on her shoulders, like "angel wings," and appeared playful but then calmly lay on her back for a tummy rub. Everhart thought she'd be athletic, which was important because the couple hiked in the mountains around Aspen.

She looked at Dodie and saw a hardworking farm woman with a very pleasant and cheery smile, who called the pups' dam momma. She trusted her.

The couple selected the "angel wings" puppy and named her Wheeler after the opera house. They paid the remainder of the $600 sales price in cash and drove the pup home.

Everhart immediately took Wheeler for a vet examination. The pup received a clean bill of health. At Wheeler's next appointment, the veterinarian asked where the couple had purchased her and then suggested that they keep an eye on her hips. Everhart, still in "puppy mommy glory," didn't become alarmed with his "light, cautionary advice."

At another appointment, Everhart mentioned that Wheeler didn't gait normally or act as frisky as she expected. Was she overreacting and seeing things?

The veterinarian disclosed what he'd feared: Wheeler had bilateral hip dysplasia. The nine-month-old puppy might need hip surgery sometime during the next three and a half years. He'd seen a number of dogs with elbow and hip dysplasia from the kennel of Wheeler's breeder.

"Oh great," a surprised Everhart responded.

She picked up the phone and called Dodie. "I am calling you because I need to talk about my puppy."

"Okay," Dodie replied.

"I have to report what my vet is telling me about this dog." She told Dodie the pup had hip dysplasia.

"I've never had a problem."

"I am really upset. You told me these dogs had good hips." She reminded Dodie that she had given them a guarantee of sorts. "My vet told me that a couple of the dogs you bred you know had hip and elbow problems. I'm going to have to provide surgery later for her in life."

"I get my dogs tested; I've got the certifications," Dodie said.

"I don't know what you think you are certifying; you clearly have dogs with dysplasia," Everhart responded, angry and upset.

"You can get them certified, but there is still a percentage that something could happen."

"Dodie, that may have worked a few months ago, and now I am so educated now on this." She told Dodie that she was "a horrible person . . . you are affecting families . . . in about five years I'll have this little girl and I [will] have this crippled dog. You know that is going to be horrible," the now pregnant Everhart retorted.[3]

"Bring back the puppy, and I'll give you another one," Dodie said.

Everhart demanded a refund and money toward Wheeler's medical expenses.

"If you have a problem, bring the puppy back, and I'll give you another one," Dodie repeated. She refused to give a refund or funds for Wheeler's medical expenses.

Everhart wouldn't give up the pup; she was too attached. Wheeler wasn't a piece of furniture that could be returned. She vowed to do everything in her power to stop Dodie from breeding. Aspen was a small community.

She called the oldest dog registry in this country—the AKC— whose mission is to "advocate for the purebred dog as a family companion, advance canine health and well-being, work to protect the rights of all dog owners and promote responsible dog ownership."[4] Everhart hoped the AKC would act if enough puppy buyers reported dysplasia problems. A representative advised her to put her complaint in writing. She did but never heard back.

Everhart carefully monitored Wheeler and took her only on short walks. She and her husband carried her upstairs to sleep at the foot of their bed.

About a year after she bought Wheeler, Everhart discovered that her neighbors' yellow, male Labrador, also purchased from Dodie, had started to have problems before she'd bought her pup. He had elbow dysplasia. She wished she had talked more to his owners before she contacted Dodie.

Everhart's disclosure of Wheeler's hip dysplasia meant that Dodie now knew that McDougal was a hip dysplasia carrier. He'd produce dysplastic pups if bred to another carrier or dysplastic mate. She'd have to stop breeding him to be sure that he wouldn't produce any dysplastic puppies. Instead, she continued to use him as her main yellow stud dog.

The same summer that the Everharts purchased Wheeler, Dodie told Susan Burke that she was interested in getting into chocolates and wanted a show quality chocolate puppy. She neglected to mention that she had a chocolate stud dog and just the year before purchased a female chocolate puppy whose parents didn't have OFA hip clearances or any known eye certifications.

In July, during the parvo outbreak at her kennel, Dodie deposited $100 with Burke for a chocolate puppy expected to be born in late August. She also bred one of her females to Burke's chocolate show dog and paid the $400 stud fee.

Months later, Dodie paid Burke an additional $400 and brought home the pick-of-the-litter male puppy. Burke gave a written hip dysplasia guarantee. If OFA found the dog's hips dysplastic based on x-rays taken by the age of thirty months, she offered another puppy upon proof the dysplastic dog was neutered. Burke also retained the first right to buy back the dog, a provision lacking in any version of Dodie's puppy contracts.

Although Dodie lessened any contact with her artist friends and dog breeder acquaintances, she still found time several times a year for visits from her twin James. A divorced James had moved to the Denver area and celebrated Thanksgiving at times with her. Their mother as well as younger brother Doug and his family now lived in California. Dodie saw Doug and his family when they traveled to Colorado for ski vacations and other visits. But the family and extended family gatherings remained a bit tense. No one ever knew when Dodie would explode about something in the news or someone she didn't like.

The family knew that Dodie lived in her own world and found it difficult to operate within the norms of society. Kathleen, Doug's wife, observed that Dodie had a "great work ethic" and "when she was good, she was good and when she wasn't, boy, she wasn't." And Dodie was very self-centered.

But Dodie remained the saleswoman when she met prospective puppy buyers even though her canines' living conditions weren't as pristine as they once had been. At times, potential customers, including Barbara Shoemaker, felt taken aback by those conditions.[5]

Shoemaker felt her hair stand on end as she saw way too many dogs in way too small an area. She gaped at the horde of puppies in pens and cages, some with their dams, others without them, all in a covered patio area. Adult Labradors watched from crates stacked on top of each other on that November 1993 day.

The extremely overweight puppies probably didn't get exercise, but the dogs looked fairly healthy. There really isn't a reason not to buy a puppy but . . . , Shoemaker thought. She and her husband settled on an eight-week-old chocolate puppy and drove home to Wyoming. The sweet, happy, energetic puppy slimmed down to become Shoemaker's hiking partner.

Dodie continued to breed as many dogs as she pleased because the county didn't check her numbers, which far exceeded that allowed by her kennel permit. At the same time, she continued her quest to produce black and white paints and bred several mares to Nuestro Peso, Shirley Gonzales's stallion. She built a second horse barn to accommodate her growing equine population and bred her mares each year or every other year. If the breedings were timed correctly, some mares conceived every year.

Her confidence in her horse business grew when she was offered $8,000 for a black and white paint that she'd bought as a colt from Shirley and trained for hunter-jumper classes. Shirley warned her that one didn't make money breeding horses. Although Shirley more than broke even, she had a steady clientele with her foal sales, boarding facility, and stallion stud service. She'd bred for years, and she and her father were well known in the paint horse circles. Dodie didn't have those connections, reputation, or exposure to the public. Shirley wondered if Dodie thought that she made more money than she did because of her large home and property. Shirley's masonry contractor husband supported their lifestyle.

Raised in the paint horse business, Shirley understood the importance of selling foals just after they were weaned. Otherwise a breeder faced the high overhead costs of feeding, training, and generally caring for the foals for two and a half more years before they'd be salable again. It was better to sell low or even give young horses away to avoid these costs, she advised. But Dodie chose not to listen. Instead, she failed to consider what people would pay and didn't change her mind when she decided how much to charge for her horses.

Dodie used her artistic talent to promote her equines. She designed colored flyers to advertise her "sport horses, bred for competitive English riders" and asked thousands of dollars for solids and paints of color other than black and whites. Her prices reflected her stock's age and training. She overpriced her horses and sold mostly foals. The limited sales failed to deter her from searching for new horses to buy and looking for new studs. Dr. Culver knew that only feed suppliers, farriers, and veterinarians made money on horses.

CHAPTER 11

Collision Course

One of Dodie's puppy owners called Labrador breeder Susan Burke in the spring of 1994. Due to changed circumstances, the owner no longer could care for his ten-month-old puppy sired by Burke's Ben-Hur. Dodie refused to take back the puppy, and he'd relinquish him to the pound unless Burke immediately retrieved him.[1]

"I can't believe that you breeders aren't responsible," the owner said.

"I beg to differ," Burke replied. She'd shown dogs since she was a child and bred canines for fifteen years.

Burke drove about seventy miles that night to pick up the puppy.

"I can't believe that you guys deal with this lady."

"What do you mean?" Burke inquired.

"She is nothing but a puppy mill." He said the kennel conditions were deplorable; dogs were everywhere. That was the first that Burke heard there might be a problem with Dodie.

The next day, she called Linda Vaughn, the Lab Club member whom Dodie had used as a reference. She reported her conversation with the puppy owner, and Vaughn acknowledged that she'd heard "rumblings."

Burke drove to Dodie's kennel and knocked on the farmhouse's front door. No answer. She walked in and froze when she reached the dark kitchen. Her eyes focused on Labrador dams and puppies in filthy conditions living in kitchen cabinets.

An angry Burke stormed outside. Dogs ran around everywhere in runs and yards. Poop was everywhere. "The conditions were horrible." She strode farther back on the property until she spotted Dodie in a field. Burke relayed the disgruntled puppy owner's conversation and how he'd quoted Dodie as saying that the puppy wasn't her problem.

"That is not the way you are supposed to do business; you are supposed to be responsible and accountable," Burke said. "If somebody has to give up a puppy, you take it back and find another home."

Dazed by an estimated forty to fifty dogs on the property, she stared at Dodie. "I thought you said you'd had only one or two litters. How many dogs do you have?"

Dodie "kind of stumbled over herself" and became "very defensive." She asked Burke to leave. Burke complied.

Troubled by what she had seen, Burke telephoned Vaughn and asked the Lab Club to investigate. She didn't belong to the club but knew Vaughn was a prominent member. Vaughn, who wasn't an officer at the time, believed that the club didn't have any "police power" to investigate and could only have denied membership to Dodie, who hadn't applied.

Burke also reported the conditions to Weld County Animal Control.[2] A representative said that she wasn't the first to complain. Burke never heard back from animal control.

———

The Lab Club didn't investigate Dodie's practices or contact the AKC. Members seemingly weren't made aware of Burke's request or, if some were, they'd forgotten that the club had asked the AKC to investigate another complaint in 1987.

At that time, the owner of an Iowa-born Labrador, with temperament and physical problems, sought help from the club. A Denver pet store had sold the dog. Club members unanimously authorized then-president Donna Stacey to ask the AKC to investigate. The AKC said that it lacked authority over sales of purebred dogs and only inspected kennels for compliance with its recordkeeping and inspection requirements. However, it could schedule a kennel for an inspection if it had information about "problems." At the time of Burke's request, Stacey was no longer a club member. There is no way of knowing whether the AKC would have acted had it been notified about the condition of Dodie's dogs.

Months after Burke's request, the Colorado legislature passed its first law to regulate the small pet industry. The Pet Animal Care Facilities Act authorized the Colorado Department of Agriculture to enforce minimum standards for physical facilities, sanitation, spatial and enclosure requirements, and recordkeeping regarding health care as well as transactions of dogs and other pet animals. It prohibited the sale or transfer of puppies younger than eight weeks of age and required licensing of persons operating a pet animal facility involved in selling, transferring, and breeding dogs. One veterinarian and two field inspectors would conduct announced and unannounced inspections throughout the state to enforce the new law.

Colorado joined other states when it authorized government representatives to inspect medium- to large-sized kennels, but, unlike some states, it failed to mandate such inspections, which meant little if authorities allowed poor conditions to exist.[3]

Dodie paid $175 for a one-year small dog breeder's license in March 1995. That license allowed her to transfer or sell no more than ninety-nine canines a year. She'd wait to see if the state was as lax as the county in enforcing its regulations.

A partial answer came the following year when the state inspected her kennel for the first time. The inspector found the need for "more regular removal of fecal material," and indoor bare wood surfaces require paint or seal. Nearly a year later, the same inspector discovered "several days/weeks accumulation of fecal material in outdoor kennels. This must be remedied. Daily removal will be needed regardless of weather conditions." He failed to issue a citation after either inspection and didn't contact Weld County about the conditions or the number of dogs, undoubtedly well over the permitted sixteen. And the county didn't inspect Dodie's kennel even though it could have revoked her permit if she'd refused to comply with its dog limitation.

Although the county and state didn't interfere with Dodie's booming puppy business, her spending habits undermined any financial security. She built a two-car garage-type structure with a high roof and decorative windows. One side housed her prized English racing green MG sports car. The other, a sitting area, doubled as space for her older, retired female Labradors to enjoy themselves apart from the general dog population and led out to a fenced-in run.

She didn't save but took advantage of the wave of lenders approving loans to unqualified applicants. She'd use one loan to pay off another and then return to primarily one bank for yet another loan, sometimes to refinance her farm or for "personal reasons." By 1996, she had a nearly $58,000 mortgage on her farm and continued to juggle her finances to try to meet expenses.

Dodie also looked to family for assistance. She asked James for loans periodically and always repaid him. Their mother supplemented her income for years. She knew that her daughter was troubled and asked Doug and James to look after their sister when she passed. Dodie received about $15,000 from her mother's estate in 1996 and then turned, for the first time, to Doug for monetary assistance. He'd built a very profitable, diversified real estate company in Southern California.

Instead of using her inheritance to pay off bills, Dodie purchased an old Class C mini motorhome and stored it in her stable of vehicles. At one time, she owned eight vehicles, including a 1982 Nissan 280 ZX, the MG sports car, a truck, a van, and a horse trailer.

Equine costs increased in tandem with her growing horse population; she kept unsold foals and occasionally bought a new horse. She spent much less on her Labradors—nearly $3,400 in veterinarian bills and probably between $11,500 and $16,000 on dog food, depending on its quality, in 1996. There were other canine expenses as well: the state kennel license fee, AKC registration fees of $18 per litter, newspaper advertisements, and upkeep of her dog runs and yards as well as cleaning and other supplies.[4]

Dodie expended a large sum when she took Charmin', her longtime favorite and Max's grandmother, to CSU's veterinary hospital for cancer treatment. A surgeon removed part of the dog's rib cage to try to save her. Although Charmin' later succumbed, Dr. Culver knew her client had spent a fortune trying to save her.

In the face of mounting debt, Dodie opted to craft the same pottery that she'd made for years instead of making changes to keep up with her competitors.

At one annual Art in the Park summer festival in Steamboat Springs, she joked with friend and fellow potter Nancy Zoller when they weren't busy with customers.

"God, everybody's buying your pottery and not mine," Dodie said.

Yes! Yes! You have been my model for all of these years, and now I've made it, Nancy thought.[5]

She encouraged Dodie to update her pottery by adding more color as she and other potters had done. Her friend disregarded her advice.

Nancy also urged Dodie to craft more of the small sculptures that had marked a departure from her typical work and led Trimble Court to name Dodie as its featured artist of the month. Once again, Dodie rejected Nancy's suggestion.

"Wow, I make so much more money selling dogs. This pottery thing is over for me. I am just going to raise dogs," Dodie confided to Nancy one day. And, she didn't need a man; she had her dogs.

Dodie sold as many puppies as she chose because the county and state failed to enforce their permit requirements. Then in April 1996, the AKC adopted a policy that seemed to require breeders to maintain sanitary kennel conditions. The Care and Conditions Policy, which "wasn't a minimum standard for breeding facilities," provided a basis for "helping individuals correct specific deficiencies found during routine inspections." It generally required that dogs have adequate food, water, housing, and exercise. "Feces should be picked up and disposed of as frequently as necessary so as not to pose a threat" to the dogs' health.[6] Dodie was subject to the AKC's policies because she certified that she'd comply with all its rules and regulations when she applied for litter and individual dog registrations.

Additionally, the policy required AKC inspectors to promptly notify agencies with proper jurisdiction if they found dogs in conditions placing them in immediate danger. In Colorado, that meant a call to a municipal or county animal control office or the state veterinarian's office. If dogs were in a "clearly compromised condition," such as severely dehydrated, grossly underweight, or with serious untreated injuries or severe external parasitic infestation, the AKC could place an individual's AKC privileges on hold. Failure to correct such deficiencies could trigger a disciplinary process that could lead to reprimands, imposition of fines, and/or suspensions of all AKC privileges. A suspension of privileges meant that an individual couldn't register any puppy or adult dog with the AKC or compete in AKC events.

Previously, AKC field inspectors only reviewed breeders' records and verified dogs' identification by tattoos, name tags, or plates on collars or pens to assure a buyer that a dog's parentage was as represented.

So far, the AKC, state, and county hadn't curtailed Dodie's puppy business. That allowed her to raise even more litters in an attempt to support her horse business as she eased out of the pottery profession.

Dodie picked up a spiral-bound journal. Headshots of one yellow and one black Lab graced its cover. She turned to the first page and wrote, "Thoughts Moments Memories-Gratitude's." Next, she penned "Feb. 1997" and dedicated the journal "to my Labradors who have kept me sane in this World of Insanity . . ." She didn't write anything further until early March when she described an upbeat day: a puppy sale, playtime with four litters of pups, and the adoption of Sebastian, a shy chocolate six-month-old male. "Hope he works out. A good boy, tho. I pray for him. Thank you Lord."

When Jon McClain and his wife purchased their $500 puppy Montgomery that October, Dodie no longer offered any hip guarantee due to "the unpredictability of all genetic disorders." Her sales contract promised that "we will continue to selectively breed OFA certified sound, athletic and healthy dogs. The dogs are bred under the guidance of a veterinarian." But Dodie knew the pup's sire, McDougal, was a carrier for hip dysplasia, and the pup's dam and her parents lacked OFA hip clearances.

The late-twenties couple sought an AKC pup because AKC meant "everything was legitimate" and "good."[7] They wanted a shorter, stockier yellow "English" Labrador puppy from the same litter as a coworker's new family member. The puppies and house appeared clean even though the couple smelled a strong dog odor when they played with four two-and-a-half-month-old pups in Dodie's kitchen. They fell for "a super cute" lighter yellow male pup with a black nose and rims around his eyes and darker yellow-colored ears. He looked smaller than the others and didn't resemble the puppy owned by McClain's buddy. McClain wondered if the pup was really from the same litter.

Nearly six months later, eight-month-old Montgomery was diagnosed with OCD (osteochondritis dissecans), an inflammatory condition occurring when abnormal cartilage grows on the end of a bone in a joint and then separates from the underlying bone. OCD often causes lameness and pain. When McClain learned that OCD was genetic, he called Dodie about the diagnosis. He thought it odd when she said that she'd never heard of the condition.

Montgomery underwent surgery on both of his hocks and endured casts for several weeks. The McClains then swam and regularly walked him but didn't allow him to run. He could hike for twenty or thirty minutes, a bit longer in the snow.

Days after the McClains bought Montgomery, the state conducted its third inspection of Dodie's kennel, following up a week-old complaint about "very unsanitary conditions" and dogs kept in "traveling crates," including a pregnant female who'd be crated until she whelped.

The inspector found the "animal enclosures" adequate and all crates with dogs relatively clean. He discussed "the importance of regular cleaning," preferably daily, with Dodie after he discovered about two weeks' accumulation of fecal material in several outdoor runs and pens. Even though this was the third time the state found an excessive amount of feces, the inspector only issued a warning and stayed a $200 fine provided that wastes were removed each week.

About four months later, the same state inspector returned to Dodie's kennel after a second complaint about feces on puppies and adults. He again instructed Dodie to pick up feces more often, "if possible," after he observed adult pens with "several days of accumulation of fecal." He noted that the puppy runs looked as if they'd been recently cleaned and once again didn't issue a citation.

The state inspected 1,300 pet facilities in 1997–98. It also required breeders to report the number of litters and dogs sold each year when they applied for the renewal of their kennel license.[8] Starting in 1996, Dodie reported that she sold ninety-three dogs in three successive years, with declining numbers of litters: eighteen, fourteen, and ten. The state never questioned her tallies even though Labradors often have eight to ten puppies in a litter. Dodie underreported the number of litters and sales for March 1997 through February 1998. Her veterinarian's records showed that she had at least twenty litters instead of fourteen, and 135 puppies, not 93.[9] The state never told Weld County how many dogs she had, nor did the county check with the state or visit Dodie's kennel.

CHAPTER 12

Quest

M ax needed a title other than official greeter or official beer-guzzling dog in 1996. So, I decided that our Killkenny's Maximilian should earn his Companion Dog (CD) obedience degree, which Molly had easily acquired the previous summer.

At the time, I had no idea that Dodie lacked interest in showing or doing much of anything with her Killkenny Labradors except breeding and selling them. That's what Labrador enthusiast Marney McCleary had recognized years before Max was born. And, as her canine numbers grew, Dodie lacked time to train her dogs for the conformation or performance ring.

Knowledge of Dodie's disinterest in working with her dogs wouldn't have deterred me from training Max. I learned that he had some basic obedience training when I perused the documents that John had given us. The AKC transferred Max's ownership to us, so I only needed to train our boy to perform in the ring.[1] That would be fun and a bit of a challenge, I thought, and looked forward to competing at a few of the 2,400 AKC obedience trials conducted each year. I knew that obedience, a sport introduced to this country in 1933 by Mrs. Whitehouse Walker of Carillon Kennels, a standard poodle breeder, was the only AKC performance event conducted at dog shows.[2]

———

To earn a CD degree in 1986, a dog needed to score at least 170 out of a possible 200 points and earn at least 50 percent or more in each Novice exercise at three AKC obedience trials under three different judges. The Novice exercises were Heel on Leash; Figure Eight (on leash heeling around two human "posts" in a figure-eight pattern); Stand for Examination; Heel Free (off leash); Recall (come when called); the Long Sit; and the Long Down. All the exercises were performed individually except for the stays, which were done with about twelve to fifteen other canines, all off leash. To pass the Long Sit, each dog needed to sit in a row with other canines for one minute while their owners glared, sent up silent prayers, and/or counted to sixty from across the ring as they hoped that their charges wouldn't move, change position, or disturb another canine. The Long Down required each dog to lie down on command and remain in place for three minutes while their owners faced them from across the ring.[3]

Max could earn his CD without much difficulty, or so I thought, because he knew the basic sit, stay, down, and come commands. We attended drop-in classes in Parker, about ten miles north of our Franktown home, where I'd trained Molly the previous year. The instructor, Rosemary Logrie, a jolly breeder who competed with her Mardi Gras cocker spaniels in conformation, obedience, agility, and tracking, knew that I had obtained obedience titles on several dogs.

I briefed her about Max so that she'd understand that he was a pretty energetic dog. He progressed steadily from acting very nervous to settling down in class. Jake, a large, overexuberant German wirehaired pointer, thought Max was a female. Max wasn't thrilled but ignored him once he realized that Jake was just overly friendly and a bit gender challenged.

We trained daily in our backyard: heeling on and off leash and coming when called. Max learned to stay in a stand position while I walked six feet away from him, turned, and waited. Dave approached Max and ran his hand down the canine's back before I returned to Max's side. Our adoptee also remained in a sit or down position while

I walked around the yard, kicked balls, or clapped my hands to simulate distractions. To reinforce our training, we practiced in parks and competed in a practice obedience trial. Max needed more work. We continued to train.

By early fall, I believed Max was ready to compete. I knew from previous experience that if I showed him too soon and he didn't qualify, he'd learn that I couldn't correct him in the ring. The inability to give corrections usually perpetuated mistakes, which generally worsened.

I remembered my first obedience dog, Peanut, who sailed through the Novice classes to earn her CD. We next competed for a Companion Dog Excellent (CDX) degree. One of the exercises, the Drop on Recall, required a dog to come on command and then drop to a down position when the owner said or signaled down upon the judge's indication. Once the dog dropped to a down, the judge motioned the handler to call the dog.

The judge signaled drop as Peanut barreled toward me during a hot summer show in Great Barrington, Massachusetts.

"Down," I shouted.

Peanut stopped and eased herself toward the ground. I exhaled and blinked. My heart sank a second later when I opened my eyes. Peanut almost grinned as she sat and stared at me from the middle of the ring. She knew I couldn't correct her or give another command to down. That exercise became her downfall; she only earned two qualifying scores amid several disqualifying performances, always failing the Drop on Recall exercise.

Moira, one of my parents' short-coupled yellow Labradors that was a bit too smart for my own good, taught me a lesson about bored dogs. I accepted the challenge of training Moira and her blocky-headed, none-too-smart brother David because I hadn't found a summer job before my junior year of college. That summer I experienced the privilege of wearing braces on my teeth. I was speech challenged and a bit embarrassed when sit came out "shit." It was an excellent time to train dogs at home.

As my departure for college approached, I entered David in four shows because I thought he probably wouldn't qualify at least once. I entered Moira in only three shows as I believed the quicker learner would easily qualify each time she competed.

David earned his CD in three straight shows and placed third once. Moira qualified handily at her first two shows. At the third, I caught her scrutinizing a small pond as we waited to enter the ring near the end of a hot August afternoon. My confidence grew as I felt Moira at my side during the initial stretch of the Heel Free exercise. I looked straight ahead, marched around the ring, and only looked down for Moira's eyes when I heard the judge say, "Exercise finished." Moira wasn't at my side. She lay in the shade under the judge's table across the ring. At least she hadn't gone for a swim.

Max certainly was capable of the antics of Peanut and Moira. I weighed the risk of showing him too soon against boring him with repetitive training. He needed additional practice to qualify in style and not scrape by with a 170 or 171 score. I decided to gamble and entered our Killkenny adoptee in two obedience-only trials in October 1996 with the idea that I'd later enter him at the Lab Club show the following month. Max would earn his CD if he qualified at all three trials. I'd trained about eight dogs to compete for their CD; only Moira needed an extra trial to earn that title. I hoped Max wouldn't join her ranks.

Dave decided to attend Max's first obedience trial. Max was entered in Novice B. AKC rules required me to show him in that class because I'd handled other dogs to their obedience titles. The Novice

A class was reserved for those handlers who hadn't owned or shown a dog to a CD.

We arrived in ample time before Max's scheduled class in the Pikes Peak arena in Colorado Springs. I exercised Max outside to make certain that he wouldn't relieve himself in the ring. He'd be disqualified if he did. The walk also served to calm Max's and my nerves.

Once inside, we surveyed three large rings in the middle of the expansive dirt arena. We sauntered around the outside of the rings and past bleachers on the building's south side to give Max time to acclimate to the new sights and smells. He sat when I paused. The dirt floor didn't bother him. That was critical because the heeling exercises required Max to sit parallel to my left knee each time we stopped.

Max and I joined Dave on the bleachers, about twenty feet away from our ring's entrance, to wait for our class to begin. Dave agreed to climb higher up in the bleachers when Max entered the ring to avoid being a distraction.

I watched several dogs perform their individual exercises before I took Max outside for one more stroll. Then I gave him a couple of heel commands as a last-second warm-up. We entered the ring.

"Are you ready?" the judge asked.

"Ready." Max looked up at me.

I hoped for the best.

"Forward."

"Max, heel." I strode out on my left foot. Max focused on various sights instead of me but stayed in position during the Heel on Leash and Figure Eight exercises. He stood motionless, except for a slight tail wag, for the Stand for Examination. Next, the judge positioned us for the Heel Free exercise.

"Forward."

"Max, heel." I marched forward. Max trotted beside me as he held his head high and gaily wagged his tail.

"Left turn."

I felt Max's head at my left knee. Good sign.

"About turn."

I held my breath and turned around to the right. I again felt Max's head at my knee.

"Halt," the judge said.

I stopped. Max sat.

"Forward."

"Max, heel," I said. My boy started up. We're halfway through the exercise and have a good shot at qualifying, I thought.

"All dogs to Ring 1 for the Long Sit and Down," boomed a voice over a loudspeaker. Startled, I looked down at my left side. Max wasn't there. I looked up as he galloped toward the ring's exit.

"Max, come." He veered from the exit and galloped on around the ring once, then twice.

"Max, COME!" Finally, he trotted to me and sat. I grabbed his collar and looked at his face. Eyes of a deer in headlights stared back.

The judge approached us and gently advised that we could attempt the final individual exercise, the Recall.

"Max," I said.

His glazed-over eyes refused to focus.

I thanked the judge but declined her offer and explained that we had many things to learn about our adoptee. But I also feared Max wouldn't stay until I called him or, even worse, might bolt out of the ring. Max's first attempt to qualify was over.

Dave greeted us as we scurried from the ring. He'd seen the scenario develop and realized that the loudspeaker might startle Max but hadn't known what to do. He said he wished that he'd asked the announcer to delay his announcement. Me, too.

We tried to calm Max, and then the three of us meandered around the inside of the building. I wanted to make sure Max didn't fear the arena or its sights because he was scheduled to compete the next day. Dejected, I drove home with Dave and our adoptee.

Dave remained at home the next day. Max seemed happy and less nervous than the previous day during our walks around the arena. As we waited at ringside for our turn to perform the individual exercises, I prayed the loudspeaker wouldn't be used.

I felt less confident than the previous day when we entered the ring. But Max focused, heeled close to me, sat straight, and wagged his tail. The judge, a portly lady who I'd heard was a fan of sporting dogs, beamed at Max at the end of his individual exercises. The audience clapped.

Max only needed to pass the Long Sit and Long Down to qualify. No loudspeaker so far.

We were the second to last of the fifteen handler-dog teams to re-enter the ring for the group exercises. The steward lined us up, and the judge stood near our end of the ring.

"Sit your dogs."

"Sit!" the handlers said in unison.

"Leave your dogs," the judge said.

"Stay!" the handlers commanded and walked to the opposite side of the ring. We turned and glared at our dogs.

Max sat statue-like, straight and tall.

I stared at Max and willed him to remain in place. He stared back. Sixty seconds seemed an eternity.

The minute evaporated.

"Back to your dogs," the judge barked.

Max jumped up and then looked aghast as if he realized his goof. My heart sank as I walked toward him.

"Oh, Max, how could you!" the judge said.

How could the judge, who had judged more than forty dogs, including twenty-seven in Max's class that day, remember our boy's name? I wondered.

The ordeal wasn't over. The Long Down came next.

"Down your dogs," the judge bellowed. For the first time, my ears picked up her loud tone.

"Down."

Max lay down.

"Leave your dogs."

"Stay," I said.

"Max, STAY. You STAY!" I heard as I took my second step away from him. I'd never witnessed a judge give a stay command to my dog or any other canine. Her command undoubtedly gave him the confidence to stay in the down position for three minutes. Afterward, I surmised that she hadn't wanted Max to acquire a bad habit. The rules technically didn't permit her to give such a command, but I remained grateful. She became Max's favorite judge.[4]

Max was the first dog that I had owned, much less handled, that failed two Novice obedience trial classes. He also was my first adopted dog. Therein lay the difference, I rationalized. But I likewise knew that some adopted dogs performed flawlessly with their new owners. I needed to learn more about our boy.

After the Colorado Springs trials, Dave and I watched Max more closely to ascertain any phobias besides loudspeakers. We learned that he feared knives, flashlights, door openers, and slim to medium-built, dark-haired men who smoked.

I conferred with Rosemary, our obedience instructor, when we returned to her drop-in classes for Max's remedial training. She played tapes of loud, barking canines at dog shows and used a bull horn to desensitize Max so that he wouldn't bolt. She wore different hats just in case a judge donned one. Thankfully, she didn't smoke.

Rosemary and I discussed whether Max would be ready to compete again in early November at the Lab specialty. I'd planned to enter him, but now he needed to qualify not only there but twice more. Two all-breed shows, where any breed can compete in conformation and obedience classes, were scheduled for the two days following the Lab specialty at the same location. Those shows would be rowdy. Would it be too much for Max to compete at three back-to-back shows?

On the plus side, we had a few weeks to work on loud noise issues, which appeared as Max's main problem. After the three November trials, the next shows were all-breed events in February inside the noisy Denver Coliseum. February was months away. Winter driving conditions might prevent us from attending Rosemary's classes. By February, Max would be totally bored. I shuddered as I recalled my experiences with Peanut and Moira. I already had difficulty keeping Max's attention. Food wasn't the incentive it had been for my other Labs. He was the pickiest eater that I had ever owned and really couldn't be bribed with a treat to perform. Max worked only occasionally for special treats or only when he wanted. That made training much more difficult.

On the con side, Max might be too tired and unfocused to qualify at three back-to-back shows. I didn't know what to expect because I'd never asked a dog to compete for three days in a row in obedience. I'd be asking an awful lot of him.

My fear of utterly boring Max won out. I entered him in the three November trials and looked for other practice venues. We trained at different parks and at an outdoor outlet mall that blared music to shoppers as they walked store to store. Max heeled, sat, and downed. Shoppers watched and smiled. A few patted him while he sat on the Long Sit.

Killkenny's Maximilian was ready to compete.

CHAPTER 13

The AKC Threat

The AKC randomly selected Dodie's kennel for an inspection in 1998 under its new DNA Compliance Program, which the AKC Board of Directors adopted to strengthen the integrity of its dog registry. The new policy authorized suspensions of breeders if DNA disclosed that a dog's lineage wasn't correctly represented. Suspended breeders couldn't legally sell their canines as AKC stock.

The program empowered AKC inspectors to collect DNA of the sire, dam, and puppies of a litter owned by a randomly selected breeder who registered seven or more litters in a year. If DNA results showed a discrepancy with the breeder's representation of a litter's parentage, the AKC notified the breeder of its findings and investigated. After an investigation, the AKC's Management Disciplinary Committee could fine and/or suspend the violator's AKC privileges. However, the suspected violator could request that a trial board, usually with an attorney as its chair, conduct an administrative hearing on the allegations.

In the program's inaugural year, fourteen AKC inspectors conducted more than 5,200 inspections of kennels, pet shops, auctions, and distributors across the country. They collected more than 6,500 random DNA samples during kennel inspections and found 693 incorrectly registered litters.

When the AKC inspector collected DNA samples from Dodie's puppies and adults, he undoubtedly examined her records and may have inspected her dogs' living conditions. The AKC could sanction breeders for substandard kennel conditions if an administrative body or court found animal neglect or cruelty and/or for substandard recordkeeping.

At best, Dodie's recordkeeping was haphazard. She wrote an individual dog's name, date of birth, sire and dam names, and tattoo number, if any, on the outside of letter-sized envelopes, one per dog. Inside, she typically stored the dog's pedigree or its parents' pedigrees; copies of or original AKC registrations and OFA certificates, if any; and copies of photographs of the dog and its parents. She also kept pedigrees and photos of some of her dogs in a three-ring binder.[1]

Her records weren't always accurate. Dodie named two dogs Killkenny's Donovan McDuff. One was born on January 7, 1990, the other supposedly on January 7, 1997. She altered the first McDuff's OFA certificate to create a copy for the second dog. OFA has a record only of the original Donovan. Even Dodie seemed uncertain of her dogs' parentage at times. She listed two sires for one dog on one envelope and used identical photos to represent two full siblings and their dam.[2]

Dodie didn't attract the AKC's full attention with her poor record-keeping practices or the questionable living conditions of at least some of her dogs. That happened when she represented the parentage of two litters that DNA proved otherwise.

She identified the sire of one of those litters as owned by Linda Vaughn. An AKC representative inspected Vaughn's kennel and took a DNA swab of the purported sire. Test results proved the dog wasn't the sire. Dodie hadn't bred any of her dogs to one of Vaughn's studs in nearly a decade.[3]

An enraged Dodie telephoned Vaughn when the AKC disclosed its DNA findings. She accused Vaughn and the Lab Club of trying to "get her."

That wasn't the case, Vaughn replied. She'd had no choice but to allow the AKC inspector to collect DNA samples from her dogs.

Dodie explained the sire mix-up to Dr. Culver. She'd forgotten that she'd placed a puppy or two from one litter in with another litter to nurse. Dr. Culver had recommended that Dodie allow a couple of puppies from a larger litter to nurse a dam with a small litter to supplement their milk intake because she refused to bottle-feed pups. She instructed Dodie to clearly mark these puppies and keep good records so she'd know they weren't the surrogate dam's offspring. Once weaned, Dodie could return the pups to their own litter.[4]

Even though she gave an outward appearance of confidence, Dodie wrestled with self-doubts about her life. She picked up her journal for the first time in eighteen months in late September 1998. "After just reading that one entry, I feel so sad & depressed at where I am today." Dogs meant more to her than she thought; she loved having litters and finding just the right homes for the puppies.

"Now with my problems with AKC—I don't know what to do. Should I continue breeding—without AKC? People seem to want 'papers.' Half the time they don't seem to use or reg. their dogs. And yet they want the papers!! What a mess my life is right now. And yet— other than moments of sadness—at what has happened—I feel a strange sense of Peace. What does it mean?

". . . I have sold over 100 pups since Mar of '97. People seem to like my dogs. I must write to everyone to see how they all are doing!!!

"I love my dogs! Oh God!! What have I done?

"Dear Lord—Why has this happened? What does this mean? What should I do? What is your message?

"This is happening for some reason. To teach me some lessons. Please open my heart & mind and help my soul grow.

"In the last year, I have been 'burnt-out' on the dogs! Having too many—I haven't even had the time to do any pottery. I have yelled & complained and the result is that now I have caused this to happen to me. I am in trouble Big Time, and don't know what to do. At this point, I guess I will continue w/AKC and ask for a formal hearing—I have sent them a letter yesterday—requesting such."

In a more upbeat tone, Dodie wrote about her horses: she bought Legacy, a gray thoroughbred gelding, and hired two CSU students to help with the equines. The following summer, she employed two different CSU students who painted the farm because they weren't good riders and installed new landscaping. When the students returned to college, she realized she needed assistance with the horses. "When one Door CLOSES—Look for another DOOR to Open!"

In mid-October, Dodie picked up her journal again. Her mood seemed more upbeat as she expressed gratitude that one of her Labradors had nine beautiful yellow puppies, all her dogs had been "good & healthy," mortgage interest rates went down, and three kittens lived in her new hay barn. She'd moved forty boxes of new clay into her studio and mailed letters to prior dog customers to keep her puppy business afloat. Puppy owners sent back glowing reports. She placed these letters, and previous correspondence from happy puppy buyers and pictures of their new family members, in a three-ring binder.

Dodie looked to horses as a way out of her mounting financial problems. The possible AKC suspension, which could destroy her puppy business, hung over her head.

She didn't curb her spending. Instead, she purchased Native Jet Son, a four-month-old APHA foal, mostly black with some white markings, from a Loveland rancher. To pay his several-thousand-dollar purchase price, she refinanced her farm for $170,000-plus, at a lower interest rate than her previous $160,000 mortgage, which she'd negotiated just fifteen months prior.

"I love him! Maybe He is my new opportunity for the future?! Who knows—but I must go on and try to do the best I can—because today is the 1st day of the rest of my life." She knew that once the gentle, easy-to-handle colt matured, he could eliminate her need for and the cost of breeding to outside stallions, and his stud fees could bring in good money.

Dodie resumed journaling in late January 1999.

She vowed to set aside time each night to write "thoughts and words" and list her daily gratitudes. "I am grateful for the natural beauty of Colo. that I sometimes I forget how lucky I am to live on this beautiful farm located so I can see the snowcapped Rockies everyday-all-day as I do my chores . . . work in the studio or ride the horses."

She thanked the Lord that she was still healthy and able to ride her thoroughbreds. "I know I complain about taking care of them, but really, when I do ride, I know how lucky I am to have lived over 18 years on this beautiful farm!! I have worked so hard since I was 19, 20 yrs old to have this lifestyle—and I now—just in the last year or two have been able to finally take some time to enjoy it. Thank you, Lord for allowing me this 'time-off' to just enjoy life—instead of just work, work, work.

"Please Lord help me to appreciate all my blessings and 'simple joys' in my life."

She wrote about her canines: "I love my dogs. Not all of them. Some of them I just hate. But my favorite ones, I just love more every day! Prince, Sophia, Kelly, Victoria, Ronika, Kersey, Secret, Rhumba, Misha, Journey, Titan, McDougal, Megan, Thunder & Donovan. I love when I am raising a pup up into the Killkenny family. I love when I am bonding & the new pup is turning out well & looking good. I do have such a sense of pride & joy—I know I am doing the 'right thing.'

"Not all the dogs are good & perfect—Some are just 'breeding-stock,' but the joy I receive every day from my favorites is worth it. Please, Dear Lord, help me to appreciate all you have blessed me with Every Day!!"

On Valentine's Day in 1999, Dodie opened her journal again. She recounted a "horrible conversation" with the wife of a puppy buyer who didn't understand her contract. She'd stayed mellow as she explained the terms of her contract and the reasons for her "no money back" and "no guarantees" bill of sale. "I love it . . . it works for me.

"These people have a stupid & horrible veterinarian, who now has caused large 'doubt' with these people. Ick! Ugh! I am going to stick to the terms of my contract & see what happens. I went to bed Fr. Nite thinking 'God' was giving me more 'hints' to quit breeding. But then on Sat—things got good again!!!"

She'd talked at length with a man about "Labs & Quality & Linda Vaughn" and the "Lab Club." He bought a female chocolate puppy. "It was one of the best 'appointments' & 'showing' I've ever had! . . . a perfect match. I love it when things go this well."

Dodie vowed to write about the "good" things and the "good" days to remember them on "bad" days. She hoped to become more "kind and gentle, quiet, poised, proud and not too defensive," and knew she shouldn't get so defensive about her dogs as they "speak for themselves."

Then she penned, "they're not all good—I really should get rid of the ones I don't like."

The AKC's South Central Trial Board, comprised of three non-AKC employees, convened on September 29, 1999, to consider the allegations that Dodie falsified two litter registration applications. The AKC's staff would present sworn testimony and other evidence at the hearing even if she didn't attend. Dodie told Dr. Culver that she'd gone with her lawyer to the hearing, although their attendance couldn't be verified. She didn't write about the proceeding in her journal, and the AKC declined to comment.

The trial board concluded that Dodie "submitted or caused to submit two litter registration applications which she knew or should have known contained false certifications."[5] It recommended a ten-year suspension of all AKC privileges and a $500 fine. The hefty sanctions confirmed the likelihood that Dodie had incorrectly listed the wrong sire and/or dam on both litter registrations. Several other breeders also accused of submitting two false litter registration applications received an identical penalty that same year.

The AKC Board of Directors voted to accept the trial board's recommendations and suspended Dodie on October 11, 1999.[6] That meant that she couldn't register her dogs or litters with the AKC for ten years. She didn't appeal her suspension to the AKC's Appeals Trial Board.

Instead, she continued to sell puppies and often as AKC pups. She gambled that her customers wouldn't call the AKC to inquire whether she was in good standing or would read about her suspension in the December 1999 issue of *The AKC Gazette*, a monthly periodical. She also gambled they wouldn't ask for proof of her breeding stock's health clearances.

Dr. Culver noticed that Dodie no longer sought OFA evaluations of her dogs' hips well before the AKC suspension. That meant her client saved an estimated $100 per dog for radiographs and OFA's examination fee.[7]

"That's just not a very good idea," Dr. Culver said. She counseled her "at length" about the importance of OFA hip clearances.

"Well, I'm not going to. I'm not going to guarantee anything," Dodie responded.

She told her friend Carol Mayberry-Sanchez that she didn't need OFA hip clearances because her line didn't have a hip dysplasia problem. Dodie knew otherwise. Her records reflected one puppy born in June 1993 had hip dysplasia. Kristen Everhart had told her about Wheeler's hip dysplasia diagnosis that same year.

As of August 1999, and spanning about twenty years of breeding Labradors, Dodie had owned a minimum of eighty adult Labradors. Only twenty-six had an OFA fair or better hip rating.[8]

Dodie's decision to forgo health clearances ran contrary to the practices of many reputable breeders who tested their Labradors not only for hip dysplasia and eye diseases but also for elbow dysplasia in the late 1990s.[9] Her decision increased the odds that she'd breed dogs with serious health issues and sell unhealthy puppies to unsuspecting buyers.

Eye exams were especially crucial in Labradors because in the 1980s, a prominent stud had repeatedly been bred before it was discovered that he carried the PRA gene when some of his offspring went blind. His PRA carrier status hadn't been detected earlier because of the lack of a genetic test for the eye disease.

That changed in the late 1990s when Gregory Acland and Gustavo Aguirre, both then Cornell University veterinary ophthalmologists, teamed up with Jeannette Felix and Kunal Ray, human geneticists, and developed the first blood marker test for the eye disease. They formed OptiGen, Inc., which offered the first PRA genetic test for Labradors in 2000.

The $260 blood test determined if a dog was PRA-free, carried the PRA gene, or was affected by PRA. The canine would go blind if affected. OptiGen tested blood samples from an estimated 600 Labradors for PRA in 2001. About 2 to 4 percent of those dogs were affected, and more than 20 percent were carriers.[10] A carrier bred to another carrier or an affected dog produced carriers and affected dogs. But a clear dog bred to a carrier produced clear and carrier offspring.

The test provided breeders a tool to make more educated breeding decisions and a chance to eliminate PRA. Some breeders only bred PRA-clear dogs to each other. That trend changed when good characteristics, such as excellent movement or body structure, were bred out of a line. Now many breeders breed PRA-clear dogs to PRA carriers.

Dodie evidently didn't take advantage of the OptiGen test even though she knew the grandfather of McDougal, her most prolific stud dog, was a PRA carrier.[11] Nor did she evidently have McDougal's eyes examined by an ophthalmologist. Fortunately, her dogs may have sidestepped the PRA gene.[12]

She dodged more trouble when a state inspector arrived at her kennel in March 2000, the first time in nearly two years. He noticed a buildup of feces in a large exercise area that required daily cleaning and maintenance at "an acceptable level." The inspector also instructed Dodie to provide cleanable surfaces underneath her second level of crates in two "primary enclosure rooms." Even though the state had observed excessive amounts of feces on each of its five inspections, it again failed to fine Dodie for unsanitary conditions or seek a court order to shut down her puppy business.

Instead of hiring kennel help, Dodie had built a fourteen-by-fourteen-foot "away room," with skylights, where she relaxed at night in the nicely furnished space with a few invited Labradors. And she secured yet another loan, this time for $34,000.

Dodie accurately predicted that many puppy buyers weren't interested in registering their new wards with the AKC. That was true of Joan Tilden and her husband, both engineers. In May of 2000, they just wanted a healthy puppy and inquired about any hip issues because they'd previously owned a Lab with hip dysplasia. Dodie assured them that there weren't any, but she knew differently.

The couple and their two sons, ages ten and thirteen, played with the four- to five-week-old, light-yellow Labrador puppies in the farmhouse's kitchen. Dodie picked up the smallest pup from the old linoleum floor and pressed its lips until it yelped. She pressed the pup's lips again.

Tilden gasped. "Is that okay? Is the pup all right?"[13]

"They are dogs; they need discipline," Dodie gruffly responded.

Tilden was taken aback by the change in Dodie's voice and actions. Just seconds before the breeder had spoken in a very pleasant, friendly manner.

She and her husband noticed a home-for-sale sign as they turned into Dodie's driveway and sensed something was odd. They felt puzzled that the breeder didn't ask about their home, yard, or where they would keep their new family member. The puppies, dam, and sire looked healthy, so they placed a $300 deposit on the largest male puppy that had taken to the children.

Ten days later, the family paid an additional $300 and drove home with their pup Chief and the pedigrees of his parents, McDougal and Killkenny's Becca O'Leary. Becca's sire was Prince, a McDougal son. That meant Becca had been bred to her grandfather, McDougal, a dog that Dodie knew was a hip dysplasia carrier. The breeding increased the risk that some of the litter would be dysplastic because McDougal's carrier gene(s) might have passed to his son and then on to his granddaughter. Dodie ignored the risk and even penned "OFA good" next to Prince's name, although OFA hadn't certified his hips.

The family quickly learned that Chief had a very sensitive stomach and tried several premium dog foods until they found one that didn't make him throw up. Chief started to limp that fall, but the Tildens' veterinarian assured them that their five-month-old puppy was just going through growing pains.

Years before the Tildens bought Chief, Dr. Culver vaccinated dogs at Dodie's kennel because it was easier than handling them in her office. Dodie showed her an accounting of how much she made per hour on the Labradors. The veterinarian noted that Dodie calculated time for feeding and cleaning but none for playtime. "You gotta leash train them, you gotta pet them, you gotta work them," she told her client.

By 2000, Dr. Culver saw that Dodie couldn't handle all of her dogs and encouraged her to place some of them. The veterinarian believed that one person could properly care for only twenty adult dogs and/or puppies six months or older.

Her client refused to relinquish any to a humane society because she feared they'd be euthanized. She reluctantly agreed to turn over two six-month-old puppies to a "no-kill" shelter after Dr. Culver arranged for the relinquishment. Then Dodie changed her mind and kept the puppies. After that, she didn't ask Dr. Culver to make any more house calls and took her dogs less frequently to the vet hospital.

Money was tight, so Dodie refinanced her farm again in December of 2000. Principal owed increased to nearly $230,000, up from the $172,000-plus mortgage she'd acquired in November 1998.

A friend called Marney McCleary for advice about buying a puppy from Dodie. McCleary learned that the litter's dam and sire didn't have OFA hip clearances and advised against the purchase. Irritated that her former friend wasn't doing hip clearances, she picked up the phone.

"Why aren't you doing clearances?"

"I don't have to do anything I don't want to," Dodie retorted. "They're my dogs."

CHAPTER 14

The Equine Money Pit

Dodie eyed her mostly paint colt, Native Jet Son, as her ticket to becoming a successful horse breeder. But he needed a more "regal" name as did her farm before she advertised his services. She dropped his "too cowboyish name" and re-registered the two-year-old colt as Lord Liberty with the paint association. Next, she advertised him standing at stud for $1,000 at Valley Ridge Farm and insisted he'd impregnate mares only by artificial insemination.

Shirley Gonzales, her horse breeder friend, warned that people wouldn't pay such a high stud fee or foot the cost of artificial insemination. Her registered paint stallions' stud fees ranged from $250 to $350.

"People aren't going to take a chance; they don't know what they will get," Shirley said, referring to the unpredictability of producing paints of color. "They aren't going to pay that kind of stud fee and get a solid baby that they'll get $1,000 out of or maybe less."

Dodie settled on a $750 to $850 stud fee. She promoted Lord Liberty with flyers and business cards featuring her artistic, water-color-like images of the stallion running through clouds or trotting across a field with white-capped mountains in the background. Lord Liberty's photo graced the cover of the May 2001 *New Mexico–Colorado Horse Trader* free magazine circular. Copy highlighted his "Size, Style, Stamina" and his dam's "Kentucky race bloodlines." But her advertising campaign netted only a handful of stud fees in 2001. She bred him to five of her own mares that year.

Lord Liberty's stud fees didn't ward off Dodie's troubles. She took out a $40,000 loan secured by her farm. When she failed to respond to two collection companies' lawsuits, default judgments totaling nearly $2,000 were entered against her. Earlier in the year, she'd been charged with misdemeanor harassment after she shoved a process server.[1] She pleaded guilty to the charge, but the case was dismissed after she completed twenty hours of community service.

These financial setbacks and legal entanglements didn't deter Dodie from advertising for part-time help to train her horses in the summer of 2001. Twenty-two-year-old Mary Gates responded.[2] She'd worked around equines since she was six years old and broken green horses but hadn't trained jumpers. Mary thought Dodie sounded classy and worried that she wouldn't get the job. But a friend assured her that she would because her prospective employer wasn't as she appeared. Dodie hired Mary on the spot for $8 an hour.

Mary looked around and saw about twenty-five horses, some in the two pastures, and others in fenced-in runs outside of two barns. She noticed foals and their dams as well as yearlings; two gray thoroughbred geldings, London Fog and Legacy; and a stallion, Lord Liberty. Some of the older horses were for sale from $5,550 to $7,500, a bit steep, she thought, and foals for $1,000 to $1,500. Potential buyers looked but no one bought.

Three times a week, Mary and a college student groomed and exercised most of the horses but rarely rode the two thoroughbreds. They saddle-broke Lord Liberty and other horses and trained the two- to four-year-olds that had been broken to a saddle but needed additional work to become marketable. Sometimes Dodie coached Mary to ride and train her jumpers. Because of a knee injury inflicted by a colt, Dodie only rode occasionally to demonstrate a technique. On some days, Dodie lacked patience with the horses. On other days, she'd hug Lord Liberty, which caused Mary to tense because she knew stallions could be unpredictable. She'd then relax when the 17.1 hand, 1,200-pound stallion rested his big head on his proud owner's shoulder.

Mary noticed that Dodie had high and low days. The young women wouldn't see her at all on some days, but on others, she'd appear with a glass of wine in tow for a late afternoon chat but never seemed tipsy.

Dodie didn't want them to help with the dogs or to "waste her money" to pay them to clean, feed, or water the equines. She'd do those chores. When she failed to wash the horses' water buckets, mold and sometimes drowned rats accumulated. So, one of the young women acted as a lookout while the other scrubbed and filled the buckets with fresh water. Dodie mucked the individual stalls perhaps once a week. Manure in outside runs and pastures went untouched for months until she had it hauled out to a big pile in a rear field. Only Mary continued to work in the fall and only when Dodie could pay her.

Dodie's finances dwindled as she poured money into her horse business and ignored many of her state kennel license requirements. The state had instructed Dodie to improve her kennel's sanitation five times by the summer of 2001 but never cited her for subpar conditions. In August, the state issued its first citation to Dodie: for failure to renew her kennel license. It fined her $75 and assessed a $22.60 late fee. A day later, the state issued a second citation for an excessive amount of feces and flies following a complaint, and it levied a $300 penalty. The inspector noted that the same violation had been ongoing and directed that feces be "removed weekly or as needed to control odors."

Just five days later, the state received a complaint that Dodie bred unhealthy and sick dogs. The veterinary records of the complainant's pup disclosed that the seven-and-a-half-week-old female chocolate had an eye discharge and adult roundworms the day after her owner brought her home. Three days later, a large lump developed over one of the pup's eyes, and her feces contained a "heavy load of coccidian," a parasite. For the next month, the puppy fought off a variety of worms and other parasites as well as itchy skin conditions.

Although a state inspector validated the complaint three weeks later, he didn't issue a citation and found that the puppies and adult dogs "appear healthy." The facility's sanitation had greatly improved, he wrote in his report, but noted that increased sanitation would help prevent the spread of parasites and worms. Once again, the state didn't contact the county about the condition or number of Dodie's dogs, and the county didn't inspect Dodie's kennel for compliance with its permit. Dodie continued to run her kennel as she pleased.

In the fall of 2001, Kelly Henderson decided not to wait until her aunt Pat Cooke, a Lab Club member, had a litter before she bought a Labrador puppy.[3] She and her family selected a Killkenny "white" pup for $600 cash even though they harbored concerns about the puppies' condition and Dodie. Their pup Bella's clean-looking fur smelled. The pup appeared younger than her age and acted as if she'd never been outside on the lawn. Henderson noticed that Dodie didn't cuddle the puppy or her littermate but picked them up as if they were "rocks." The family met the puppy's well-nourished chocolate dam in the "horribly" smelly farmhouse. Dodie refused to produce the sire because, she said, they didn't need to see him. Instead, she pulled out a three-ring binder filled with photographs of Labradors and pointed to the yellow sire's picture.

The couple had no way of knowing that some of the photos weren't of canines owned or bred by Dodie, or even of stud dogs that she'd used. She'd inserted several pictures from *The Labrador Quarterly*, then a Colorado publication that primarily featured conformation show Labradors. From the Winter 2000–2001 issue, she'd cut out the cover photo of two very light-yellow champions and, from the Spring 2001 issue, photographs of a stunning black champion and a chocolate female.

Dodie assured the couple that she'd mail Bella's AKC registration papers to them upon proof that they'd spayed the puppy. A few days later, the family picked up Bella, and the family's veterinarian gave the pup a clean bill of health.

Henderson called her aunt.

"Where did you buy the puppy?" Cooke asked.

"Dodie Cariaso."

"Oh my god, I wished you had told me."

Henderson's stomach fell. Oh, no. Her family had fallen in love with Bella and would never return her.

Dodie wasn't a reputable breeder and had been in trouble with the AKC because of multiple sires, Cooke told her niece. Had Dodie promised to give AKC registration papers for Bella?

Yes, as soon as Bella was spayed.

Cooke assured her that wouldn't happen.[4]

Months later, Henderson telephoned Dodie after Bella was spayed to ask for registration papers. Dodie said that she no longer provided them. Bella later was diagnosed with hip dysplasia.

Henderson didn't complain to the state about Dodie's misrepresentation, but other buyers reported problems. In January 2002, a woman alleged that she paid $600 cash for a five-plus-week-old chocolate puppy, purportedly sired by twelve-year-old Thunder, Max's sire. The pup had seizures. The state only issued a $300 fine to Dodie for selling the underage puppy, although it knew that she'd previously sold another pup under the state law's minimum sales age of eight weeks.[5]

Despite mounting complaints against Dodie, the state failed to question her litter and sales reports: eleven litters and eighty-two sales from March 2000 to March 2001, and eight litters and sixty-nine sales from March 2001 to March 2002. And it didn't contact Weld County.

Three complaints filed in late June and early July 2002 attracted more state attention. The complainants all thought they'd bought AKC puppies, and their new family members all had orthopedic problems that required surgery.

Neal and Paula Stack produced the March 2, 2002 *Denver Post* ad that had brought them to Dodie's kennel: "LABS, AKC, OFA, yel/wht, Eng. Am. Can. Show ch ped, bred for qual conf & temp, wide, blocky, kind. Guar $500–$600 970-613-1191."

Undeterred by the urine and fecal smell permeating Dodie's house, the young couple fell for the social, light-yellow boy that they named Riley.[6] Like so many other people, they thought an AKC puppy would be healthier and "better somehow." About two months later, five-month-old Riley underwent surgery for bilateral (both) elbow dysplasia.

At the surgeon's office, Paula Stack met an owner of another Dodie puppy that had "extreme elbow and hip dysplasia." That pup also underwent arthroscopic surgery on both elbows. Dodie failed to return calls from both puppy owners. She also didn't respond to the Stacks' request for reimbursement of more than $3,167 in expenses for Riley's elbow surgery and related costs.

The contracts for both puppies, born just three and a half months apart, listed nearly eleven-year-old McDougal as their sire and Becca as their dam. If true, that meant that Dodie had again bred McDougal, a known hip dysplasia carrier, to his granddaughter Becca, whose sire lacked an OFA hip clearance. Becca and McDougal also lacked OFA elbow clearances and were elbow dysplasia carriers, as demonstrated by producing Riley and/or the other puppy that Paula Stack met at the surgeon's office. Most Labrador females come into heat every six months, and their gestation period is sixty-three days. Becca couldn't have whelped both puppies given their purported birth dates. Had Dodie deliberately falsified the puppies' parentage, or had she just lost track of the various dams and sires because she was breeding so many dogs? Unknown to the puppies' owners, her recordkeeping had virtually stopped.

Both puppy owners complained to the state as did a Crested Butte couple after their puppy, sired by McDougal, underwent $1,500 surgery for bilateral elbow dysplasia. They'd responded to an ad nearly identical to the one read by the Stacks. The puppy later was diagnosed with hip dysplasia. His dam lacked OFA hip and elbow clearances.

The three complainants received the same contract, which stated, "no AKC papers issued" and no guarantees for any genetic disorder. But all believed they could register their puppies with the AKC. Dodie also gave the Stacks a copy of a letter addressed to new puppy owners from the AKC's Board of Directors' chairman. It stated if they hadn't received their "purebred puppy's official registration papers" from the AKC, "you will be receiving them shortly."

As a result of these three "false advertising" complaints, the state only issued a warning and stayed the $250 per complaint penalty. It directed Dodie to remove AKC from her advertisements or "to be totally clear that AKC is referring to the parents and not to the puppy." The state also required disclosure of the possibility of elbow dysplasia if she bred the parents of the complainants' puppies to each other and mandated that she take "reasonable care" to sell only those dogs that "are free of undisclosed . . . abnormality."

The state didn't know that earlier that year, the Tildens' Chief, whose friendly disposition and good looks won him many friends, was diagnosed with elbow dysplasia after he developed pronounced lameness following a winter hiking expedition. During the arthroscopic procedure, a surgeon removed tiny bone fragments from the right elbow of the less-than-two-year-old Labrador. The $1,881 bill didn't include subsequent indoor swimming physical therapy or acupuncture treatments. Chief's sire and dam were reportedly the same as the puppies owned by two of the June complainants. The purported sire, McDougal, died that year.

A full-blown drought hit Colorado in 2002. Hay prices soared, in some cases doubling from previous years. Dodie's badly overgrazed pastures couldn't support her twenty-five horses in a wet year, much less a drought. Her vet and farrier costs increased because of her equine numbers and inflation. Farriers now charged about $40 to trim hoofs and upwards of $80 to shoe one horse. Dodie's annual horse expenses easily could have reached $55,000 to $65,000, presuming she eliminated purchases of new tack and riding clothes. That amount excluded Mary's $10 hourly wage and unexpected veterinarian bills.[7]

Dodie's debt mounted. At the beginning of the summer, she took out a $20,000 loan from a finance company. Just a year before, she'd received an $80,000 revolving credit loan from a bank. She refinanced her farm mortgage once again, for nearly $234,000 with a $1,528 monthly payment, for a three-year term.

She didn't reduce her money-draining equine population. Instead, she cut back on canine vet bills. In lieu of paying Dr. Culver, she removed infant puppies' dew claws and administered shots. That year, Dodie spent $2,400 on vet bills, $622 of that on Prince, her very favorite Labrador, for tumor removal and hospital stays. She incurred numerous late fees on those bills.

Mary quickly realized that her employer couldn't afford to keep so many horses but had no idea that Dodie paid for loads of hay with checks from a closed bank account that fall. She only knew that a good number of horses were for sale but none sold. Only foals had sold since she had started to work for Dodie.

She offered suggestions but only when Dodie was in a good mood. The mares' hooves were growing out and their weight was dropping, she told Dodie. She suggested taking some mares to auction or finding homes for older mares that wouldn't be bred again. "They need more care and you can't provide it right now," Mary said.

Dodie gave a bay and white paint horse, with his registration papers, to Mary after several prospective buyers balked at his $7,500 price tag. She didn't want to sell him "to one of those greedy buyers." She enjoyed watching Mary train and show him.

"Maybe you can't afford all of these horses. Maybe you have got to look at what you can really afford to do, what quality of life and lifestyle you really can afford," Doug and Kathleen told Dodie over the years.

Set in her ways and living in her own world, Dodie rejected her relatives' advice. Now Doug saw Dodie's farm heading toward foreclosure. She needed to downsize to live within her means. He contacted a "very dear" Winter Park childhood skiing friend, now a prominent attorney in Denver, to help out. His friend agreed to assist free of charge and needed to meet with Dodie to review documents.

Doug requested that his older sister meet his friend in downtown Denver. She called for directions as she drove to the lawyer's office.

"That asshole rich brother of mine, I don't want to deal with any of you god damn lawyers," she shouted into her cell phone.

"Dodie, I'm not dealing with you," the lawyer responded. "I am done. That asshole, rich brother of yours is the only guy in America that is willing to help you."[8]

Finally, Dodie listened to Mary, who convinced her to downsize her equine population and persuaded her to bring a few mares to an auction in January 2003. When the two women arrived, the auctioneers chastised them for the horses' condition.

Why couldn't the auctioneers be nicer and realize that selling the horses would be best for these animals? Mary thought as she wept. Instead, the auctioneers made an ordeal out of the sales.

Dodie walked away with $1,154 after selling two mares. A private party purchased another broodmare and a filly from her that same month. One of her original mares, nearly nineteen years old, sold in another auction. But some of Dodie's horses didn't sell at auction because her minimum price wasn't met.

After Dodie stopped paying her mortgage for a year, Doug bailed her out of foreclosure. Other debts mounted. She owed $10,000 to the state as well as a total of nearly $11,000 to banks, a finance company, and a horse veterinary service when she failed to respond to their lawsuits.[9] She didn't pay a $9,000 bill from CSU's veterinary hospital where she had taken a foal injured at birth.[10] In late June, foreclosure proceedings began anew because once again, she'd stopped paying her mortgage.

While Dodie ignored these bills, she successfully deflected even more complaints about her dog care. The previous December, a state inspector invalidated a complaint about unsanitary conditions and a urine-reeking kitchen. The complainant, who had bought a puppy with a bladder infection, quoted Dodie as saying the vet gave her Amox, an antibiotic, by the 100s that she dispensed as she saw fit. Dodie told the state inspector that she'd advised the buyer that she'd medicated the puppy for the suspected infection, and the puppy couldn't be registered with the AKC.

Three months later, a prospective puppy buyer complained about a "horrible urine odor" and reported that three Labrador pups, in a small travel crate, "are lacking muscle development from being in the crates so long and were covered in feces." A six-month-old dog "wouldn't" walk on its own. The state didn't investigate, nor did it ask Weld County to look into the matter.

Weeks later, the state received an anonymous complaint that the stench of urine and feces was overwhelming at Dodie's. "Conditions were absolutely filthy." Four days later, the state invalidated the complaint apparently because its inspection, three weeks prior, failed to reveal any sanitation violations. "Animals appeared in good health. Pens & cages were within standards." A month later, the state instructed Dodie to cover two holes in the walls of one building after a routine inspection.

Dodie's all-time favorite Labrador, Prince, died in the spring of 2003. He'd been a favorite of Dr. Culver's as well. She'd treated him for parvo when he was a puppy in the summer of 1993, and he'd received lots of socialization at her vet hospital.

"I have been so depressed after Prince died . . . everything seems so useless and unfulfilling . . . I just miss him so much," Dodie journaled.

Dodie tracked down the Hurleys in Georgia to ask if she could use their black Labrador, Murphy, as a stud dog. She'd sold him as a pup in 1993. When the surprised Hurleys said that Murphy had been neutered years before, Dodie became angry, as if she didn't believe them.

Then in July, the Weld County District Attorney charged Dodie with felony and misdemeanor theft, and fraud by check, alleging that she'd paid for hay with checks on a closed bank account the previous fall.

Earlier that month, Dodie had cut back even more on dog expenses. She'd stopped taking her dogs to Dr. Culver after she'd spent $1,698 on vet bills that year. Over the next seven months, she bought $245 worth of medications and vaccines for kennel cough and other maladies from the veterinarian but rarely paid on time. She purchased dog food at Sam's Club, paying $6,268 for about 56,600 pounds in 2003. Each fifty-five-pound bag cost just over $11.

Carol Mayberry-Sanchez, her longtime horse and corgi friend, met Dodie for lunch at a Longmont restaurant. She listened to her friend explain that she'd just breed more litters to get out of her financial pinch. Dodie's eyes brightened as she mentioned her puppy prices. She'd place an ad in the *Denver Post*, and "people would just run up to my place and buy them because they were so good."

Carol felt put off by her friend's comments. Was she letting the dollar become "a little more important" than the dog? She knew that Dodie "in her right mind" would care for and love her dogs but wondered if she had forgotten to do so because of her financial situation.

Mary Gates listened to Dodie fret about the foreclosure of her farm and hint at suicide. Dodie confided that her brother offered to set her up in a little house if she didn't have her animals, but she'd rather run away. She talked about reestablishing herself in Missouri or escaping to a beach to sell art.

During the summer, Mary broke her clavicle after she was bucked off of one of Dodie's horses and couldn't work until she healed. She lacked health insurance or funds for medical treatment. Dodie paid her medical bills. That fall, she called Mary and offered to compensate her if she'd visit and chat over a glass of wine. Mary sensed that Dodie needed to vent to a friend and visited every couple of weeks but declined any payment.

The two women went to the movie theater to see *Lord of the Rings, Part 2*. Dodie dressed up, tied a fancy scarf around her neck, and attached a fake ponytail and ringlets to her hair. During the movie, she yelled at other patrons to turn off their cell phones. Mary cringed with embarrassment and decided that was the last movie they'd see together. Other days, the two women scouted for places for Dodie to live after her farm was foreclosed and drove to Boulder to visit Dodie's old haunts.

At times, Mary witnessed Dodie's anger at a disgruntled buyer who'd complained about his dog's hip dysplasia. Dodie's face contorted. She clenched her fists as anger ran through her body. A few minutes later, Dodie's foul mood passed. Mary withstood Dodie's moods and criticisms because she wanted to help her former employer and the horses. She urged her again to reduce the horse population that slightly increased after her employer took in a mare and her foal, sired by Lord Liberty, when their owner unexpectedly moved to Florida. Dodie also purchased a thoroughbred mare only later to discover that the horse was lame. Mary reached out to friends to try to find homes for the twenty horses.

On October 9, 2003, the Weld County District Court found that Dodie owed more than $260,000, including $17,000 in interest, on her farm mortgage. Could she dodge foreclosure a second time?

CHAPTER 15

On The Radar

An overwhelming stench of urine and feces blasted the furnace repairman as he stepped into Dodie's farmhouse on Sunday, November 30, 2003. The twenty-eight-year-old quickly retreated to his vehicle. He put on a gas mask and re-entered the farmhouse.

The repairman saw multiple dogs crammed together in crates in the kitchen. He heard but couldn't see other canines. The next day, he reported what he had seen to the Weld County Sheriff's Office.

Eight days later, Weld County Animal Control officers Andrea Milne and Gary Schwartz investigated the repairman's complaint. After Dodie granted permission to enter, the officers walked into a very unkempt and cluttered house that reeked of urine and feces. They counted five crates in the kitchen. Two crates each contained two puppies, both about six months old. Others housed multiple dogs. One dog lay on a chair. All the blankets in the crates were soaked in urine and coated with feces.

The officers continued through the kitchen to a back room littered with excrement. They counted ten to fifteen additional crates that housed primarily young feces-covered puppies. Dodie said she had cleaned the crates on Saturday, four days previous.

Five or six older puppies were contained in a small enclosed "extremely dirty" area just outside the back door. The officers heard dogs barking in several outbuildings and asked to see them. Dodie refused. She seemed agitated and less cooperative once Milne explained that she was investigating a complaint.

Schwartz, a ten-year animal control officer veteran, counted twenty-five to thirty dogs, some in separate pens in the backyard, on the property. The canines all had dog houses for shelter. Dodie's assertion that she cleaned the puppies' quarters daily was "highly doubtful. There was no way she could really take care of all of the dogs; she was by herself." The task, Schwartz believed, wasn't humanly possible.[1]

Dodie handed the officers a report from a state inspector who had visited the kennel just six days prior to follow up a mid-October complaint. An anonymous complainant had reported feces and tick-covered puppies with profusely bleeding toenails, and a tired and overbred dam with visible cuts. The state inspector smelled a strong odor of urine and feces and found sanitation "below standards." He failed to issue a citation and only instructed that cleaning "be done as often as necessary" for "the health of the animal."

That meant that the state had found violations at Dodie's Killkenny kennel thirteen times yet only cited and fined her three times, including once for late payment of her kennel license.

Milne contacted the state inspector, the first communication between the county and the state regarding Dodie's kennel, and learned about numerous problems. In her written report, Milne suggested that animal control consider filing possible animal neglect charges.

Five days later, Schwartz returned to Dodie's farm. A county health department representative and Chris Gathman, a county planner, accompanied him. Dodie gave the trio permission to inspect her property and dogs and ushered them into the kitchen. There they saw three Labradors and a springer spaniel, all looking healthy and well fed.

In the back-porch area, the trio smelled a strong odor of feces, urine, and ammonia. They observed numerous canines: eight- to ten-week-old puppies and a variety of other ages of Labradors in about eight crates, some with three to a crate. All the canines appeared "fat and healthy." Feces and urine covered the floors of their crates.

Dodie said she'd cleaned the crates and given all these dogs baths just three days before their visit. She tried to wash the crates and change the animals' blankets every two to three days.

At first, Dodie said she had about sixty dogs, including puppies, and then revised the number to forty. She'd had difficulty selling the adults because of a "glut" of Labradors on the market. Gathman informed her that she had many more dogs than allowed by her county kennel permit and needed to come into compliance.

Dodie asked for help to find homes for some of her adult dogs. She wanted to keep the puppies because they were the source of her income. Schwartz arranged for the Weld County Humane Society to accept a few dogs a day until about twenty to twenty-five canines were removed. Dodie and Schwartz agreed that he'd pick up a predetermined number of canines at prearranged times, and she'd relinquish their ownership to the Humane Society.

The next day, Dodie led six elderly Labradors, some with health issues, one by one out of her home. She sobbed as she handed over two twelve- to fourteen-year-old canines. Schwartz recalled later that was the only time that she cried during the relinquishments. Over the next two weeks, Dodie surrendered more adult Labradors, and Schwartz drove them to the Humane Society for placement in new homes. Three dogs were euthanized.

Gathman regarded Dodie as "fairly open" during his initial visit and didn't think that she'd hidden any dogs.[2] However, he also believed that she wouldn't reduce her canine population to sixteen, the maximum number allowed by her kennel permit. He scheduled a hearing for the Weld County Board of County Commissioners to decide whether there was "reasonable evidence" to conduct a second hearing to consider revoking her kennel permit for excessive dog numbers and accumulation of animal waste.

Like many local entities, Weld County chose to enforce its zoning regulations as a means of protecting animals instead of charging Dodie with animal abuse.

———

Just two days before the January 7th hearing, Gathman called Dodie to reinspect her property. Although the house looked cleaner, he counted twenty-two adult dogs and about seven to ten puppies less than six months old that were kept in one area of the home. Dodie claimed that she only had thirty dogs.

Two days later, Dodie stood before the county commissioners to outline the history of her kennel. She said that she first raised Labradors as a hobby, a side business to her pottery enterprise. She bred "show champion bloodlines," not field trial dogs. Her "excellent" breeding program expanded over the years to accommodate increased requests for puppies. She kept all of her eight- to ten-year-old healthy dogs because they were too much like family to be euthanized just because they reached a certain age. Her voice cracked. She admitted that she exceeded her permit's limit of dogs but assured commissioners that she had the money and facilities to care for them.

But she didn't have the money, nor did she breed show champion bloodlines. She'd overbred and neglected health clearances by using her own stud dogs. She'd misrepresented OFA certifications and her puppies as AKC registerable and falsified breeding records. Did she knowingly lie, or had she lied so many times that she believed what she told the commissioners? No one challenged her representations.

County Attorney Bruce Barker advised the commissioners that Dodie's permit and the Weld County code referenced the permissible number of dogs without distinguishing between adults and puppies.

Therefore, he said, the permit's limit, unless amended, was sixteen dogs.

Dodie's voice cracked as she said that she'd given away thirty-three Labradors. She wanted to keep thirty canines, including ten older dogs. Then she broke down and sobbed.

"I have been breeding so long; any breeder, they go over (the limit) quickly," she said, and puppies were difficult to sell after ten weeks of age. She had thirty-two puppies when county representatives visited in early December but now was down to seven. She'd move by June 1st because her property was in foreclosure and wanted "the opportunity to keep the dogs I have, I love."

Commissioners granted Dodie time to apply for a permit amendment by scheduling a second hearing for February 18th, when she needed to show why they shouldn't revoke her permit.

Before the hearing concluded, Schwartz reported that he'd visited Dodie's property about six times. He confirmed that she'd given up thirty-three dogs. While the county footed the bill of several thousand dollars (to care for the dogs), he said that Dodie "has been very cooperative."

The original problem related to some of the dogs' extremely bad living conditions, not the large numbers of canines, Schwartz said. "Those conditions have improved," and she'd been better able to care for fewer dogs.

He expressed concern if she was allowed to have more canines. "What happens two years from now or five years from now? Are we going to be dealing with this same issue where we are going to have to go in and have problems again?"

Later that month, a classified ad for Labrador puppies caught Schwartz's eye. He recognized the phone number as Dodie's.

He believed that she'd recognize his voice, so he asked a friend to call and pose as a prospective puppy buyer. Dodie asked $800 for a puppy before she lowered the price to about $250. His friend didn't visit Dodie's kennel.

A young Colorado couple did visit after they decided against purchasing an out-of-state "silver" Labrador. The breeder claimed the $1,000 puppy could be registered with the AKC and guaranteed her hips and eyes. Then Sara Bensman's boyfriend spotted Dodie's ad.

Dodie correctly advised that Labradors were only black, chocolate, and yellow. She encouraged the couple to check out a puppy in person and buy from a reputable breeder, such as herself. Her puppies sold for $500 cash only.[3]

But Dodie also spun her pups as AKC stock: she could register the couple's chosen pup Gaia, but the couple couldn't because people were breeding Labradors with hip dysplasia, and she didn't want any of hers bred to dogs with bad hips.

Dodie guaranteed Gaia's hips and represented that the puppies' sire, an out-of-state, black champion show dog, and the chocolate dam that wasn't on-site, were AKC registered. And she produced the parents' OFA hip certifications and pedigrees.

The couple quickly learned that their lively chocolate pup, with dull brown fur and a pointy nose, had diarrhea caused by parasites. Gaia was later diagnosed with hip dysplasia.[4]

———

Gathman, Schwartz, and a county health department representative noticed a "for sale by owner" sign as they turned into Dodie's driveway eight days before the commissioners' February 18th hearing. The property looked cleaner.

Dodie washed crates as she talked. She had about thirty-two dogs, and upkeep had been easier since she relinquished some of her Labradors to the county. Unless she found a way to avoid mortgage default, and that was unlikely, she said, she'd probably move before June 1st.

County staff met with Dodie immediately before the February 18th hearing. Both sides agreed to a four-month continuance so she could remove her kennel, downsize to sixteen dogs, or seek a permit amendment to allow more canines. Dodie left the hearing room to attend to a "dog emergency."

Commissioners conducted the hearing in Dodie's absence. They listened to a neighbor complain about the conditions of Dodie's dogs and horses. He and another neighbor also griped about barking dogs. Commissioners continued the hearing until March 3rd to allow Dodie more time to come into compliance.

The day before the March hearing, a Dodie puppy buyer asked the Denver Dumb Friends League to "get the word out" about the breeder so she "no longer breeds or has endorsements from any professional organizations such as the AKC or Labrador groups."[5] The League forwarded his email to the state, which labeled the complaint "a civil matter at this time" and didn't investigate.

The man also contacted the Lab Club to ask that members not refer potential puppy buyers to Dodie. When he purchased his yellow pup from Dodie the previous November, he'd wondered if the pup's black sire was really Ch. Cameo's Great Expectations, known as Dickens. Dodie claimed that Dickens and Becca, the yellow dam, were off-site but produced photos of them as well as copies of their pedigrees, registrations, and OFA hip certificates.

In fact, Dickens couldn't have sired the yellow pup because his gene color was BB (black-black), meaning that he could only produce black offspring even if bred to a yellow. Dickens was bred occasionally on the East Coast but only to carefully selected females and never to a Colorado mate. His owner routinely sent copies of Dickens's pedigree and clearances to individuals who inquired about his stud dog. Dodie had cut out Dickens's photo from the cover of *The Labrador Quarterly's* Spring 2001 issue and inserted it among photos of her dogs in a three-ring binder.

At just four months of age, the man's pup was diagnosed with severe bilateral hip dysplasia. The estimated $10,000 to $14,000 cost of surgical options, including hip replacements, was prohibitive. "I just wasn't going to spend $14,000 on a $400 dog." Instead, the pup received Rimadyl or over-the-counter medications for his pain.

When the man called Dodie to look into his pup's dysplasia, she accused vets of being out to get breeders and suggested that he euthanize the pup. She refused to refund his puppy's purchase price but offered a replacement pup. He declined her offer; he wasn't willing to risk a second unhealthy puppy.

———

Commissioners convened their March 3rd hearing in Dodie's absence. Gathman produced two letters solicited by Dodie. One neighbor wrote that she'd never seen Dodie's horses or dogs loose and only heard dogs barking for their food.

A state inspector, the second letter's author, reported that he hadn't found any violations related to overcrowded conditions or escape of dogs when he reviewed his office's file. Dodie complied with or exceeded the minimum square footage requirements per animal and could sell up to ninety-nine puppies a year. State law, he wrote, didn't govern the number of animals that a facility could house. "I have not known you (Dodie) to wholesale puppies to pet stores or other retail outlets, nor have I known you to board any animals." He failed to mention the state's numerous findings of filthy conditions and complaints lodged against Dodie.

Two neighbors again complained about barking dogs, burgeoning manure piles, and improper care of horses. One claimed that Dodie fed and watered only half of her horses and reported her twice to the county for failure to water them.

Dodie finally arrived at the hearing. She stood to address the commissioners and jumped from one topic to another. The breeder described the background of her Killkenny kennel operation and deflected her neighbors' complaints. Her Labradors were "very well taken care of animals" and "clean, healthy, wonderful dogs. These are AKC Labradors, companion dogs, show pedigree, not field, so they are not high-strung; these are mellow, sweetheart dogs." Her chronic barkers were debarked, and all her Labradors slept inside or in crates at night.

She rambled on and sometimes spoke in incomplete sentences as she explained her dog population.

"Why shouldn't I be allowed to keep my old dogs? I would be a puppy mill if the day they are done breeding when they are six or seven, okay kill them, they aren't breedable anymore."

The huge manure pile was from her horses. Friends scooped up the manure once a year. She placed dog waste in dumpsters, which were emptied weekly.

She'd had eight dogs and made a full-time living as a potter when she applied for her kennel permit. She bred as a hobby, but her business grew as time went on. "Do you say no to a growing business?"

Commissioners listened.

"How often are you going to check on me? Are you going to come out here, or what are you going to do?" she'd asked the animal control officer who inspected her kennel during the permitting process in 1988.

"She said never unless we have a complaint; that's what she said.

"Every time people did have a complaint with Weld County, they sent Animal Control. They found me not in violation in any way. I always was willing to show them anything they wanted. But they always just came in my kitchen and looked at some of my dogs in my kitchen, and that's all they seemed to want to see, the health of the animals."

She wasn't trying "to do anything blatantly illegal." The situation just evolved as she "became a popular Lab breeder. I just ended up keeping my old dogs instead of saying you aren't breedable, and I'm going to kill you. What people don't understand, it is extremely hard as a breeder to find homes, even if they are healthy, for eight, nine, ten and twelve-year-old healthy, beautiful trained dogs, people don't want to take."

Dodie conceded that she had more than sixteen dogs but didn't want to waste $2,000 to reapply for a kennel permit because she'd probably move.

A commissioner asked if she wanted to remove her kennel, apply for a new permit, or downsize her kennel.

"I am willing to downsize."

"To sixteen dogs?"

"Okay," Dodie responded in a dejected voice.

Her tone brightened when she said if she remained on her property, she could apply to have more dogs and get her numbers up to fifty or sixty within a year. She'd previously told commissioners that sometimes she had sixty to seventy dogs.

"But you understand you can't do that without a new USR [special use permit]?"

"Exactly. I am not a stupid person. I am highly educated. I know what you are saying. I will agree to get down to sixteen until I am either off the property, or I will come in with a new amendment."

Commissioners continued the hearing until June 16th, based on Dodie's agreement to downsize to sixteen dogs by March 31st. County staff would inspect her kennel to ascertain compliance.

———

Dodie stood next to her public defender in a Weld County courtroom and entered into plea agreement stemming from charges of writing bad checks to pay for hay in the fall of 2002. She pleaded guilty to felony theft on the condition that the charge would be dismissed after four years if she obeyed the law and the terms of unsupervised probation. The court ordered her to pay $3,795 in restitution, as well as other costs and fees, and perform twenty-four hours of community service. She also pleaded guilty to misdemeanor theft and received a six-month suspended jail sentence and a $500 suspended fine.

Just the day prior, March 18, 2004, she'd been served with yet another lawsuit brought by a collection agency. She failed to respond to the complaint, and a default judgment of $1,240 was entered against her.

In early April, Dodie handed over fifteen Labradors, including a few puppies in the three- to seven-month-old range, to Schwartz on two different days. He e-mailed Gathman on April 14th: "I think this will get her numbers to be in compliance."

Seven days later, a Loveland police officer stopped Dodie for driving her Nissan 280zx sports car with expired vehicle plates and without car insurance. The plates had expired in June 2002. Dodie said that she had just taken the car out of storage and hadn't had time to obtain a current vehicle registration. The officer issued a summons for her to appear in Larimer County Court on June 29th.

That same month, James and his wife Vikki Weeks drove to his sister's home. They picked out their new family member, an eight-week-old chocolate female puppy, and named her Tess. Dodie promised a puppy to her nephew, James's son, as a high school graduation present. Vikki noticed many puppies on Dodie's farm but had no idea how many dogs were there.

CHAPTER 16

Gauntlet

The dog fancy can be a very small world. I'd wanted to attend the Lab Club's inaugural specialty in 1986 to watch the judging of Margie Cairns, an old family friend from Scotland. Although work precluded my attendance, Margie and I caught up with each other's news during her stay at my home when she arrived in Denver. I wondered years later whether I'd missed not only Margie's judging but also a chance meeting with Dodie, who may have attended as a spectator. The show was only a half-hour drive from her farm.

Ten years later, I arranged for a day off from work before entering Molly and Max in the club's November specialty. I hoped that the two best friends would calm one another's nerves. Molly would compete in the American Bred class against other females for points toward her conformation championship. In conformation classes, dogs are judged on their looks and movement, not on whether they obey commands, but certainly a well-behaved and -handled dog helps. I entered Max, our Killkenny adoptee, in Novice B obedience.

My worries about whether I'd have time to warm up Max and groom Molly before their classes evaporated when I received the judging program. I'd also have time to change clothes in between their classes. Many obedience competitors wore pants in colors that matched their dogs' fur to make any crooked sits appear a bit less obvious. The conformation ring called for a suit or dress in colors to complement the canine. I'd wear my green Pendleton jacket and green and blue plaid skirt to show off Molly's dense black fur, and khaki slacks and a dressy green sweater when I competed with Max. I'd show him first in his class of two.

When we arrived at the show in Greeley, I first exercised both dogs outside and then walked them into the spacious Island Grove Park building. I noted the hundred-foot-plus open space separating the conformation and obedience rings but also an exit door on the far side of Max's ring.

Max and I watched the other Novice B dog as he went through his paces. We edged up to ringside as the dog completed the recall.

Our adoptee wagged his tail as we breezed through the Heel on Leash, Figure Eight, and Stand for Examination exercises. So far, so good. He trotted just a step or two out of position on the second-to-last stretch of the Heel Free routine.

The Recall, the final individual exercise, came next. Max waited until I called him. He galloped toward me and sat squarely in front of me. Applause broke out.

Only the Long Sit and Long Down exercises separated Max from his first qualifying score.

The Novice A and B handler-dog teams entered the ring for the group exercises. I held my breath and stared at Max as he sat with the three other dogs. He remained in place during both exercises. Only Max and the other Novice B dog qualified.

The judge called the two Novice B teams back into the ring. We hurried in and turned to face the judge. The dogs sat; the humans stood.

"First place goes to Dog Number Four, with a score of one hundred ninety and a half out of a possible two hundred points," the judge said.

I looked at the other handler and waited for her to step forward to accept the ribbons and trophies. She didn't move. Silence.

Then I glanced down at my armband. Number Four. Max had won his class! The judge handed us a blue ribbon and pottery creamer for first place, a green qualifying ribbon, and a pottery sugar bowl for the highest scoring dog in the Novice classes.

I learned afterward that a friend had positioned herself next to the door near the obedience ring so that no one used that exit during Max's performance. She knew about our Colorado Springs debacle. Max's guardian angel had watched over him.

My attention turned to Molly. I exercised and then groomed her. And I learned the hard way that one should never wash a dog without extreme care the day before a show. Her beautiful otter tail hung limp, motionless. I'd used a hose for bathing her and apparently sprayed ice-cold water on glands near her tail. She didn't get a look from the judge.

We didn't stay for the rest of the judging. Max needed to get home to rest up for the next two days of shows.

Max hesitated to jump out of his crate when we arrived the following morning at the Boulder County Fairgrounds in Longmont. He crowded me as we entered the show building and weaved our way through hordes of people and barking dogs.

I tried to relax. The competition was stiff; thirty-one dogs of various breeds were entered in Max's Novice B class. I just wanted our boy to qualify; placement in the ribbons seemed out of the question.

Max performed smoothly although not phenomenally during the individual exercises. Applause broke out as we finished. So far, he was qualifying.

Fifteen dog-handler teams lined up for the Long Sit and Long Down. We were near a Bernese mountain dog that had already failed the Heel Free exercise and his last sixteen classes. I vowed to give up long before that many attempts.

Max held on the Long Sit.

"Down your dogs."

"Down," I instructed as I gave Max the down hand signal. A verbal command and hand signal were allowed if done simultaneously.

Max just looked at me.

I couldn't give him another command if he were to qualify. I stared daggers at his sweet face for what felt like an eternity.

A second or two later, Max slurped my face, which was bent over near his head. He lay down. His eyes smiled.

"Leave your dogs."

"Stay," I said, praying that he would.

He did. I hugged him. He had two qualifying scores and only needed one more for his degree.

Max received a 190 score that left him out of the ribbons. He'd nearly given me heart failure, but we had a fun day. We drove a quick hour and a half home.

On Sunday, the third show day, Max really needed to perform. We both felt tired. Doubts crept into my brain.

Maybe I should consider retiring him if he doesn't qualify today, I wondered. His unpredictable behavior wasn't going to change. He'd already given me sufficient heart trauma in this quest for a CD.

Max seemed more relaxed than the previous day. He wagged his tail at spectators as we waited for our turn to compete. Twenty-five dogs were entered in his class.

He heeled quickly into the ring.

"Are you ready?" asked the judge, a rather stern-looking woman from the East Coast.

"Ready."

"Forward."

"Max, heel." We started forward, but Max didn't look at me. His near precision heeling was no more.

"Halt."

He sat but only after some reflection.

Max wagged his tail during the Stand for Examination exercise and remained in place. The Heel Free exercise was next.

"Forward."

"Max, heel." Off we went.

"Halt."

I stopped. Max sat a bit forward on my left side, a step ahead of me and slightly out of position.

"Forward."

"Max, heel." We started forward.

"Halt."

I stopped. Max continued on around me to my right side. He sat, facing the opposite direction.

This is going to be a real challenge when we start forward again. Will he heel on the right or left side? I hoped for the best.

The judge frowned. "Forward."

"Max, heel." Max swung around behind me as he returned to the proper position on my left side and started to heel. Then he gazed up at pigeons flying in the rafters. The pigeons were fascinating.

"Halt." Max walked slightly ahead, stood directly in front of me, and scratched his belly with a rear foot. Then he sat.

"Forward." My ears detected a harsher tone.

"Max, heel." He did and sat perfectly by my left side on the final halt.

The Recall was next. Max bounded to me, sat squarely in front of me, and, on my command, jumped into the heel position on my left side.

The crowd burst into applause. How could anyone applaud such a performance? I was confident that Max had flunked. My friends weren't so sure and offered me words of encouragement.

Max held on the Long Sit and Long Down. He even dropped quickly to the down position. We waited to see who was correct: my friends or me.

Our luck and training paid off. Max qualified, with a 179, the lowest score a dog of mine had ever received. But he'd earned his CD degree. I decided the judge didn't want to see our goofy boy in the ring again, so she qualified him.

The next month, Dave and I sent our annual Christmas card to John, Max's former owner, and enclosed a picture of Max next to his ribbons and trophies. We wrote about Max's new degree but omitted details of his declining performances. John wrote back to thank us for giving Max a good home.[1]

I framed Killkenny's Maximilian's AKC Companion Dog certificate and hung it in our home. It listed his breeder as Catherine W. Cariaso and the date of his degree as November 9, 1996. Max turned six that day and had given himself a very commendable birthday present.

CHAPTER 17

Denial

Thirty-year-old Erin Furman and her fiancé arrived a half-hour early to look at Labrador puppies in April 2004, the same month that the county found Dodie in compliance with her kennel permit. The couple spotted Dodie on her front porch, blow-drying the fur of three yellow puppies.

The five-week-old female Labradors, crammed into a Tupperware container, shivered. Probably more from the experience of the hairdryer than the fifty-degree temperature, Furman thought. The dental hygienist smelled urine on the fur of the healthy-looking pups.

Dodie snapped at the couple; she'd expected them later. She protested when Furman asked to see the rest of the litter to observe the other puppies' looks. They'd said they wanted a yellow female; it was too much trouble to show them the other puppies. "I am in the middle of moving. Stuff is everywhere."[1]

She let out of the house a very excited, light-yellow female about five to six years old when Furman requested to meet the puppies' parents but refused to produce the sire. It was too much trouble, the breeder repeated.

Dodie failed to show any official OFA certificates as proof of the parents' elbow and hip clearances and didn't mention eye tests. Instead, she displayed photocopies of pictures and pedigrees of random dogs. Furman noticed "OFA Good" penned in with a Sharpie next to some names of dogs.

The couple chose a red fox-colored pup. Dodie agreed to hold the puppy until after the couple's wedding, less than a month away.

"Would you like to meet Levi?" Furman inquired after she paid the $300 non-refundable deposit for the $600 cash-only pup.

"Sure." Dodie ambled toward the couple's Blazer. Furman opened the door to the backseat closest to where Levi sat. The dog moved to the far side when Dodie approached.

"Typical [Rhodesian] ridgeback," Dodie grumbled.

"You are the first person that he has acted that way toward," Furman retorted. She knew her very friendly dog loved people.

The couple thought that Dodie appeared a bit bizarre and unfriendly. Furman knew that most breeders wanted to show off their dogs, not hide them. The couple's excitement over finding a puppy pushed away any red flags.

Several days later, Furman called Pat Cooke, the Lab Club's membership chairman, to learn more about the club. A member since 1991, Cooke had bred numerous litters, shown in the conformation ring, and participated in field events. Her niece, Kelly Henderson, had bought a puppy from Dodie. Furman told Cooke that she was getting a Labrador puppy.

"Great. Who are you buying from?"

"Dodie Cariaso."

 Silence.

"Hello?" Furman asked.

"Did you say Dodie Cariaso?"

"Yes."

"When are you getting the puppy?"

"Next month."

Had she been promised (registration) papers?

She had.

Did the pup's parents have health clearances?

No. Furman knew Sharpies didn't count.

 Cooke learned that Furman bought the Killkenny puppy because her mother and sister purchased a dog from Dodie about seven years previously.

"Okay, that makes sense. I really advise you not to get a puppy from this woman."

That floored Furman.

Cooke said that the AKC had problems with Dodie. "There were other things going on, and there were health issues." She offered to refer Furman to several Lab Club breeders whose dogs were pregnant.

Furman accepted the referrals. Soon after, she and her fiancé visited Dorsey Johnson at Dos Rios Labradors in Berthoud. Johnson produced the extremely pregnant dam and the sire when Furman asked to see them.

Johnson displayed the sire's and dam's pedigrees, OFA elbow and hip clearances, and CERF paperwork. The sire was an OptiGen A, she said, and that meant that the puppies would never go blind from PRA. Furman didn't know about eye clearances and felt pleased that Johnson educated her.

The breeder accompanied the couple to a well-maintained kennel to show them eight very clean and happy adult Labradors. She identified all of the dogs who were related to the soon-to-be-born litter.

The couple made their decision. Furman gave Johnson a "ridiculously low deposit, about $100," which was totally refundable or could be applied toward another puppy in a future litter.

Johnson accepted Furman's invitation to meet Levi waiting in her Blazer. The ridgeback licked the breeder's face.

The next day, the couple's puppy Reese came into this world. They paid $700 for their new family member.

The couple decided to ask Dodie to return their deposit.

Furman telephoned Dodie and asked for her deposit back because they decided not to get a puppy. Dodie said it wasn't refundable. Furman requested that she reconsider because it would help with the upcoming wedding.

"I'll see what I can do," Dodie responded.

Reese became the couple's $1,000 puppy when Dodie didn't call.

Dodie bred even more Labradors to meet ever-mounting bills, and her canine numbers far exceeded her county permit's sixteen-dog limit.

At the same time, Mary Gates continued her crusade to find homes for her former employer's horses. She found it challenging to convince Dodie that prospective new owners only wanted to care for the equines and didn't want to make money off of them. Dodie accepted Mary's landlord's $2,000 offer to buy the colt and his dam that she had taken in the previous fall. In May, Mary convinced her to give Legacy to friends, who estimated that the tall thoroughbred gelding was 500 pounds underweight. Another friend agreed to take London Fog, the other thoroughbred gelding that also had shed way too many pounds.

Dodie needed to relocate before the bank evicted her. She rented a newish ranch home on ten acres, just a mile and a half south of her farm. Mary visited and noticed the orderly look of the rental, which was fixed up "really nicely." Dodie's dogs stayed behind at the farm; some of her older canines would join her later.

One Saturday night, Dodie sat on the large home's expansive porch and resumed writing in her journal after a more than five-year hiatus.

"I must say that because my life has spiraled into total turmoil in the last 2 years. . . I don't know where to start. My Dogs. These beautiful Labs . . . just started taking over my life . . . in a very BAD way. Complaining people. Dog fights. Vet Bills. Too many other Lab breeders. Too much Dog poop. Too much Barking. My beautiful old foundation dogs have all died. I started selling fewer pups a couple of years ago. Money got tight—Colo had a terrible drought in 2002. I had 18 horses to feed.

"I have now made so many bad decisions . . . due to all the money and dog-stress and Horses too!! My beautiful farm is in foreclosure again! Here it is May 7th—I probably have to be off the property in June or July—I don't even know—because I don't have a lawyer. They are just too expensive—and all the lawyers I've met in the last few years have been total Ass-Holes."

Dodie described her $2,000-a-month rental home: "It is beautiful and quiet here—perfect for my last days on this earth . . .

"Of course, I can't pay this unless some miracle from you, or . . . happens!" She wanted to start over her Lab breeding business and build a new kennel but estimated startup costs at between $8,000 and $10,000.

"Please, Dear Lord, Please, Please, Please . . . Help me, Help me—Show me what you want from me! I am so confused. I need to do the right things—And I don't know what that is!"

She moved back into her farmhouse after a two-month stay in the rental because she hadn't paid her rent.

On June 16th, Weld County commissioners resumed their hearing on Dodie's kennel permit without Dodie in attendance.

Gathman, the county planner, reported that Dodie was in compliance with her permit in mid-April. County staff hadn't visited her farm since then. He didn't know if she'd moved from the farm, now owned by a bank. Her kennel permit required her to own the farm; it couldn't be transferred to another owner or another location, he said.

Commissioners specifically found Dodie in compliance with her permit on April 14th. After some discussion, they revoked her county kennel permit for good cause: she no longer owned the farm.

Six days later, the Weld County District Court ordered the sheriff to evict Dodie from the farm. The eviction date was scheduled for June 29th, the same date as her court appearance for the April traffic ticket.

As eviction crept closer, Dodie hunted for a new home for her dogs and herself. She responded to an ad in the *Thrifty Nickel* and spoke with Carl Cushatt, whom she described as a sixty-two-year-old single, quiet gentleman. The over-the-road trucker wanted a renter to share his home on ten acres southwest of Berthoud and to look after his place when he was away.

Two days later, Dodie met Carl and his girlfriend, "a very nice older woman," at his farm. Dodie wrote later in her journal that she introduced herself as Kate, "my grandmother's name because I was named after her and I've always loved the name. I was beginning a whole new life. I felt like I was to start over. Carl and I got along well . . . He seemed to take to me. I told him I was a Labrador breeder and wanted to build a kennel. He walked me around the property and we agreed that behind his horse barn . . . away from the sight of his favorite neighbors to the East . . . was a good place."

Dodie told Carl that she'd get rid of most of her dogs before she moved. She'd bring only a few Labradors and one litter to his property. She learned that Carl was a truck driver and on the road for days and weeks at a time. He discovered that they both were "kind of religious," which "kind of put her over the top" of the applicants. Carl thought Dodie seemed like a "nice person" and had no other place to go. "The more we talked, the more I liked her."[2]

On the road in California, Carl received a telephone call from Dodie.

"What do you think, Carl, do you think we can get along?" Dodie asked.

Carl chuckled. "Well, you don't seem like too bad a gal." He believed the arrangement would work: Dodie would live rent-free in his home in exchange for some light housekeeping duties, generally looking after his house, and feeding his two horses on the weekends when he traveled.

"Can I start moving some things in?" Dodie inquired. "I won't move anything into the house, but I did want to move a few things over there."

Carl agreed. She'd move into his guest bedroom on July 1st and occupy that room until his renter moved out, probably mid-July.

Dodie continued moving preparations. Her farrier trimmed the hooves of seven horses. She paid him cash and then several hundred dollars more to board Lord Liberty and three mares, including the lame thoroughbred.

She sold some of her antiques for about $8,500 to a relative of Mary Gates's boyfriend. An estate broker firm purchased "decent" antiques, pottery, and other household goods. Firm representatives planned to clean up the goods before they auctioned them off at the "Cariaso Living Estate" on July 11th.

Dodie felt displeased with the amount of money she received for her antiques. And desperate. She rented a Loveland-area storage unit for her remaining furniture, artwork, and other personal property and stored her MG sports car.

On June 28th, the day before the scheduled eviction, Dodie called Animal Control officer Schwartz to relinquish a few more Labradors. He arrived early in the afternoon to accept seventeen Labradors, mostly puppies between four to eight months of age.

Mary hadn't heard from Dodie and knew that her former employer, who still had three horses on her property, was focused on her dogs.

She drove her truck and horse trailer to Dodie's farm so she could take the equines and find homes for them. Dodie agreed.

As Mary drove off with the mares, Dodie and her nephew washed dog crates and fence panels. They worked until dark and then hauled the kennel fencing to Carl's to build three separate runs.

Dodie arose early the next morning on Tuesday, June 29th. It was her final day at the farm. She fed, watered, and exercised all of her dogs before she loaded them into crates that she'd stacked in a horse trailer. The dogs acted nervous and anxious. They "knew something awful was happening. They were all scared and shaking."

Two horse trailer loads later, all Dodie's dogs were situated at Carl's. Then she learned that four canines had escaped from their crates; two had chased Carl's horses to a neighbor's house.

Dodie called the canine escapees; three returned and were crated. She found the fourth, a chocolate female, shaking and standing, frozen in place, in a neighbor's front yard. The dog had never been out of her yard or home, her "safe area." She carried the Labrador partway back to Carl's property. Then she and a neighbor captured and returned Carl's horses to a corral.

When Carl telephoned later, Dodie assured him that all was under control. No animals or people were hurt. He said he'd return the next day at about 6 p.m.

Dodie took her springer spaniel, Ebony, over to play with a German shepherd that she'd spotted with a man sitting outside a trailer behind Carl's house. She asked if the Labradors' barking bothered him. It didn't.

She started to cry; she felt scared and feared the situation wasn't going to work out. The man assured her that it would work out; she was just tired from moving. Rest and you'll feel better the next day, he told her.

Dodie called Vikki, her sister-in-law, to say that she'd moved. Vikki heard worry and concern in Dodie's voice as she related how she'd let five or six of her dogs out of their crates at a time to exercise and how upset they seemed.

Carl returned home the following day, Wednesday, June 30th, and found Dodie behind his barn. His jaw dropped as he looked at eighty-some Labradors in crates and pens.

"You cannot bring in animals like this because they are going to bark, and these neighbors are close. I am going to have them all down my throat."

Dodie said she'd stay in her van to be near her canines and agreed to get rid of 90 percent of them.

Carl, a trusting soul, believed her. "These Labs, they shouldn't be too hard to get rid of them, give them away if nothing else." He said that he'd drive to Dodge City, Kansas, the next day, Thursday, July 1st, and return late on the 2nd.

Dodie, her twin brother James (l)
and younger brother Doug
(James Wilson courtesy photo)

Dodie and Fred
(Wilson courtesy photo)

The newlyweds with Dodie's mother and father
(Wilson courtesy photo)

Dodie astride her part-thoroughbred
Witchy Blue next to Liebchen
(Wilson courtesy photo)

Dodie at work
(Wilson courtesy photo)

Dodie's foundation Labrador, Samba (l), and her daughter
(Wilson courtesy photo)

Dodie's paint horses
(Wilson courtesy photo)

Charmin' Find, Max's grandmother
(Wilson courtesy photo)

McIvory
(Bland Nesbit courtesy photo)

McDougal
(Nesbit courtesy photo)

Yellow mother with nursing pups
(undated photo)
(Wilson courtesy photo)

Dodie and a favorite yellow pup
(Nesbit courtesy photo)

Young puppies
(Wilson courtesy photo)

Liberty, one of the abandoned Labs, with puppy Owen.
Leslie Brown, co-founder of Safe Harbor Lab Rescue, adopted her.
(Brown courtesy photo)

Max in his first owner's home
(John Ulrich courtesy photo)

Max and Molly above Square Top Lakes

Max with Cary on his first 14er summit, Mt. Sherman

Max with his "niece" Brew and her mother, Molly

Max and his great "niece" Taz

Dave and Max on LaPlata Peak's summit

Max on his last 14er summit, Mt. Shavano

CHAPTER 18

Survivors

A shaken James arrived home on July 3rd from the rural field where Dodie had left dozens of Labradors. He described to his wife Vikki the chaotic scene at Carl's and the discovery of the body bags containing some of his sister's dogs.

Vikki picked up the telephone. She reached Dodie on her cell phone in Missouri and broke the news about what had happened.[1]

"My dogs! My dogs! What did they do to my dogs?" Dodie cried out. She said she'd thought Weld County would just take and find good homes for her dogs as it had in the past. But she'd left them in Larimer, not Weld County.

Vikki knew that Dodie loved some of the Labradors as pets, and while others weren't pets, they all had names.

James telephoned his younger brother Doug. He told him about the abandonment and promised to stay in touch. A shocked Doug and his wife Kathleen went online to learn more about what had happened.

———

Tim Kloer, a Larimer County Humane Society employee, put on plastic gloves before he clutched each animal while Dr. Spindel examined them. His white T-shirt quickly became caked with feces. A coworker photographed each canine next to a white sheet of paper that bore a number for identification purposes.[2]

The young veterinarian recorded her observations. The weights of the three-week-old or younger puppies were slightly below average.

The puppies older than three weeks, and the majority of nursing mothers were underweight. Four of the ten weaned puppies, all eight weeks or older, had significant health issues.

But the weights of the adult males and non-nursing females ranged from ideal to obese.

At times, the on-scene veterinarian couple helped Dr. Spindel reach medical conclusions as to whether individual dogs could be saved. Those that could and were of sufficient age received a vaccination for distemper, hepatitis, and the parvovirus and deworming medicine.

Dr. Spindel opined that every animal exhibited behavior that would "unquestionably" deem them "unadoptable" in an animal shelter. The dogs panicked when out of their crates. They weren't leash trained. Many bit through leashes; some required the use of catch poles to restrain them so they could be examined. Several dogs required sedation. The dogs were in various states of distress and unable to "engage in normal activities such as feeding, drinking, grooming, and socially interacting." Dr. Spindel concluded that they experienced stress from "fear, hunger, dehydration, anxiety, boredom, separation, and their physical environment."[3]

The young veterinarian relied on Neira for his assessment of the dogs' behavioral problems and whether those problems, with work, could be overcome so that the animals could be adopted. Other workers assisted with this behavioral assessment. They considered how far away a dog stayed from humans, how accepting it was to touch, if it "freaked out" when put on a leash, and, generally, the overall body posture of its ears, tail, and lips, and its eye expression.

Neira found the hard part of the rescue was that many of the friendly dogs were unhealthy, and the aggressive or extremely frightened dogs were in good health.[4]

Of the eighty-four Labradors encountered by the Humane Society, only nine adults and twenty-one puppies survived on July 3rd. The survivors were canines that the Humane Society workers thought could be nursed back to health and sufficiently socialized to find forever homes.

Three eight-week-old puppies were released on-site to Carl or his family after the new owners promised to bring them to the Humane Society for vaccinations. Carl wanted to keep the light-yellow adult male that the workers had first noticed in his yard. But he changed his mind when the dog repeatedly fled from the backyard to return to his crate. He traveled too much to deal with the escape artist.

Carl agreed to use his horse trailer to transport the crated survivors to Cloverleaf Kennel Club's facilities. The facility had an on-site caretaker and adequate kennels to temporarily house the Labradors. That gave workers time to create space for them at the Humane Society's shelter apart from the existing population, to prevent the spread of any illness.

At Cloverleaf, Carl saw that the facility had room to house all eighty-four Labradors. Earlier in the day, he'd questioned why so many of the dogs were put down. A worker told him that they just didn't have room. But they did, he thought, as he looked around. And why couldn't some of the dogs have been taken to shelters in Greeley or Denver? he wondered. When he'd fed and watered many of the canines that morning, none seemed "vicious" or so sick that they needed to be euthanized.

About 10 p.m., Neira drove his vehicle, with the bodies of the euthanized animals, from Carl's to Colorado State University's veterinary school in Fort Collins. That night, some of the workers experienced nightmares about what they had seen. Neira couldn't get the yellow puppy with his nose and upper muzzle torn away from the bone out of his mind.

For the next several days, Humane Society workers took shifts to care for the twenty-seven Labradors. These dogs are just a few of the estimated 825,000 purebreds in this nation's shelters.[5] That figure is a fourth of the total shelter population figure of 3.3 million dogs.

The survivors included four nursing dams and their litters, and three older yellow puppies. Only one adult male survived: the young yellow that Carl had fancied. Four other females, two yellows about four to five years old and two older dogs, a chocolate and a yellow, also lived.

Only the two older females had tattoos. Workers estimated the age of "Lucca" at twelve years old, but she was only nine. Registered as Killkenny's Kersey O'Shea, Lucca was the daughter of the puppy that Dodie bought from Susan Burke in 1993. The older yellow, "Daisy," registered as Killkenny's Charlilly Charm, was nine and a half years old and a half-sister to Max.[6]

The abandoned dogs lived in two dorm-style buildings with separate areas for the adults. They received antibiotics to treat coccidiosis, an organism causing diarrhea and obtained from eating feces. Puppies received treatment for worms and additional vaccinations.

Workers fed, watered, and bathed the Labradors. They supervised the adults and weaned puppies when in a communal run. And they monitored the animals' weight gains.

Christine Samuelian, director of the Humane Society's behavior and training, smelled an awful stench when she first approached the rescued animals at Cloverleaf.

"It still stays with me, the god-awful smell; smelled like parvo," she recalled years later.[7] She learned the dogs didn't have parvo, but their diarrhea, which they rolled and walked through, smelled as if they did.

Samuelian called home after her first Cloverleaf shift to ask her husband to leave a towel in their garage. When she arrived home, she stripped, wrapped herself in the towel, and stepped into the house.

The next day, she dressed in the same smelly clothes before she left for Cloverleaf. She knew that she'd throw out the clothes because they'd never come clean.

Several days after the abandonment, Neira and Samuelian stopped on their way to Cloverleaf at a 7-Eleven convenience store about a half mile from the Humane Society. He waited in the vehicle while she entered the store.

Minutes later, Neira noticed Samuelian in the checkout line. He switched his gaze to the woman standing behind her. The woman wore a wig, a hat, and large sunglasses. He stared harder before he realized that the woman was Dodie, who he'd suspected was hiding in the area. Neira thought there was an outstanding warrant for her arrest but knew he lacked the authority to execute it. He called the sheriff's office.

Samuelian returned to the car and an animated Neira. She couldn't believe that she'd stood next to Dodie and then realized that she'd never seen her photo.

Neira and Samuelian helplessly watched as Dodie walked out of the store and drove off. After their Cloverleaf shift, they returned to the shelter. Samuelian described her near encounter with Dodie and the wanted woman's get-up to the receptionist.

"Oh, my God! She was here!"

A woman sporting a wig, sunglasses, and a hat had walked into the shelter earlier that day and asked to see the abandoned dogs. She left after the receptionist said no one could see them. And, Samuelian surmised, the woman drove around the corner to the 7-Eleven. The Labradors were watched more closely after that day.

James looked up from planting trees in the backyard of his Denver home. He studied an individual who climbed over his back gate and walked toward him. That's when he recognized his sister. She wore dark glasses and a hat as an apparent disguise.

"I'm Jesse McClure."

"Dodie, what are you doing here? You know that they are looking for you. You are on the front page of the paper; you are on the news."

"I need help and a place to stay."

James thought quickly. "Wait here." He retreated into his home. "Dodie's here."

His wife of eight years looked at his pale, drawn face. "Yeah, right."

"No, really. She's in the backyard and wants help."

"Oh, my God."

The couple discussed what to do. They didn't want to harbor a fugitive.

James stepped back outside.

"Dodie, this is not a good place for you to be. You need to turn yourself in. It's not a huge thing now, and it will work itself out. This running thing is not a good thing." He knew his sister already had previous bad experiences with the law, mostly self-inflicted and related to her finances. She won't turn herself in, he thought.

"You can't stay here. You need to go."

A "wild man look" came over her face as she internalized anger. She turned and stormed away, through the backyard gate and down the alley out of sight to her parked Toyota 4Runner. James walked back into the house. He didn't pick up the phone. Dodie was his twin.

The Humane Society shifted dogs around its shelter and placed others in foster homes to make room for the Labradors. Only Dr. Spindel interacted with the Labradors for two weeks to avoid any cross contamination with other shelter dogs. She drew blood from five Labradors as a "representative sampling" and found evidence of anemia, probably due to stress. The dogs gradually gained weight.

The public reacted swiftly to the widespread television and newspaper accounts about the abandoned Labradors. Donations poured into the shelter. A few individuals offered to foster the dogs. An estimated 600 persons, including several who previously purchased puppies from Dodie, wanted to adopt the surviving Labradors. Others contacted the Humane Society to relate their experiences with Dodie, including an individual who'd bought a puppy from her just three days before she left the farm.

The Lab Club e-mailed its members to seek aid for the Labradors. It offered to collect necessary supplies for the animals, send members to help socialize the dogs, and educate prospective adoptive families about the responsibilities of Labrador ownership.

By July 21st, the Humane Society had received more than $10,000 in cash donations from the general public, including Lab Club members. Some contributions were for as much as $500 and $1,000.

The Humane Society faced an enormous challenge when it screened applicants to permanently adopt the Labradors because of the dogs' health issues and socialization problems, with people and, sometimes, with other canines.

To facilitate the screening process, the Humane Society scheduled an informational session at the county fairgrounds. During the July 28th night meeting, a crowd of want-to-be Labrador owners watched a PowerPoint presentation that contrasted the behavior of a healthy Labrador with one of the abandoned dogs.

An estimated 200 people listened as CEO Olsen and Samuelian explained the amount of care that the animals needed. They emphasized that the adults required even more socialization than the puppies. Their goal was to pare down the applicants to those able to care for and handle the adults that exhibited seriously altered behavior, such as cowering at the sight of a leash. At the meeting's conclusion, thirty-five individuals applied to adopt one of the Labradors. All but one wanted a puppy. Workers followed up with telephone interviews before they chose the successful applicants.

Lauren Kloer, the Humane Society's foster program director, e-mailed more than 200 volunteers to foster the healthier adults and non-nursing Labrador puppies. The animals were unsocialized and unhealthy, and required continuing medical care, she wrote.

The Humane Society wanted the Labradors, as soon as medically and behaviorally cleared, to live in foster homes to accelerate the socialization process. The animals needed to learn basic commands such as sit, come, and heel (on a leash) as well as to wait before they entered doorways and to stay off counters. This constant care and training would be essential to their development and preparation for their adoptive homes.

The foster volunteers were asked to record their canine's preferences and dislikes, any cowering issues, and house-training progress. The Humane Society sought to transfer as much information as possible from the foster to the permanent home.

The Labradors received weekly medical checkups and evaluations for progress, if any, with social skills. Lauren Kloer noticed many appeared to be deformed and walked with a funny gait.[8] The adults exhibited more behavioral issues than the puppies and stayed longer at the shelter to receive additional socialization. By mid-August, several of the Labrador adults lived with their new families, and many of the puppies resided in foster homes.

A month later, most of the abandoned Labradors had found homes. All of them were spayed or neutered before they were released to their permanent owners. Four adult females considered the more difficult behavioral cases still hadn't acquired new owners. All but one had nursing puppies when rescued. Safe Harbor Labrador Rescue, a nonprofit organization, accepted these Labradors to try to find them forever homes.

———

Nine days after Carl discovered the Labradors, the Larimer County District Attorney's Office charged Dodie with sixteen counts of cruelty to animals: fifteen for animal abuse/neglect and one for animal abuse/abandonment. Specific dogs weren't named as victims.

A sheriff's investigator, in an unmarked black pickup truck, staked out Carl's property on the afternoon of July 12th. Authorities thought Dodie might return to pick up her prized Nissan 280zx sports car. About 3 p.m., the investigator noticed a taxi and its female passenger, outfitted in a wig, hat, and sunglasses, approach Carl's farm. He pulled over the cab as Dodie urged the cab driver not to stop. The investigator arrested her on two warrants—one for animal abuse and another for failure to appear in a traffic court case on the day that she moved to Carl's.

He gathered up Dodie's purse and miscellaneous pieces of clothing and bedding as well as three half-full bottles of Armor-All Protectant, commonly used to clean car interiors, from the taxi. Next, he drove her to the Larimer County jail in Fort Collins. There, a deputy inventoried her other property, including more than $3,266 in cash.

In response to routine screening questions during the booking process, Dodie reported that she wasn't suicidal and listed a knee as a physical handicap or impairment. Later that day, she walked out of jail after Vikki posted the $10,000 animal abuse case and the $1,000 traffic case bonds.

On July 27th, Dodie appeared in the county court's magistrate division to be arraigned on the animal abuse charges. She wanted to hire a lawyer, so her case was transferred to county court and scheduled for a pretrial conference for possible plea bargain negotiations.

Deputies then arrested her for failure to comply with the terms of her probation in the Weld County felony theft/bad check case. A judge had issued an arrest warrant after Weld County prosecutors filed a complaint that alleged the noncompliance. Hours after her arrest, Dodie posted a $5,000 bond.

Homeless, Dodie slept in her van and then in a stable's tack room in the Estes Park area. She called Vikki more frequently.

"Why don't you buy a place in Estes Park? It would be a good investment, and you could rent it to me," Dodie told her sister-in-law.

Vikki declined. She knew she'd never be paid. That's why she'd taken possession of Dodie's Toyota 4Runner and its title as collateral for putting up bond money. When Dodie said that she needed money, Vikki lent her funds and put the 4Runner up for sale. After she sold the SUV, she gave Dodie about $8,000 and kept $4,000, the amount that her sister-in-law owed her, from the proceeds.

Vikki went out for lunch or dinner with Dodie when work brought her to Estes Park. One day, she stopped in to visit and saw a cute light-yellow Labrador puppy running toward her. Dodie said she'd used an alias to purchase puppy Ben at just eight weeks of age. That upset Vikki, who understood that a court order barred Dodie from pet ownership. And Dodie had used part of the money that Vikki had loaned her for living expenses to buy the puppy. Ben turned two months old on July 20th.

CHAPTER 19

Battle Lines

The Larimer County District Attorney's Office assigned Dodie's case to a dog-loving prosecutor who owned a black Labrador named Lucy. Deputy District Attorney Jennifer Lee had hoped for the assignment. In her three years with the office, the thirty-two-year-old prosecutor had the most trial experience in misdemeanor and traffic cases of any nonsupervisory deputy district attorney then assigned to Larimer County Court.

Lee read the district attorney's case file once, then twice, which she usually didn't do because of the hundreds of cases she prosecuted each year. But she wanted to be well prepared for the August 31 pretrial conference; she was outraged when she heard about the abandonment.[1]

She cried as she scrutinized more than a hundred on-scene photographs. Anger welled up inside her while she stared at countless images of emaciated, sick, and filthy Labradors and euthanized Labradors of all ages.

Tears streamed down her face as she read about the dogs' physical and environmental conditions. She'd reviewed appalling photographs and read awful accounts of crimes before but very few seemed as horrendous. In her mind, crimes against children and animals were some of the most horrific because the victims were so helpless. She felt convinced that the Labradors' conditions had not occurred over a few days but over a much more extended period of time.

Lee conferred with Neira, the Humane Society investigator. They'd worked together on other cases. She considered him a fair, compassionate person who took his job seriously without being overbearing. They discussed how Dodie could have prevented much of what had occurred if she'd relinquished her dogs to authorities before their conditions deteriorated.

Neira helped Lee understand the "astronomical costs" of the case: the rescue operation, the abandoned animals' continuing care, and the case prosecution. They recognized that money used in connection with this case would be taken away from other worthy projects that involved lost or abandoned animals. Neira recounted how the abandonment took its toll on the veterinarians and other on-scene rescuers. Many had recurring nightmares over what they had seen that hot July day. You couldn't help but be upset over what was witnessed, Neira told her.

The extensive news coverage of the abandoned Labradors prompted current and past owners of Dodie's dogs to telephone and e-mail the Humane Society and district attorney's office. Some were shocked. Others lauded Dodie and their Killkenny Labradors. Still others related the numerous health problems their pups had experienced.

At least two owners, including Jon McClain, who'd bought his now seven-year-old, even-tempered Labrador, Montgomery, as a pup, offered to testify. He'd spent an estimated $10,000 on Montgomery for vet care, including surgery to correct an orthopedic disorder and two mast cell tumor surgeries by the time the dog was just fourteen months old.[2] The district attorney's office asked McClain to submit a written statement and Montgomery's medical history and bills for the case file.

Lee gave Dodie the nickname of Cruella De Vil, the self-centered, mentally unstable character in the *101 Dalmatians* movie, to help her cope with the case. She was reminded of Cruella's villainess because of "the hoarding of dogs" and her perception of Dodie's abuse, "whether it be actual physical abuse or neglect" of her canines.

Although Lee believed that Dodie's actions were inexcusable and should have constituted a felony, she knew that felony animal abuse could be charged only if Dodie had intentionally inflicted harm, such as burning an animal. And that was true in this nation's other states—Dodie's actions were only misdemeanors, although penalties varied.[3]

The evidence only supported the Class 1 misdemeanor animal abuse charges of neglect and abandonment. Each charge exposed Dodie to a possible sentence of six to eighteen months in the county jail and/or a fine ranging from $500 to $5,000 and/or probation of up to five years. That meant that the judge could sentence Dodie to a maximum of twenty-four years in jail if she were convicted of all sixteen counts and sentenced consecutively on each count.

In Missouri, where she fled after the abandonment, Dodie could have spent only fifteen days in jail and fined $500 per charge for the same offenses.

But Dodie faced accountability in Colorado and a hard-nosed prosecutor.

"I knew that I wasn't cutting her any break. She had to plead straight up." The images of the dead and dying dogs remained etched in Lee's mind. The prosecutor wanted Dodie to serve jail time to feel like the canines depicted in the case photographs. She wouldn't agree to dismiss any of the counts but thought an offer to limit jail time to sixteen years was reasonable.

Although a sixteen-year sentence from chief county court judge Ronald L. Schultz, who presided over Dodie's case, was "not necessarily realistic," Lee thought that it wasn't "out of the question with any judge given the horrific nature of the crimes." Schultz, a judge since 1974, had private practice and prosecutorial experience. Assigned to his courtroom for a total of about eighteen months, Lee regarded Judge Schultz as a fair judge who respected those within the criminal justice system and maintained a good judicial demeanor. He also seemed approachable and human.

However, Lee knew that Judge Schultz was a reputed lenient sentencer. If she tried the case, he'd hear vivid accounts of the horrors inflicted upon the Labradors. She thought that testimony coupled with any public outrage might influence him to impose a stiff sentence: jail time and restitution.

She also wanted to try the case to send the message that neglect and abandonment of animals were unacceptable. Dodie's type of behavior, she thought, could lead to much worse. She believed that some of the most heinous crimes started with animals, and some of the worst serial killers began their careers by torturing animals. Although Dodie didn't directly torture the canines or engage her animals in dogfighting, Lee believed that the Labradors' physical conditions, caused by neglect, were torturous regardless of intent.

———

Television crews and print media waited in the hall outside of the conference rooms on the courthouse's second floor to catch a glimpse of Dodie as she walked to and from her pretrial conference. As the day wore on, Lee wondered if Dodie would even show up. Sometimes defendants unwisely failed to appear for their pretrial conferences. When that happened, the judge issued a bench warrant to arrest the defendant for failure to attend the conference.

Would Dodie make a scene? Lee wondered. She noticed numerous deputy sheriffs in the courthouse ready to maintain order if necessary.

Lee looked for Dodie when she greeted other defendants and defense attorneys before their pretrial conferences. She recalled from photographs that Dodie had medium-length light-colored hair. But she didn't see anyone who resembled her, either standing outside of the two conference rooms or sitting on the partially occupied benches in the adjacent hallway.

Then her eyes were drawn to a woman who wore large sunglasses and a dark-colored, shoulder-length wig that sat at an angle on her head. She seemed to be talking to herself. Lee stared harder at the almost-comedic, casually dressed woman in the haphazard disguise. The prosecutor realized that she was scrutinizing Dodie, who seemed to be "sort of courting the press" and "came off as a bit unstable." My nickname of Cruella De Vil is perfect, she thought.

Lee picked up a file from the conference room table and stepped to the doorway. "Catherine Cariaso."

Dodie walked into the small conference room and sat down across the table from Lee. She seemed nervous, loud, and "brassy." Dodie had an "air about her of a mentally ill person covering with overconfidence"—someone who couldn't focus and just wanted to end the meeting, Lee recalled later.[4]

Then Dodie told the five-foot-one prosecutor, who always wore three-inch heels to see over the podium in the courtroom, that she wanted a public defender. That meant that Lee couldn't ethically discuss a possible plea bargain with her. She noted Dodie's public defender request and obtained a date for Dodie's next court appearance from the court clerk. Her encounter with Dodie had lasted about two minutes.

In September, the public defender's office approved Dodie's request for free legal representation after it decided that she met its requirements: a monthly income of about $1,000 or less and the fact that prosecutors were seeking jail time in her misdemeanor case. She swore, under penalty of perjury, on her public defender application that she was jobless and homeless and listed total assets as $3,500: a 1982 Datsun car (presumably her 280zx sports car) with a $1,500 value; $200 in cash; no banking account; "NO MONEY"; and three horses for sale. She didn't mention her furniture, artwork, or MG—all in storage—or her van.

Norm Townsend, who headed the Larimer County Public Defender's Office, filed a court pleading to announce that he represented Dodie. She pleaded not guilty to all charges and asked for a jury trial.

About the same time, Lee accepted a new job but found her decision difficult because she loved her work as a prosecutor and had become "emotionally attached" to Dodie's case.

Lee wanted to leave the case in good hands and in the best possible posture, so she spoke to Neira again. She learned that Dodie had boarded a horse, which had difficulty standing and walking, with an individual who claimed that she refused to provide for the animal. Neira contacted Dodie, who said she didn't have money to care for the horse and agreed to relinquish him to the Humane Society even though the investigator advised that the animal might have to be put down.[5] Neira thought that Dodie had a disconnect from reality about the horse's condition and didn't seem to comprehend that he was the lead investigator in her dog abuse case. However, he'd identified himself by name and organization.[6]

Next, Lee met with Townsend to try to settle the case. Townsend said that he wanted Dodie to accept a plea bargain, but his client adamantly desired to go to trial. Lee left with the impression that Dodie thought the situation was everyone else's fault.

Lee also conferred with Susan Ermani, who was inheriting Dodie's case, and Todd Field, who she thought would assist the younger, inexperienced prosecutor. Both were dog lovers: Ermani owned a bichon frise and Field, a three-legged rescue dog named Jake.

Ermani, a petite twenty-six-year-old, had been hired as a deputy district attorney about four months prior, after her admittance to the Colorado bar. She'd interned in the office as a University of Colorado law school student and considered Field her mentor.

When Ermani looked at the on-scene photographs, the four-foot-nine, dark-haired prosecutor became upset when she saw so many healthy-looking puppies that had been put down. She met with Dr. Spindel, the thirtyish veterinarian who euthanized the fifty-four Labradors, including thirty-two puppies.[7]

They talked and reviewed the photographs on Ermani's computer screen in the prosecutor's office. Dr. Spindel related that she'd seen dogs that were fearful and fought on leashes, dogs with old infected bite wounds, puppies on top of each other in crates because of lack of space, dogs with respiratory infections, emaciated dogs, and a nursing female with feces on her nipples. She said that the Humane Society released one puppy, with ocular, nasal, and respiratory discharges, on-site because Carl had promised the dog to a family. That puppy died a week later.

Why had she put down the dogs? Ermani inquired. She felt terrible when she asked the question because she sensed that Dr. Spindel was very caring but felt uncomfortable.

Adult by adult, puppy by puppy, the veterinarian explained why each animal, sometimes for health and other times for aggressiveness toward people or extreme fearfulness, was unadoptable and, therefore, euthanized. Ermani believed that Dr. Spindel had thoroughly thought through whether each animal could or could not be saved or adopted. The prosecutor left the meeting impressed with the veterinarian and convinced that the Humane Society workers "really had done a very good job of saving those they felt they could rehabilitate or adopt out."

Confident that she was on the right side of the proceeding, Ermani met with her supervisor, Chief Deputy District Attorney Cliff Riedel. They crafted what she thought was a fair plea bargain.

She conveyed the offer to Townsend at an October 22nd pretrial conference. Dodie didn't attend the conference, which was customary in Larimer County because a lawyer represented her. If Dodie pleaded guilty to five counts of cruelty to animals, Ermani wouldn't seek more than seven and a half years in the county jail. However, the judge could impose probation without any jail time.

Ermani believed Townsend appeared pleased with her offer and didn't want to try the case. She knew that Dodie needed to accept the plea bargain, and the judge needed to approve it. The two lawyers obtained another court date in January. At that hearing, Ermani expected Dodie to plead guilty to five animal cruelty counts and she'd dismiss the remaining eleven charges. She presumed that Townsend would call her as soon as his client accepted the plea bargain.

———

In stark contrast to Ermani's minimal legal experience, Townsend had practiced criminal law for more than twenty-seven years and handled two cases before the US Supreme Court. The former Green Beret, who had gone to Vietnam a conservative and returned a liberal, graduated from George Washington University Law School in Washington, DC. With two classmates, he opened a criminal law defense practice in northern Virginia, where he remained for seven years. Next, he taught at the University of Georgia Law School before he migrated to Colorado. He passed the Colorado bar in 1986 and joined the public defender's office in Steamboat Springs, where he rose through the ranks to head the office. Next, the state office promoted this five-foot-eight, medium-build trial attorney to the Fort Collins office to lead six attorneys, two investigators, and other staff.

For the first year or so in Fort Collins, Townsend handled some felonies but also assigned himself to all the misdemeanor cases so that he would know what his lawyers faced in county court. He still handled misdemeanors when Dodie's case came into his office. Although district attorney and public defender offices usually assigned their least experienced attorneys to misdemeanor cases, Ermani faced a defense attorney more than double her age with decades more legal experience.

Townsend saw an angry person who didn't believe that she had done anything wrong when he first met Dodie. He perceived her as a very bright woman who didn't wear makeup or pay much attention to her appearance and dressed with a western flair. He learned that every day of her life, she carried "100 pounds of dog food into her home in the morning and every night carried out 100 pounds of dog shit, not literally but that was her life." Her sole livelihood was breeding dogs and selling puppies. "She was a working girl," lived an isolated life, maintained a small circle of friends, and had some issues dealing with men. However, he believed that she was a good, decent person who loved her dogs that were "her children."[8]

He learned that Dodie looked down her nose at those who showed dogs. She identified three types of dog owners who fought amongst each other: breeders, puppy mill operators, and lapdog owners. The fifty-eight-year-old attorney with graying hair quickly realized that he needed help from someone who understood the dog world. Although he grew up with a beagle as a child, he hadn't owned an animal other than a cat when he was married. He asked Pam Buffington, an investigator with his office for more than fourteen years, for help and insight into the dog world. He assigned Jennifer Stinson, a twenty-five-year-old Tulane University Law School graduate and a recent bar admittee, to assist him as his mentee.

Buffington owned and loved dogs all her life.[9] In 1995, she bought her first borzoi as a pet but soon was smitten by the dog show world.

By 2004, she'd competed in the show ring for about eight years, first with borzois and then salukis, and exhibited two to their conformation championships. Her show experience gave her an understanding of rivalries and infighting that sometimes occurred in the dog fancy. She'd also bred one saluki, so she'd dealt with puppies and puppy buyers. And she'd worked on two non-canine animal abuse cases.

She saw a train wreck of a woman when she met Dodie. Buffington thought that Townsend and Dodie didn't speak the same language: Townsend "didn't understand where Dodie was coming from."[10] But Buffington believed that Dodie identified with her because they were both divorced, showed horses, and bred dogs. She also thought Dodie didn't have anyone else to talk to, so she carved out time for long conversations when her client called.

At times, Buffington spoke alone with Dodie and, other times, joined both defense attorneys when they met with their client. Dodie talked copiously, making it difficult for others to speak. She appeared high strung and often volatile. Buffington surmised that Dodie alienated and drove away friends and family. "To Dodie, it was my way or the highway."

Townsend liked Dodie, although she was a difficult client. He felt sympathetic toward her but recognized that she harbored some denial about the farm foreclosure. She'd probably dragged her feet to find a new place to live with her dogs. He concluded that his client's downfall began with the economy when the price of hay doubled. At that time, her only source of income was selling Labradors. However, puppies were marketable only for a certain period of time. If Dodie couldn't sell them, she kept them, causing her Labrador numbers to grow. She bred more and more dogs as she tried to make ends meet.

Doug and his wife Kathleen again tried to help Dodie. They wired money to assist with living expenses after she'd called for help. She moved into a motel near downtown Estes Park. Kathleen mostly talked to Dodie; she tried to connect on a "woman-to-woman level." [11]

The couple wanted to provide a place to live and income for Dodie and offered to buy a house with sufficient space for roommates. Dodie would have difficulty finding employment because she had trouble working with people, they thought, so rent from roommates would provide a means of support.

Doug and Kathleen flew in from California to look at homes with Dodie and a realtor. Dodie found a house that she loved—one with several bedrooms and a small barn on an acre on the outskirts of Estes Park. Doug and Kathleen wanted assurance that she wouldn't "trash" the house or resume her dog and horse breeding businesses. Doug hired an attorney to draw up a lease agreement. Dodie could live rent-free at first if she found roommates to pay rent. She could have four dogs and two horses but couldn't build additional fences or corrals. Dodie reviewed the agreement and crossed out all of its essential provisions. Completely frustrated, Doug and Kathleen didn't close on the house but continued to send monthly checks to help pay Dodie's motel rent. Dodie also defrayed some of her living expenses by selling her treasured MG.

After the pretrial conference, the ordinarily feisty Ermani lost all confidence in the plea bargain offer she'd made. She dissolved into tears as she walked into her supervisor's office. She'd offered much too lenient a deal because the plea bargain, she believed, had been accepted so quickly. How could she have let the woman off so easily, she wondered. How could she have made such a horrible mistake? She was beside herself for the next month.

Unbeknownst to Ermani, Townsend thought the prosecutor hadn't made much of an offer. He called Dodie. She had no intention of accepting the plea bargain. She proclaimed her innocence and wanted to go to trial to be vindicated. She hadn't done anything wrong.

For about a month, Townsend and Dodie talked about the plea offer. He believed that she had a defense to the abandonment charge because she left a note for her landlord, Carl, to call the Humane Society to take her dogs. She thought the Humane Society would find homes for them just as Weld County Animal Control had done so many times before. She never believed that any of the dogs would be euthanized.

Dodie also faced fifteen animal neglect charges. Townsend recognized that a jury might convict his client of some of those counts. Acceptance of a plea bargain eliminated the risk of twenty-four years in the county jail because of Ermani's offer to cap the jail time to seven and a half years. Dodie remained adamant that she wanted a trial.

The defense team questioned why so many of the Labradors had been put down at Carl's property. Based on media accounts, they first thought that many of the dogs were so sick that they were going to die anyway, and others were so violent that they couldn't be adopted. But when they scrutinized the dogs' photographs, they saw many healthy Labradors. Was it just easier to euthanize them on a holiday weekend? Had the Humane Society become overwhelmed by the numbers and conditions of the canines? Wasn't there a place to take all of them? Why couldn't many of the puppies have been rescued and adopted?

Buffington recognized that although the photographs of rows of dead puppies looked like they could be saved, she hadn't seen the animals in person, hadn't touched their fur or looked into their mouths. She couldn't say for sure if they were viable. But she wondered what had happened when she learned that Cloverleaf, where the surviving dogs had been taken, had enough space for all the Labradors.

Townsend decided to put the Humane Society "on trial" to deflect attention from Dodie. Would his strategy work?

———————

In her spacious ground-floor motel room, Dodie sat down and opened her journal on November 10th. She hadn't written in it since May. The motel, situated on riverfront property, was just off the main road to Rocky Mountain National Park and a little over a mile from the center of Estes Park.

Two Labrador puppies lived with her in the two-queen-bed room, complete with a kitchenette: Ben, the pup that she bought in July, and Bernitta, a yellow female that she purchased from an Estes Park breeder. Both puppies were from different lineages but close in age.

"Well, it has been months since the terrible tragic day of Death and Slaughter by the Larimer County Humane Society," she penned and marked a large X across Humane.

"I had decided to only take my Best & Favorite & special dogs over to Carl's. Charlie (10r old yel fe), Kersey (11 yr old Choc fe)—80 lbs big the best choc fe I've ever produced), Rhumba (a big, beaut white fe only 6 years—still had 3 pups on her), Tandicca, Rusha, Mambo-B-Jambo—a big 75 lb-white fe—only 5 yrs—produces big white pups—pregnant was due to welp [sic] within days—They probably MURDERED HER!! TOO!!

"Those ASSHOLES!! I hate them all for their rash and uncalled for behavior! I can't write anymore right now!! Because I am so filled with anger and hatred!"

Four days later, Dodie resumed writing. "Ok! Today's a better day!" After a few more days, she penned, "Things are going good these days," and there "is a lot of fun stuff . . . free live music, concerts—also some great local community events. I think I'm going to like living up here a lot." She enjoyed walking her two puppies on Knob Hill across from the Stanley Hotel.

"I'm really falling in love with this beautiful little park right in the middle of Estes. It sits up high with a good panoramic view of the town, lake & mts. Wow! Every day—I take the dogs for a 'free'-walk (off leash) so they can run & run & chase each-other around! They are in heaven up there, and I just love watching them run & play & grow. Neither one is limping, or hopping, so I think they're going to have 'good-hips.'

"I want, so much, for my future up here in the Mts to work out. To be happy & good. For the dogs and I to adjust and be happy!" She'd made some useful business contacts and located a great retail spot. "I love Dogs! I love Dogs! I love Dogs! Love, Love, Love—All we need is Love! John Lennon . . ."

———

A couple of weeks after the pretrial conference, Ermani left messages for Townsend to confirm Dodie's acceptance of the plea bargain. Irritated when he didn't return her calls, she revoked the plea offer on the day before Thanksgiving and asked that a jury trial be scheduled. The court clerk later set Dodie's animal abuse case for a three-day jury trial beginning on April 11, 2005.

On the day after Thanksgiving, Vikki opened an envelope postmarked two days before. It bore the return address of Dodie's farm, where her sister-in-law hadn't lived for more than five months. She read the letter once, then twice, and reached for the telephone. Dodie's answering machine picked up. Vikki called again and again. No answer.

She'd never received such a letter from Dodie. Her sister-in-law penned that she considered her an honest, sincere individual giving much to others and didn't seem to judge. These traits, Dodie wrote, were "not inherent to my personality." She referenced her "perfect life on her farm" but wrote she could no longer live in this world. "I just cannot adjust . . . I cannot change. I say goodbye . . . So I can rest in peace."

A worried Vikki called the Estes Park Police Department at 8 p.m. when she still hadn't reached Dodie. She reported her concerns and that Dodie previously had threatened suicide by cop.

When asked if Dodie had any weapons, Vikki repeated what her sister-in-law had said: she'd buy a toy gun. Then Dodie had laughed.

Estes Park police officer Walker Steinhage drove to the motel to check on Dodie. He learned from the motel's emergency contact that Dodie didn't appear to be acting strangely, had one yellow Labrador, and drove a Nissan 280zx as well as a tan and beige van.

Dodie looked perplexed when she opened her motel room's door and stared at two officers. She invited them in and asked why they were there.

Steinhage and the other officer explained the purpose of their visit. When asked, she said she didn't have any weapons and wasn't thinking of hurting herself. She was scared of "having to live on the streets" and hoped she'd soon find a job. She struggled financially and had recently lost her farm. Her family wasn't helping her and blamed her for her life. She'd been a financially successful and famous artist, she said, and pointed to several pieces of artwork on one wall.

Dodie admitted to writing the note to Vikki but had done so several weeks ago. She'd been gone all day and hadn't received a message to call her sister-in-law. She confirmed that she'd told her brother and Vikki several times that she was going to commit suicide and did so only to manipulate them. She said she had an appointment to see a counselor and was "not bi-polar and not on medication."

"I am fine and doing well—thanks for checking on me—Love to you all," she wrote in a statement for the officers. They concluded that she wasn't a danger to herself or others and wasn't "gravely disabled."

Steinhage telephoned Vikki. A relieved Vikki said although she'd never before received such a letter, Dodie had "cried wolf" about ending her life many times. Dodie often called her and her husband to ask for money. They'd stopped giving it because they had already forked over so much. "We all have tried to help her," but she continued to get into financial trouble.

Dodie didn't threaten any peace officers in her letter and didn't indicate that "she wished to harm us or other peace officers" when he met her, Steinhage wrote in his report. He didn't take further action.

Two days later, Dodie resumed writing in her journal.

"Sunday! It's SNOWING!! Yeah! I love snowstorms! It makes everything slow & quiet! Especially up here in Estes, where there are beautiful rocks, & hills & tall trees to gently cover with beautiful white halos. 'Love can change Everything!' Love leads us to Heaven on Earth! Comfort & Joy! Boughs of Holly! Joy to the World! It's Christmas-Time-Excitement all around!"

She began to pen her thoughts in a stream of consciousness:

> Snowstorms & Hot Chocolate
> Merry Measures
> Dogs & Horses—
> Hounds & Foxes
> Fox Hunting & Turkey Dinner!
> Peppermint Schnapps!

She listed her puppies Bennington and Bernitta before the names Linda Vaughn and Diana Richardson, two Labrador breeders she'd known. She referenced actors "Tom Selleck & Tom Hanks—Nice Guys & Nice Smiles! Good Hearts & Kindness!" and "English & Irish! Irish Forever! . . ."

> Lexus & Lincolns!
> Jaguars, Jaguars, Jaguars!
> Christmas is a Gorgeous Time.
> Colored lites, ornaments
> Children laughing!
> People Hugging!
> Strangers Hugging!
> People Toasting!
> Toasting to Joy—
> Toasting to Happiness.

Then she switched her focus and named some of her favorite horses: London, Legacy, Meriah, and Witchy Blue Lady as well as

> Lord Liberty!
> What a guy!
> What a Stud!
> Paints x Thorobreds [sic]! Paints Forever!

And then her dogs:

> Labradors are The Best!!!
> Samba, Coco-Joe, Kelly, Charmin', Sophie & Athena,
> Nadeen, Prince of Charmin',
> Christie & Thunder, Victoria,
> & Brittania, Ronika, Wistie,
> Devon, Kersey, McIvory
> McDougal O'Keefe
> Casey!! Loved her!
> Nexus & Samba, Donovan,
> Sebastian & Remington &
> Finnegan. Appollo [sic]
> O'Leary—Becca O'Leary

Killkenny Retrievers

I forgot—Burbury Belle—
AKA "Bobbie"
Mambo & Java-Joe &
Bianca Jean & Tandicca
& Haven-Ridge &
Mahagony [sic] & Ebony & Ivy League

I sure miss you all so much.
I can't wait to be with you all again Soon!
Here's to Killkenny Labradors!
The Greatest Labradors there ever was—or will be!!

Two days later, Dodie listened to Jimmy Buffett sing on the *Today Show*. "Wow! He has really aged well . . . very handsome 50+ man. I sure wish I could find an older (my age) talented, wise man! Hip! & Cool!"

That same month, Stanlyn Johnston, who now lived in Oklahoma, sent a Christmas card to Dodie, her former neighbor, to give her moral support. She'd read about Dodie in newspaper stories that had been sent to her. Dodie was so caring toward her always clean and healthy dogs, Stanlyn recalled. Her card, mailed to Dodie's farm, came back after it wasn't picked up.

Dodie pasted a picture of her favorite Labrador, Prince, in her journal. The photograph captured his light-yellow face framed by his cocked, darker ears as he rested his front paws on a wooden fence. She penned "Prince My Love" across the photo, and just above, "He could see right through you." He "was the love of my LIFE for over 10 years. He was big, strong, handsome, sweet, smart, Athletic-Kind & Loving! He was the Best!!!!"

That night, she watched a *60 Minutes* interview with former Miami Dolphins star running back Ricky Williams. "Wow!! What a Neat! Smart! Guy!!" He'd quit the team and left behind a huge salary "to go find his own personal space & <u>freedom!</u>" Dodie journaled. "If you want to know how I feel about Life. Look at this interview on Sun. Dec. 19th at 6 pm—on *60 Minutes*. With Rickie [sic] Williams . . . I totally agreed with EVERYTHING he had to say in his interview! Wow! Cool! Wow!"

During the interview, Williams said money had made him miserable and couldn't buy happiness. So, he quit football and ran away to Australia to seek balance while he lived in a tent community for seven dollars a day, he said, because he couldn't deal with the public humiliation after he failed a third drug test.

"Dec was a terrible month of no money, no job," Dodie lamented in her journal on January 13, 2005. Next, she complained about Vikki, the woman who just weeks before she'd praised for her kindness, honesty, and sincerity.

CHAPTER 20

The Search for Molly's Mate

When I was nine, my parents gave me my first Labrador, Thumper, a stocky yellow with a blocky head and outgoing personality. I'd loved yellow Labs ever since.

Decades later, my mother coached me on the importance of temperament, body structure, and hip and eye clearances as Molly drew closer to possible motherhood. My mom's guidance contrasted sharply with Dodie's practice of obtaining only hip clearances on only some of her breeding stock, and mostly during the early years of her puppy business.

In early 1996, I located a suitable stud for Molly: Froggie, a medium-colored, short-coupled yellow with nice movement and a happy personality. He had his eye and hip clearances.

The breeding would produce only black puppies because Molly was black, as were her parents. A Molly-Froggie daughter, carrying both yellow and black genes, bred to a yellow stud would produce yellows and blacks. That meant that I'd have my yellow again after two generations.

Our new Castle Rock vet x-rayed Molly's hips to ascertain if our black beauty was good breeding material. OFA certified them as good. In March, a dog ophthalmologist examined not only Molly's eyes but also Max's because we wanted to establish a baseline in case he later developed optic problems.

The ophthalmologist proclaimed Molly's eyes free from cataracts and PRA and filled out the CERF paperwork. He found small hereditary cataracts in both of Max's eyes but thought they wouldn't impact our adoptee's quality of life. We agreed to bring him back for another exam in a year, or sooner if his sight began to fail. The doctor suggested that I notify Max's breeder about the cataracts, so I wrote Dodie. I wasn't surprised when Dodie didn't respond even though I knew nothing about her.

A year later, the same ophthalmologist re-examined our wards' eyes. Molly again passed her eye exam. Max's cataracts hadn't grown.

Next, I telephoned Froggie's owner to check on the stud's latest eye exam. That's when I learned that Molly's prospective mate had been sold for $10,000 to a party in Japan.

I clutched the phone, unable to speak.

Froggie's frozen semen was available, the breeder said.

I found my voice. "Thanks, but I'd like her bred the old-fashioned way." I was sure Molly would agree.

So began my second hunt for Molly's mate. I recalled a chunky-looking yellow male at the previous summer's Cheyenne show where I'd competed with Molly in conformation. I learned that the Virginia dog, Allegheny's Sharper Image (SI), still lived in Berthoud with his handler Susan Burke. Next, I telephoned Burke to discuss Molly and arrange a visit with SI. In passing, I mentioned Max.

Burke greeted us when Dave and I stepped out of our SUV at her kennel after our two-hour drive from Franktown. Molly and Max remained in their crates. Max accompanied us because he'd be the honorary uncle to Molly's pups.

Was Molly the Killkenny dog that I had mentioned in our telephone conversation? Burke inquired.

"No," I said. "Max is the Killkenny dog. We'd had him neutered soon after he joined our family because we didn't think that he was a suitable mate for Molly. She is from my parents' Walden line."

Burke relaxed and told us that she didn't allow any of her studs or SI to be bred to Killkenny dogs. Max's breeder, Dodie Cariaso, she said, kept dams and their puppies in kitchen cabinets. I cringed at the image of a teeny Max living in a dark cabinet in a dimly lit kitchen during the first weeks of his life.

Dave and I met SI, a medium-colored yellow with dark pigmentation around his eyes. Burke showed us his eye and hip certifications. His laid-back, kind personality won us over.

We handed over a copy of Molly's hip and eye clearances and pedigree. Molly met with Burke's approval. We only needed to test Molly for brucellosis before she could be bred to SI for a $500 stud fee.

Burke's comments were our first glimpse into the conditions in which Max may have lived as a tiny puppy. While she hadn't characterized Dodie's kennel operation as a puppy mill, we left with that impression. Maybe that was why we never heard back from Dodie after I notified her of Max's cataracts.

———

Early one morning in July 1997, Dave, Max, and I set out from Franktown to drive to the base of Mt. Sherman, Colorado's reputed easiest-to-climb 14,000-plus-foot-tall mountain, just east of the Continental Divide. We'd never climbed a fourteener with our adoptee. He deserved some special attention because we constantly doted on our very pregnant Molly.

Max trotted close to us and greeted other hikers as we hiked up the trail that led to the top of the popular mountain. Once on the football-field-length summit, Dave and I took pictures of one another with Max. We ate lunch and savored the view of surrounding mountains and Turquoise Lake far below near Leadville. Then we headed back down the mountain, first along a narrow, rocky ridge.

At the saddle, we had two choices: glissade down a very steep 1,000-foot wall of snow or traverse down on the rocky trail to the bottom of a bowl where scattered flowers emerged from the tundra.[1] I settled on the rocky trail because of previous neck and shoulder injuries and assumed Max would follow me.

Instead, he trotted next to Dave, who chose the more adventuresome descent. They traversed to the top of the snowfield and paused on the cornice above a very steep slope. Dog and man stepped off the cornice. Dave hesitated as he reconsidered the wisdom of his decision. Max's feet slid, with the steep incline propelling him head first, spread eagle down the snowfield.

"Look at the dog! Look at the dog!" onlookers shouted from the base of the snowfield.

Dave realized that he had little choice but to follow. He took a step and then slid on his rump down the slope. Max reached the bottom of the snowfield first, stood up, and wagged his tail vigorously as he sauntered over to Dave, who had slowed to a stop. Nearby hikers applauded Max and perhaps Dave.

We'd had a perfect day for Max's first fourteener climb. Max slept on our SUV's backseat as we drove home toward Denver along the winding, two-lane Highway 285. The line of Sunday traffic abruptly stopped. Dave and I looked at each other. We knew that a very pregnant Molly was inside our home. She likely needed to relieve herself. The line of traffic inched forward. We finally spotted a pay phone at a Conifer gas station. We called our neighbors, who answered and agreed to rescue Molly. Disaster averted.

Less than two weeks later, on July 15, 1997, Molly treated her family kindly by waiting until 9 a.m. to whelp her first puppy. My parents' dogs always delivered their puppies late at night or in the early morning. I'd never understood until adulthood the nicety of daytime whelpings.

Molly's maternal instincts didn't kick in when the first puppy was born, so Dave cut the pup's umbilical cord. Molly then took over. Max watched from the hallway just outside our guest room-turned-whelping room. Within an hour, Molly had two daughters, Miss Green and Miss Red, so named because we painted their toenails with nail polish to differentiate the small black blobs.

Molly delivered five live black puppies and one stillborn. The smallest was Blaze, so named because of a white mark on her chest. We called the fourth puppy Miss Pink and dabbed her nails with pink nail polish. The fifth puppy was nail polish-free because she was the last born and easily distinguishable from Blaze. It also was simpler to paint the nails of only three squirming puppies. Within a week, we had Blaze, Miss Green, Miss Red, and two Miss Pinks. The nail polish wore off quickly. Over and over, we painted the nails of two puppies pink because the real Miss Pink and the Phantom Miss Pink looked so much alike.

We called the alpha of the all-female litter Bruiser. She declared that she owned me at six weeks of age during my, Dave's, and often Max's nightly play/socialization time with the puppies. That night, Bruiser rested her head on my thigh while I sat on the floor. The rest was history. Luckily, Bruiser, whom I renamed Brew, was the conformation pick of the litter.

Friends purchased Miss Green and Blaze. That left the two Miss Pinks to sell. We listed them in the Lab Club's newsletter, *The Retriever Believer*, and ran a Denver newspaper ad. Jan and his son, who wanted a hunting dog to join their chocolate Lab named Duke, responded. They selected the Miss Pink that already loved to retrieve small balls.

Dave renamed his favorite, the other Miss Pink, "Wiggles" because she loved to wiggle. Molly preferred Wiggles to Brew, Max's favorite. Uncle Max played gently with the pups and tolerated their attempts to climb all over him.

Molly, however, was ready for another puppy or two to leave home.

Dave was out of state on business when a couple called one Saturday morning in response to our newspaper ad. They had the mandatory fenced-in yard and owned an intact Killkenny dog that they wanted to breed in the future. I gave them directions to our home. They'd immediately drive down from their north Denver suburban home.

The contents of our conversation sank in after I hung up. Their dog was a Killkenny male, the same kennel that produced Max, who had hereditary cataracts. Dodie, Max's breeder, failed to respond when I wrote her about his cataracts. Burke wouldn't let her dogs be bred to a Killkenny canine and told us that. Killkenny puppies were raised in kitchen cabinets. The en route couple would want to breed Wiggles one day to their Killkenny dog. I shuddered and realized that I wouldn't sell Wiggles to them. But I couldn't call them back because I'd neglected to ask for their phone number. I waited in dread.

When the couple arrived, I ushered them inside our home to our dining room table, where I set out Max's pedigree and eye exam. I explained what we knew about Max's cataracts and apologized to them for driving to Franktown. Then I said I couldn't sell them a puppy because I knew that she'd be bred to their Killkenny dog. I suggested that they have their dog's eyes examined. The wife thanked me. The husband didn't.

The Lab Club referred a woman to us several days later. Her family had previously owned a Labrador from Linda Vaughn's Simerdown Kennels.

We made an appointment for the caller and her husband to visit Wiggles. Husband Harold fell in love with Wiggles at first sight. Wife Linda wondered if something was wrong with Wiggles because she was the last puppy for sale. Linda wanted to look around more. Harold groaned. They had wisely left their three children at home.

Within a day or so, Linda called and wanted her whole family to visit Wiggles. Harold, Linda, their three children, and Harold's ninety-something-year-old grandmother, arrived on the appointed day. They left with Wiggles in their vintage station wagon.

Max's bond with Brew grew stronger. He had much to teach his "niece" and many hikes and mountains to enjoy with her.

CHAPTER 21

Case Strategies

Judge Schultz admonished the prosecution and defense to keep their tempers as he opened the March 23, 2005 hearing. Dodie sat next to Townsend and Stinson in a courtroom large enough for about a hundred spectators. Ermani and Todd Field, a Willamette College of Law graduate with three years of prosecutorial experience, listened from their seats at the prosecution table.

Both sides knew the stakes were high as they waited to argue their positions on the flurry of motions that they'd filed. Should the judge allow prosecutors to add more abandonment counts, Dodie faced a possible jail sentence of 148½ years if convicted of those counts and the original sixteen charges. If he granted the defense motion to dismiss, the case was over.

The public defenders adhered to their strategy to put the Humane Society on trial. In their motions, they accused the organization of intentionally murdering fifty-four Labradors and alleged that the animals could have been saved with proper care. They asked the judge to dismiss the case because the dogs' bodies were destroyed before a defense expert could examine them.

The defense also requested that the prosecutors identify a victim for each of the fifteen neglect counts. At first, Ermani and Field didn't know how to comply because the dogs didn't have names. Then they realized that the Humane Society had assigned a serial number to each dog, so they asked for those numbers and cross-referenced them with Neira's on-scene notes. That gave them a method to identify a specific victim for each neglect charge that alleged Dodie, "having the charge or custody of an animal, unlawfully, knowingly, recklessly, or with criminal negligence failed to provide the named animal with proper food, drink, protection from the weather . . ."

Prosecutors selected eight euthanized Labradors as neglect victims, all with horrific health issues: two ten-week-old puppies, one with a traumatic lump on its face and the other with major facial trauma; an adult female covered with feces with moist vulvar erosions; two emaciated nursing females; an eight-week-old male with punctures on his face as well as eye and nasal discharges; a seven- to ten-day-old female puppy with an ulcerated umbilical hernia; and a dying chocolate mother.

They named seven surviving Labradors as other neglect victims: a five-month-old male; Lucca, an elderly chocolate female with severe dental disease and problems with standing because of overgrown nails; a ten-week-old fearful female; an emaciated nursing female; and the starving chocolate mother found inside the horse trailer as well as two of her puppies, both with umbilical hernias.

During the process of identifying the neglect victims, Ermani and Field agreed that they were bothered that Dodie faced only a single abandonment count even though the Humane Society discovered eighty-four abandoned dogs. The concern wasn't new. The previous July, Field wrote, "DA to investigate additional counts," and that his office should meet with the Humane Society on the district attorney's case file after he noticed the single abandonment charge during his preparation for a possible court appearance.

Once Ermani and Field resolved how to identify the dogs, they decided to ask the judge to add eighty-three abandonment counts, one for each abandoned Labrador.

Their decision infuriated the normally calm Townsend, who had no way of knowing that Field considered additional counts in July when he wrote the file note. Such notes are confidential attorney work product and, therefore, not disclosed to opposing parties or their counsel.

Townsend viewed the attempt to add additional counts as punishment for filing defense motions and his client's exercise of her constitutional right to a jury trial. They're trying to scare her out of going to trial, he thought. He accused the prosecutors of acting in bad faith and in a vindictive manner. That enraged Ermani and Field.

Now, the prosecutors and defense attorneys sat quietly as Judge Schultz concluded his admonishment at the start of the March hearing in the tension-filled courtroom.

The judge asked Townsend about the materials sought in the defense subpoena duces tecums (requests) issued to the Humane Society. Townsend wanted euthanasia records. Ermani argued that they were irrelevant because they didn't pertain to whether the Labradors were more or less likely to have been abandoned or given food, water, or proper medical attention.

Dodie cried softly. She muttered as she became increasingly agitated and glared at Ermani. Townsend tried to soothe her.

"Then leave, Dodie," he whispered. But Dodie remained seated at the defense table. She cried and sniffled.

Ermani offered to provide relevant information from the Humane Society.

Judge Schultz asked Townsend if he could streamline his requests.

Townsend sidestepped the question and accused the prosecutor of arguing that Rule 17 (subpoena and subpoena duces tecum rule) was superfluous: "it might as well not be there." He labeled the arrest warrant's statement that Dodie's neglect required the killing of fifty-four dogs, "a bald-faced lie. I have the right to inquire about that on cross-examination on the issue of bias and motive. They didn't have to kill any of the dogs. It was their choice to kill, to do it and then to blame this lady for it.

"They said it in the arrest warrant affidavit . . . that this lady has neglected her dogs, made it necessary for the Humane Society to kill fifty-four, that's what they said in effecting her arrest. I have the right to inquire." Townsend's voice intensified as he stood at the podium and argued.

"Shush, shush," Stinson whispered to Dodie.

"You can't respond," Judge Schultz instructed Dodie. "You'll have to be quiet; you will have to leave the courtroom, whichever you would like to do."

"I can't handle this," Dodie sobbed. "I can't handle this." She sobbed even harder.

"Then go ahead and step outside and go to the conference room, that's fine," the judge said. "Counsel, go ahead," he instructed Townsend.

"THEY BLAMED ME FOR WHAT THEY DID. THEY BLAMED ME FOR WHAT THEY DID," Dodie wailed.

"That's my trouble; they have made it relevant, the Humane Society, not someone else," Townsend argued. He momentarily hesitated.

Dodie, engulfed in tears, walked out of the courtroom.

Townsend pushed on, ". . . swore out an arrest warrant saying this woman's neglect of her animals made it necessary for them to kill fifty-four of them and I submit that is simply not true, that there was no necessity to do so, that it was a choice of the Humane Society and I have a right to inquire into that, as a matter of inquiring into bias and motive. First of all, it is a lie under oath."

"The case is very emotionally charged as you can see by watching the defendant herself," Ermani began after she replaced Townsend at the podium. Whether dogs were euthanized wasn't relevant because the charges didn't require that the animals be killed or have died, she argued.

The Humane Society wasn't on trial. The trial concerned whether the Labradors were abandoned before the Humane Society arrived and if they had water and adequate medical attention, she insisted.

"These animals got in this condition over a long period of time." Any questions about the Humane Society's actions were for a civil court to consider, Ermani noted.

Judge Schultz switched his focus to the defense motion to dismiss. Townsend argued for dismissal because the dogs were destroyed before the defense's veterinarians could examine them to determine if they'd been mistreated, were emaciated, or should have been euthanized. No necropsies (autopsies of animals) were conducted.

"It is simply their word. We came, we showed up, we believe, and therefore she is guilty, and they want to preclude us from cross-examining about that and by their own actions they destroyed the evidence . . . I have the right to inquire into their lies, and if that means asking them, what was the basis for your killing this dog, I have the right to do that."

Ermani argued that the dogs' bodies were not absolving evidence under the US Supreme Court case of *Brady v. Maryland* that required prosecutors to turn over all exculpatory evidence to the defense. CSU's veterinary hospital agreed to keep the dogs' bodies only for twenty-four to forty-eight hours. After that, the Humane Society could have stored the bodies only in a van, and that storage would have presented a sanitary risk because of the summer heat.

"When a dog is starved," Ermani said as her voice intensified, "you can see by its body that it has not had any food because it becomes very skinny, you can see the ribs, and you can see the spine, and you can see the hips of the dog. Your Honor, there were photographs taken of these dogs, and the doctors provided their diagnoses and provided reasons as to why each animal they felt was not given proper care at that time." Case law, she argued, supported her position that the defense's expert could examine the photographs that provided comparable evidence of the dogs' conditions.

"In other words, we get to rely on the words of the people who actually destroyed the evidence, trust them," Townsend fired back. The Humane Society could have taken tissue, blood, fecal, and urine samples from the animals and notified his client that the dogs were going to be destroyed so she could have had an independent examination conducted, he argued.

Judge Schultz turned to the prosecution's request to add the eighty-three abandonment counts.

Field stood to address the judge. In a matter-of-fact tone, he argued that prosecutors have the discretion to decide what charges to file and take to trial. His office hadn't filed additional abandonment charges earlier because it was "cumbersome for everyone" and believed that the case would be resolved. However, a plea bargain wasn't reached, and his office retained the authority to add additional charges to reflect the scope and gravity of Dodie's conduct, he contended.

Townsend argued that the prosecution decided to break out the one abandonment charge into eighty-four separate counts only when his client rejected the plea bargain, set the case for trial, and filed motions.

"Nothing changed except Ms. Cariaso asked for her day in court. Having done that, then the District Attorney upped the ante. The appearance, at the very least, is vindictive. This is not a case where the District Attorney overlooked conduct and didn't charge offenses," Townsend insisted. "It is outrageous."

Judge Schultz excused himself to retrieve a cup of tea. Within a minute, he returned to the bench and sat down to read case law. He ruled a few minutes later.

First, he denied Dodie's Motion to Dismiss and noted that the prosecution complied with the law in *Brady v. Maryland*. Next, he declined to find prosecutorial misconduct and granted the addition of eighty-three abandonment charges. Finally, he sided with the defense and ruled that it was entitled to obtain the information it sought in its subpoena duces tecums. He'd ruled in just less than three minutes after he'd listened to more than fifty minutes of argument.

The defense now needed to decide how to best minimize Dodie's exposure to 148½ years in the county jail.

CHAPTER 22

Headed To Trial

The defense case changed dramatically once Judge Schultz allowed prosecutors to charge Dodie with ninety-nine counts instead of just sixteen. Townsend became increasingly invested and emotionally attached to the case. He believed that the prosecutors perceived his client as evil and thought they'd lost perspective. Although he suspected that the Humane Society whispered in the ear of Ermani that his client was a puppy mill operator, he remained angry that she'd added the additional counts. He didn't think his client was being treated fairly. And he believed that she never intended to or had abused her dogs and hadn't abandoned them under the law. He saw a woman who became desperate and overwhelmed by financial problems and dogs. That's what he had to show a jury. But Dodie had her flaws, and they had their differences.

The defense also needed to combat at least some of the public's perception that Dodie had operated a puppy mill, which the ASPCA has defined as a "large scale commercial dog breeding facility where profit is given priority over the well-being of dogs."[1] An estimated 10,000 puppy mills exist nationwide.[2]

With some investigation, the prosecution could argue that Dodie exhibited some characteristics of a puppy mill operator: she often housed dogs in overcrowded and unsanitary conditions without adequate food, water, veterinary care, or socialization; bred females at every opportunity, often in disregard for genetic disease issues; sent puppies with diseases or parasite infestations to new homes; and sold puppies that frequently suffered from fear and other behavioral problems.

Some defense team members thought that Dodie was so desperate that she believed her only option was to leave the dogs and a note for Carl to contact the Humane Society. She'd gotten in over her head and lacked the emotional wherewithal to call the authorities. Dodie needed to convince a jury that she cared for her animals so much that she tried to make sure that they would be left alone only for twenty-four hours before Carl returned home. If she had intended to abandon them, she wouldn't have left a note with instructions for their care or called to make sure Carl was driving home. She'd had an emotional breakdown.

To convince a jury of her intentions, Dodie needed to testify that she wasn't a puppy mill operator who abandoned "all these poor abused dogs" the second they became unprofitable. Only Dodie could explain her meltdown and why she left her dogs that she loved without personally surrendering them to the Humane Society. She had to justify why she continued to breed dogs after she knew her farm was in foreclosure. And she had to explain the condition of some of her dogs.

It was risky to put Dodie on the stand because of her attitude, mental state, and volatile nature. She perceived that she was the victim; the Humane Society had "murdered" her Labradors. Dodie wanted a trial to expose the Humane Society. She hated the Humane Society and Weld County, indignant that the county had come to her property and taken her "children." At least some of the defense team believed that Dodie lacked the capacity to accept any responsibility for what happened to the Labradors. Her lawyers couldn't raise any mental state issues as a defense because they lacked their client's permission to do so.

Both sides talked informally about settling the case. The lawyers knew that juries were unpredictable, no matter how strong or weak a case. A plea bargain offered some certainty.

Defense team members understood that they'd have to address some of the Labradors' conditions. They were particularly concerned about four "horribly skinny" nursing mothers named as neglect victims.

The defense team chose Dr. Culver to testify as an expert on raising dogs. Members thought because she'd known Dodie and her canines for so many years that she might be more sympathetic toward her than other veterinarians.

Dr. Culver planned to testify that four dams were woefully underweight. The defense feared that a jury would likely convict Dodie of neglecting those dogs based on that testimony and the photos illustrating the dams' emaciation. Townsend believed he could argue that while his client might be guilty of some neglect counts, she wasn't of others. However, with "the abandonment counts, she either walked away from all or none of them." The defense team knew that public opinion was against Dodie as were the odds of acquittal of all charges.

Defense team members faced the monumental task of convincing Dodie that she'd likely be convicted of some counts. Their client wanted to be left alone and questioned why she was being prosecuted. They knew the charges weren't going to evaporate, and her attitude wasn't going to help.

Buffington didn't think Dodie grasped reality and reminded her of a bipolar family member. She'd witnessed her client's extreme highs and lows during meetings in the office and from meeting to meeting. Sometimes Dodie exhibited extreme optimism coupled with inflated self-esteem. Other times she appeared hopeless and felt that her defense team wasn't listening to her, didn't have her best interests in mind, and was turning against her. No one was on her side. She became hysterical and angry and stormed out of marathon meetings.

Longtime friend Carol Mayberry-Sanchez sat in on one defense meeting. She encouraged Dodie to remain calm, but her friend lost her temper yet again.

Dodie showed photographs of some of her Labradors to Carol and asked if they looked emaciated. Some were skin and bones, creatures with jutting-out ribs, shrunken loins, and spindly legs. Carol wondered if Dodie had become delusional.

One acquaintance thought Dodie had a "disconnect with reality" when shown the same photos as proof that she'd done nothing wrong.

Dodie asked Townsend if she could be assured of concurrent sentences on each count if convicted. He couldn't because sentencing was up to the judge. However, he knew that Larimer County Court judges typically imposed only a maximum of sixty days when they sentenced misdemeanor defendants to jail as a condition of probation. But he couldn't be certain that would happen because of the extensive publicity in Dodie's case.

He believed it was "in her best interests to cut her losses" once the judge allowed the additional counts. The community wanted to "hang that lady." He "was very afraid for her." Juries were unpredictable. A plea bargain limited his client's exposure to jail. And jail, the defense team thought, would be horrible and far worse for Dodie than for the average person because of her emotional state.

Ermani and Field discussed a plea bargain. They had sticking points: Dodie's denial of wrongdoing, the sentence, and mental health issues.

Field replayed Dodie's words: "I didn't do it. I love my kids. I fed and watered them, and I left." He thought she never comprehended that what she'd done was wrong.

Ermani harbored concern about Dr. Spindel as a witness. Would the young Humane Society veterinarian, who had euthanized so many Labradors, hold up under cross-examination in a case that weighed heavily on her?

Field, Ermani, and the Humane Society "absolutely" didn't want Dodie to breed or even own any dogs. The prosecutors thought Dodie currently owned two canines. She did: puppies Ben and Bernitta.

Just five days before trial, they offered a plea bargain. If Dodie pled guilty to twenty charges, Counts 1 through 15 (neglect charges) and Counts 95 through 99 (abandonment charges), they'd dismiss the remaining seventy-nine counts. They insisted on those specific counts so that a person unfamiliar with the case could quickly ascertain that Dodie had been charged with ninety-nine counts. She'd serve no more than three years in jail, and at least one year of supervised probation, with mental health treatment if required after an evaluation. Both sides could argue about the length of probation and jail time within the stated parameters.

Prosecutors also required that Dodie agree to restitution for the Humane Society's expenses at Carl's as well as Cloverleaf's costs for housing the Labradors. They reserved the right to ask for any medical/behavioral expenses for the surviving dogs but wouldn't seek a fine or community service. Dodie was required to remain law abiding and pay all court costs and fees. She couldn't own or breed dogs.

A day later, defense team members sat down in their office with Dodie. They found it difficult to explain legal options to her. She cried, became hysterical and angry, talked rapidly, and then didn't speak at all. Townsend perceived that "she was frightened the whole time." She didn't want to plead guilty and couldn't believe that the prosecutors really would try the case.

Wasn't there another way to dispose of the charges besides agreeing to a plea bargain? Dodie sobbed. She didn't like any of her options. She didn't want to take the deal but didn't want to go to jail. She didn't want to go to trial; she wanted the case to disappear. That wasn't going to happen. The tense situation blew up.

Buffington stepped out of the room to call Dr. Culver. Would she attempt to talk sense into Dodie and convince her to accept the plea bargain? Dr. Culver agreed to try.

Dodie and Buffington chatted during the forty-minute drive to the veterinarian's office. The investigator knew that Dodie trusted and respected Dr. Culver. She just hoped that Dodie would listen.

Dr. Culver told Dodie that she would testify that four older nursing Labrador dams were woefully thin but with care might have bounced back. The four had whelped back-to-back litters, exacerbating their condition. She'd also have to testify that one person could properly take care of only about twenty adult dogs and/or puppies six months or older. If asked, she'd express concern about the lack of cleanliness at Dodie's kennel. They talked some more about what a jury might do.

"You're going to have to get this behind you; you're gonna have to go through it. It's not going away," Dr. Culver told Dodie.

Dodie refused to accept the plea bargain because she "wasn't guilty and wanted to fight the Humane Society over putting her dogs to sleep." Buffington and Dr. Culver listened to Dodie ramble and repeat herself. The veterinarian thought that Dodie wasn't making sense; she wasn't thinking straight because she was so upset.

Dr. Culver had encouraged her client to take previously offered plea bargains.

"Oh, I don't want to admit that I am guilty," Dodie had retorted.

"Well, you are guilty, so take it," Dr. Culver shot back.

Now with the additional charges, Dodie faced the possibility of a much stiffer jail sentence if she rejected the plea bargain.

"If they are offering something, you probably better take it and take what they give you because you are going to lose in court. You aren't going to win this, so get out from under this the best you can," Dr. Culver said.

Dodie finally agreed to the plea bargain. Buffington called Townsend with the news.

Ermani and Stinson stood before Judge Schultz the next morning on Friday, April 8th, to outline the agreement's terms, although a couple of details needed to be ironed out. He refused to cancel the jury trial until Dodie entered her guilty pleas. The trial remained scheduled for Monday. He'd be available until 5 p.m.

Later that day, Stinson obtained the Weld County District Attorney's Office agreement that Dodie would remain on probation in its felony theft/bad check case if she pled guilty in the animal abuse case.

Townsend and Field talked some more. They set 3:30 p.m. as the time for Dodie to enter her guilty pleas. The defense didn't show up.

About 4:30 p.m., Field left a phone message for Townsend. Did they have a deal?

Townsend called back. Dodie wanted to keep two dogs and their care needed to be overseen by the Weld County Humane Society/Animal Control, not the Larimer County Humane Society.

Ermani didn't want to agree. Field convinced her that it was acceptable for the judge to decide whether Dodie could own two dogs. He felt confident that Judge Schultz wouldn't allow Dodie to keep any animals. Ermani relented. The prosecutors, however, required Dodie to state under oath if she currently owned, cared for, had custody of, bred, or was selling any animal. She had to relinquish any animal(s) to Weld County within twenty-four hours and "may not own, care for, be in custody of, sell, breed, or give away any animal while on probation" but could keep two "current house pets" if the judge allowed.

Just after 5 p.m., the prosecutors faxed this "final" plea offer, set to expire at 5:15 p.m., to Townsend. The defense accepted. Soon after, Ermani and Field joined Townsend in Judge Schultz's courtroom to confirm the plea bargain. The judge canceled the jury trial and scheduled a hearing in its place for Dodie to plead guilty.

On Monday morning, Townsend addressed Judge Schultz. Stinson and Dodie sat quietly at the defense table. Ermani and Field listened.

"I'm sorry it took us a while to go over the paperwork. But as you can imagine, it's important that we do it thoroughly," Townsend said.

He handed a copy of the plea bargain agreement and an advisement form, setting forth what rights Dodie gave up by pleading guilty and her possible sentence, to the judge.

"Ms. Cariaso is prepared this morning to enter pleas of guilty pursuant to *North Carolina v. Alford* . . . a total of twenty counts with the agreement spelled out in that paperwork."

Townsend's statement took Ermani and Field by surprise. He hadn't told them that Dodie would enter an *Alford* plea. In the 1970 *Alford* case, the US Supreme Court upheld a criminal defendant's decision to accept a plea bargain offer of second-degree murder by pleading guilty to that charge to avoid a possible death penalty sentence while maintaining his innocence. Since then, defendants enter an *Alford* plea when they want to maintain their innocence and accept a plea bargain.

Field and Ermani sat quietly at the prosecution table. They didn't object to Townsend's announcement even though they'd only offered to let Dodie plead guilty, acknowledging her wrongdoing. By entering *Alford* pleas, Dodie only admitted there were facts upon which a jury could find her guilty. She'd maintained her innocence; she hadn't done anything wrong.

Judge Schultz accepted the signed advisement, dismissed all the other charges, and scheduled a sentencing hearing for the afternoon of June 2nd. He granted Townsend's request for a presentence report, which the Probation Department would prepare after it interviewed Dodie and investigated her family, educational, employment, and criminal history. He continued the case until the sentencing hearing.

Dodie hadn't been asked if she owned, cared for, or was breeding any animals. She hadn't spoken during the proceedings.

Ermani and Field thought most of the case lay behind them as they gathered up their file and walked out of the courtroom. They had no idea what was to come on the journey to the sentencing hearing.

CHAPTER 23

Treats In The Sky

Before we bred Molly, Dave and I agreed that we'd keep only one puppy from her litter. That way, our dog numbers would remain low and allow us to give individual attention to each of our canines. Our philosophy had been the opposite of Dodie's. Her rapidly expanding puppy business had made such attention virtually impossible because of the time needed just to feed and clean up after so many dogs.

In the summer of 1997, Dave and I kept busy as we fed, cleaned, and socialized Molly's pups. Uncle Max helped with the socialization but didn't receive much human attention. I realized that our Killkenny adoptee needed another job, but what? Could he earn a Companion Dog Excellent obedience degree, which required him to retrieve a dumbbell and deliver it to my hand? I shuddered. Food simply hadn't motivated him when he trained for his CD. And he loved to play keep away.

I'd always wanted to train a dog to compete for an AKC tracking title. Now was the perfect time to teach Max to track.

Our obedience instructor, Rosemary, had put tracking titles on many of her cockers. She drove to our home for my first lesson and watched as I fitted Max with a new black tracking harness and attached a thirty-foot black nylon line. Rosemary turned Max away from me. I placed a "start" stake in the ground and walked in a straight line for about twenty yards in our field. There I lodged a second stake in the field grass and placed a glove, covered with smelly treats, behind it. I took another step or two before easing my five-foot-eleven frame down into the tall grass and hoped Max wouldn't spot me.

Rosemary led Max to the first stake. "Go find," she said and pointed to the ground. He stood motionless and refused to sniff the dirt where I had walked just a minute before.

"Go find!" Rosemary again pointed to the ground and stepped forward. Max followed. She repeated her command and took another step forward, over and over until Max surged ahead when he spied me in the grass. Just before he reached me, he discovered the tasty treats on top of the glove and wolfed them down. "Good dog, Max," I told him as I stood up. We repeated this scenario twice more.

Another day, Rosemary hammered the start stake into the ground before she walked out about thirty yards to set another stake. She continued on a few more steps and placed the glove, again loaded with smelly treats, on the ground. This time she strode forward six feet before she turned and retraced her steps back to the start stake. Rosemary called this technique "double laying a track."

I led Max up to the start stake. "Go find." He stood erect and held his head high.

"Go find," I repeated and pointed to the ground where Rosemary had walked. I took a step or two. Max followed and stopped. I inched forward a few more steps and pointed to the ground as I reiterated, "Go find!" Max walked a couple of paces forward. We repeated this process until we finally reached the treasured glove. Then we tried the same scenario twice more with the same results.

Rosemary suggested that I tether Max to a nearby three-rail wooden fence so that he could watch me lay the double track. Then, she said, walk him to the start stake and ask him to "go find." This way Max and I could practice by ourselves.

Over the next week, I faithfully laid the double track as Max watched. But I had little success when I asked him to "go find." So, I led him deeper into our field where the grass was lusher and retained more scent. I laid another track.

"Max, go find!"

Max just stood, wagged his tail, and gazed up at me. I encouraged him to sniff the ground. He took a couple of steps to appease me. Next, he looked up at the brilliant blue sky as if to say, "My, what a beautiful day for a walk in the field. Maybe treats fall from the sky."

I sighed. Max wasn't getting it. He wasn't my tracking dog.

Mother Molly watched my futile attempts from our living room windows. I knew she craved food, so on a lark, I put the harness on her. Next, I tethered her to a fence post and double laid a track. I led her up to the start stake. She sniffed the ground and nearly pulled me over as she followed my scent to the almighty treats on top of a glove. Molly was my tracking dog and became my first canine to earn a tracking degree. Killkenny Maximilian needed some other job.

CHAPTER 24

Regrets

Dodie regretted her decision to plead guilty as soon as she strode out of the courtroom on Monday, the eleventh day of April 2005.

Just two hours before, she'd met with her defense team in Townsend's office. That's when she said she wanted a trial; she wouldn't plead guilty even though she'd agreed to do so the previous Friday. Townsend stared across his desk at his client and told her there wouldn't be a trial that day because the jury had been canceled. Stinson listened as she sat beside Dodie. Buffington watched the exchange from the other side of Stinson.

For the next hour and a half, the defense team tried to convince Dodie that the plea bargain was in her best interest. They also advised that she could ask that a jury trial be reset to another date. Dodie's emotional state varied, up and down. She became angry, cried, and "retreated physically and emotionally." Dodie was a "volatile person to begin with, but it was especially emotional that morning," Townsend recalled later.

He advised that she could enter an *Alford* plea to maintain her innocence and take advantage of the plea bargain to limit jail exposure. She listened as he explained her rights and what the prosecution must prove before a jury could convict her.

Dodie relented and signed the advisement form, acknowledging that she understood its contents. Townsend thought Dodie would have one final chance to back out of the plea bargain when the judge asked her questions about her *Alford* pleas. But Judge Schultz chose not to ask her those standard questions before he accepted her guilty pleas.

Not long after that day, Dodie informed Townsend that she wanted to withdraw her guilty pleas. He advised that she had the right to ask to withdraw her pleas and requested that she give more thought to the issue. She hadn't changed her mind when they spoke again.

———

Stanlyn Johnston read a newspaper clipping that mentioned Townsend and Dodie's *Alford* pleas. She realized that she finally had a way to locate her friend and former neighbor. So, she called the public defender's office and told an "assistant" on the case that she was very concerned about Dodie. "We are too," the assistant responded. Stanlyn asked that Dodie telephone her.

When Dodie called, the two friends talked about faith. Stanlyn learned that Dodie attended the St. Francis of Assisi Anglican Church outside of Estes Park. Dodie asked her to act as a character witness and telephone Townsend.

In late April, Dodie wrote Stanlyn to thank her for trying to reconnect "in my most dire and desperate time of my life." She thought their "little talk" helped, but "things" were still bad for her. "There are days, hours, moments that I really don't want to be on this earth anymore. I feel so depressed whenever I talk to Norm Townsend, or any of his people at the Public Defender's Office . . . I just don't think that they are on my side sometimes." She asked Stanlyn to telephone Townsend and then let her know if she thought that he was on her side.

Stanlyn wrote Townsend when she couldn't reach him by phone. She copied Dodie on her letter and enclosed a note to her. She was glad that Dodie had God in her life and would pray for her. "He never promised us a life without turmoil, but to always be there to help us thru the turmoil. But why does he allow such challenging situations [to] happen? I am sure we ought not to try to second guess him, Dodie, as tough as it can be, He is always in control. Put your trust in Him, not in the system."

Dodie wrote back. "I really appreciate your prayers because prayers are so powerful for those in desperate situations." She'd pray for Stanlyn, who had mentioned she'd had a "bad" situation of her own. "God loves us all equally and I'm sure he challenges all of us in different ways so that we can become closer to each other and better learn to love each other more every day!" She again asked Stanlyn to contact Townsend, a very busy but "nice guy."

"This is the most difficult time in my entire life . . . I have always been blessed so I guess this is a time that God wants to test me. I need to find inner strength and dignity to continue but I feel weak and vulnerable!" Dodie wrote.

Dodie attended mass several times at St. Francis of Assisi Anglican Church. She approached Father James Barlow to become a parish member and met with him at least twice. She asked him to be a character witness at her sentencing hearing.

While Dodie agonized over her future, Neal and Paula Stack knew their family member's time had come. They'd bought their yellow Labrador as a puppy from Dodie in 2002. Riley had been diagnosed with elbow dysplasia at five months of age. After surgery on both elbows, he recuperated for several months, with his puppy activities strictly limited. The Stacks gave him vet-prescribed Rimadyl as well as glucosamine and chondroitin to help ease his pain. They took him for walks around the block, but he never could do all the normal Labrador activities.

One morning, Riley walked down the stairs to their yard, lay down, and couldn't get up. The Stacks knew that they'd have to put him down that day. He was only three years old.

Two May 19th defense motions blindsided Ermani and Field. The first requested permission for Dodie to withdraw her guilty pleas. The second asked that the public defenders be allowed to withdraw from their representation of Dodie because she accused them of pressuring her into pleading guilty and that alternative defense counsel be appointed in their place. Ermani and Field didn't object to the second motion. Alternative defense counsel are private criminal defense attorneys who are paid by the state and appointed to cases when public defenders cannot represent indigents because of conflicts.

Judge Schultz ordered the appointment of a new defense attorney to represent Dodie at a hearing on June 2nd, the date initially set aside for sentencing.

Oh, Dodie, Dodie, Dodie, please don't do that, Dr. Culver thought as she read a newspaper article about Dodie's attempt to withdraw her pleas. Her client hadn't contacted her to discuss her latest proclamation of innocence.

Stefani Goldin was appointed as Dodie's new lawyer. The University of Boston Law School graduate had practiced for more than eleven years as a criminal defense attorney. When the thirty-nine-year-old lawyer first met her new client, she saw a casually dressed woman clearly distressed but intelligent and articulate. Dodie wanted her day in court.

Goldin needed more time to prepare, so she asked that the plea withdrawal hearing be delayed. Judge Schultz granted her request.

The rescheduled hearing began just after 8:30 a.m. on June 16th. Assistant District Attorney Riedel, with twenty-five years of legal experience, represented the prosecution instead of Ermani and Field, who might be called as witnesses.

Dodie sat next to Goldin. Ermani, Field, and Carol Mayberry-Sanchez, Dodie's longtime friend, watched from the spectator benches.

Goldin called Townsend to the witness stand.

He testified that in hindsight, he tried to persuade Dodie to plead guilty because he believed it was in her best interest and, in some respects, still did.

Goldin asked a series of questions to support her legal argument that the judge had failed to adequately advise Dodie of her rights and possible consequences of accepting the plea bargain.

Through Townsend, she established that the court didn't review the terms and conditions of the plea bargain or the two criminal rule advisements with Dodie.

Next Goldin asked Townsend to explain the significance of the *Alford* pleas.

"Ms. Cariaso wouldn't enter a plea at all without being able to maintain her innocence." Townsend hesitated and then continued, "she wouldn't do it otherwise. That was very significant."

Did judges usually question defendants to make sure they understood the significance of an *Alford* plea and that the plea operated as a conviction?

"Yes." Townsend confirmed that Judge Schultz had not done so.

"Was any inquiry made of Ms. Cariaso?" Goldin asked.

"No."

"Did she utter a word in Court on the day of her plea?"

"No."

Goldin guided Townsend back to the Monday morning when Dodie announced in his office that she didn't want to plead guilty even though she'd accepted the plea bargain the previous Friday.

"Were you concerned that she was making a bad choice by not following your advice?"

"Yes, I was."

"But would you concede that it was her choice to make?"

"Absolutely."

"And, in your opinion now, do you believe now that you exerted an unusual amount of pressure on her to get Ms. Cariaso to accept that plea offer?"

"Yes."

"No further questions." Goldin sat down.

Riedel stood to cross-examine Townsend. The slim, medium-tall prosecutor homed in on Townsend's eighteen years of experience with the Colorado Public Defender's Office.

Townsend acknowledged that he knew but didn't advise Dodie that Count 16, which related to the abandonment of all eighty-four dogs, could have been broken out into eighty-four individual counts.

He conceded that the additional counts didn't force Dodie to accept a plea bargain because she had the ability to say no from the "get-go."

Then he added, "That's true. I'm concerned that I forced her to. What I worry about is because they made a bigger difference to me than they did to her, that I unduly pressured her."

Asked about the Monday morning meeting in his office just before she pled guilty, Townsend agreed he'd advised Dodie that she could maintain her innocence and have a trial reset to another date. He also reviewed her rights and what she was giving up by pleading guilty.

"Would it be a fair statement that in your colloquy with the Court, you never advised the Court of any reluctance on the part of your client to accept the disposition?"

"That's true," Townsend said in a quiet voice.

He admitted that he hadn't told the court about his client's concerns expressed to him earlier that morning.

"She never expressed any concerns in the courtroom, correct?" Riedel asked.

"That's true," Townsend said quietly. He agreed that he'd explained the meaning and consequences of an *Alford* plea to Dodie before she went to court.

On re-direct examination, Townsend testified about his stress with the case.

"I've lost count of how many first-degree murder cases I have handled. I was more stressed by this case than by any of those I can recall because I believed this woman was being mistreated by the system," Townsend testified.

"And did your stress drive how you attempted to persuade?"

"It did."

"Did anything that Ms. Cariaso stated to you lead you to believe that she was not clear with the consequences of not pleading guilty that day?"

"Well, I have always wondered exactly how much she is able to understand the legal parts of it."

"Why do you think that is?"

"She is not a lawyer. She is a dog breeder."

"So, your job is to advise her of the legal consequences?" Goldin asked.

"Yes."

On recross-examination, Riedel asked Townsend if he had ever tried to change the trial's location because of his concern about the community's anger.

"No. She wanted to be tried in this community if she could because this is her home. She wanted to be vindicated in her home. She wanted the people of this community that had heard these nasty things about her to hear the truth," Townsend testified emphatically.

He stepped down from the witness stand after testifying for forty minutes. Goldin didn't call any other witnesses, and Riedel didn't call any.

The judge allowed both sides to argue.

Goldin argued that the public defenders pressured Dodie into accepting the plea bargain because they thought it was in her best interest even though she had remained steadfast in her innocence and desire for a trial. The decision to plead guilty was their decision, not Dodie's.

When she addressed Judge Schultz's failure to ask any questions of Dodie, she referred to him as the court instead of by name, probably to impersonalize her critical comments.

The court failed to be assured that Dodie understood the plea bargain and its possible consequences and couldn't rely either on the written advisements or upon her attorney's representations about his advisements, she argued. The court needed to ask, "Is that true, did your counsel advise you?" and be assured "that the accused is not under the influence of any drugs, medications, or any alcohol and simply able to understand the proceedings. None of that took place on that day."

Ten minutes into her argument, Goldin cited her first legal authority. It required the judge to have evidence of a knowing, intelligent, and voluntary nature of a plea. "To say that this plea is constitutional is stretching the limits of constitutionality."

Goldin relinquished the podium to Riedel. The veteran prosecutor argued that Townsend hadn't been asked if he'd raised his voice, threatened her, said he wouldn't represent her if she didn't take the plea or if he'd done the good guy, bad guy routine.

"Counsel talks about the persistent badgering. Where's the evidence, Your Honor? . . . The defendant did not take the stand today and say I wanted to plead not guilty, but they kept me in a room for an hour, and they just one after the other, after the other kept telling me I had to plead, I had to plead. Nothing, there is no evidence of that," Riedel argued emphatically.

Dodie hadn't testified that her pleas were involuntary, that she was distraught and didn't know what was going on, or that she had told her attorney that she didn't want to plead on April 11th, Riedel noted. Her attorneys had very thoroughly gone over the elements of the offense and required mental state, he said.

"All we have, Your Honor, is a defendant who has sort of a mercurial personality, she's up, she's down, and now she has buyer's remorse, and she wants to withdraw her plea. That's not a basis, that's not a fair and just basis for a withdrawal of a plea," he argued. He asked the judge to deny the motion and sat down. His argument had lasted less than five minutes.

Judge Schultz immediately ruled. He rejected the defense argument that the additional counts amounted to "a coercion issue."

Next, he addressed the *Alford* pleas. While the defendant didn't want to accept the disposition (plea bargain), she concluded it was in her best interest to do so, "which is exactly what an *Alford* plea is."

The judge ruled that Dodie was advised and knew all of her rights. He made court exhibits of advisement documents in his file, a somewhat unusual action. Most judges rely solely on exhibits presented by the parties or take judicial notice of portions of the court file.

In another unusual action, Judge Schultz played back a recording of part of the March 23rd motions hearing "to show the emotional and volatile way that the defendant conducted herself which relates to how my plea was taken." At the March hearing, he'd instructed Dodie to leave the courtroom after she'd screamed at the Humane Society.

Goldin sat "dumbfounded" when the judge played the recording. She thought it "was really inappropriate" and "unnecessary to flaunt her (Dodie's) emotional outburst." Dodie sniffled as the recording played.

Judge Schultz concluded that Townsend's encouragement to accept the plea bargain wasn't "coercion." Townsend was being a good attorney and advising her of her options. His client "had the best public defender available in this jurisdiction."

The judge acknowledged that he knew "very well" what he should ask Dodie and accepted her plea in the manner he did because of her "volatile, emotional or disruptive nature or behavior." He realized that he wasn't going to be able to confer back and forth with her. That's why he attached a document that set forth what the prosecution needed to prove to convict her of each charge.

He said while he preferred to use a question-answer session with the defendant, he felt it wouldn't be possible, and "that's why the elaborate set of documents were filed and handled by the Court."

"There have to be times when the Court simply can't follow all the procedures that may be best and have to try to do something else." Judge Schultz found that all of Dodie's rights had been protected and rejected Goldin's coercion argument.

"I think that counsel went above and beyond to protect his client and to try to work out a fair and just disposition," the judge said of Townsend. "He was able over the months and months to get the DA to modify their position for her benefit."

Judge Schultz denied the plea withdrawal motion because Dodie's plea was voluntary, and her rights were protected. His findings and ruling had lasted more than fifteen minutes. He ordered Goldin to confer with Townsend to determine who would represent Dodie at the sentencing hearing now set for August 22nd.

CHAPTER 25

Uncertainty

Townsend solved the representation dilemma by asking Judge Schultz to appoint Goldin to represent Dodie at sentencing because of a "conflict of interest" and "irreconcilable differences." Dodie and Townsend weren't on speaking terms.

Judge Schultz appointed Goldin, who recognized that Dodie was very suspicious of lawyers. Goldin needed to win her new client's trust and confidence, which would take time and considerable hand-holding. She had less than eight weeks to do so.

Goldin perceived Judge Schultz as a "pretty fair" sentencer—a judge who didn't want to hurt defendants but wanted them to succeed and not appear before him again. However, she recognized that he'd feel public pressure and anticipated that Ermani and Field would seek a three-year jail sentence for her client.[1]

She conferred with Dodie over the next seven weeks to prepare for sentencing in the highest-profile case that she'd handled. They met many more times than she usually did with other clients charged with misdemeanors because of the nature of the case and Dodie's emotional state.

Goldin wanted to keep Dodie out of jail or at least limit any jail time and have her allowed to own two dogs. To accomplish her goals, the defense attorney needed to show that Dodie wasn't the "monster" the media had portrayed but was instead a caring, devoted dog breeder who shouldn't be judged by one day in her life.

Dodie carried two boxes into her attorney's office. Goldin pulled out photo albums and leafed through them. She poured over photographs of Dodie as a younger woman and her dogs over the years. Then she read newspaper clippings about her client's pottery career and letters from satisfied Killkenny puppy owners.

She picked up one photograph and stared at Dodie, probably in her twenties, as she stood "spread eagle" against a six-foot-tall monument in a courtyard. Her client looked "stunningly beautiful" with a broad smile and hair that flowed down to her waist.

There was "so much calmness and happiness in that person" that it was so sad that it went wrong, Goldin said later. "It was like another person, and it just shows you that we all start off shiny and new with so much potential, and then something happens along the way. She just looked so genuinely happy, and it just seemed to me that it had been a long time since Dodie had been genuinely happy."

Goldin read Humane Society literature about the care and upbringing of dogs and learned more about her client as a potter and dog breeder. She asked Dr. Culver to write a letter for an exhibit that Buffington had initially prepared for trial. That exhibit included documentation of Dodie's food and vet care costs for her canines. According to Dr. Culver's records, Dodie spent $23,720 in veterinary care over nearly ten years. The transaction history listed charges related to more than eighty-six named dogs and countless unnamed puppies.

The defense attorney intended to introduce the exhibit to prove her client's care and love for her dogs. But those same records also showed that Dr. Culver hadn't treated any of the injured dogs discovered by the Humane Society on July 3, 2004. Dodie hadn't taken any dog to Dr. Culver's vet hospital for more than eleven months before that date and had purchased only vet supplies from her through early February 2004.

Dodie met again with the experienced Estes Park solo practitioner whom she'd hired for $800 in May to file a Chapter 7 petition in US Bankruptcy Court. She'd concluded that bankruptcy appeared to be the only way out of her dire financial situation after her unsuccessful attempt the previous November to qualify for a mortgage. She undoubtedly applied for the mortgage because she'd successfully refinanced her farm for increased amounts numerous times over twenty-plus years and received lines of credit and credit cards over the same period. Her failure to pay banks; credit card, collection, and finance companies; and numerous court judgments caught up with her. Credit bureaus awarded miserable-to-poor credit ratings to her and nixed any hope to buy a house.

Chapter 7 filings are designed for debtors lacking the ability to pay their existing debts. A debtor is allowed to keep specific "exempted" property. However, if the debtor has assets that exceed the exemption, a bankruptcy trustee takes possession and liquidates all of the debtor's property to pay off creditors according to priorities established in bankruptcy law. Most Chapter 7 filings involve debtors who don't have assets that exceed the allowed exemptions.

Dodie could start anew if the bankruptcy court discharged her allowable debts. Bankruptcy court generally didn't cancel tax debts. It could discharge civil judgments unless a lien had been filed, and then the individual or entity that held the lien would be listed as a creditor.

In her Chapter 7 petition filed on August 9, 2005, she asked the bankruptcy court to discharge more than $185,000 in debts. The petition listed thirty unsecured claims from twenty-nine different creditors. All were unprioritized, meaning one claim wouldn't be paid in advance of another. Eleven claims had been turned over to collection agencies. At least eighteen claims related to services rendered or accounts opened in 2002 or later.

The largest listed debt was for more than $92,000 owed to a bank as a home equity line of credit secured by Dodie's farm. She listed a $9,000 debt to the CSU veterinary hospital as well as $16,726 owed to Toyota Motor Credit Co. for a used 4Runner that she financed in full in March 2005. She also owed money to banks, dentists, equine veterinarians, financial institutions, debt collection agencies, Target, and Kmart as well as water, trash, and telephone providers. And, she hadn't paid $1,000 to the IRS for her 2002 taxes.

She listed more than $6,280 in judgments entered against her after she failed to respond to lawsuits brought by a collection company, two banks, a finance company, and an individual, all within the last year.

The bankruptcy petition required Dodie to disclose her personal property. She claimed a less than $1,000 total value for that property: $200 worth of used household goods, $100 of clothing, $100 of costume jewelry, $10 as cash on hand, and $500 for her Nissan 280zx. And she claimed it was all exempt property, which meant that it couldn't be taken from her or used to pay creditors. She reported a $350 rent security deposit and no checking, savings, or other financial accounts.

Dodie attested that she was unemployed and reported $1,660 in monthly expenses: $750 for rent, $100 for heating fuel and electricity, $25 for telephone, $50 for cable television, $200 for food, $50 for auto insurance, and $485 for auto installment payments. She didn't list any amount for health or renter's insurance.

She reported her aliases as C W Cariaso and Catherine W. Cariaso, aka Dodie Cariaso, aka Symposium in Mud, aka Killkenny Retrievers but failed to list Jesse McClure, the name she'd used when she bought her Labrador Ben the previous year. By signing the completed bankruptcy application, she attested to its truthfulness.

While Dodie finalized her bankruptcy application, she faced yet another legal problem. Her landlord tried to terminate her rental home lease for failure to pay rent. He cited "destruction of property, lack of upkeep and other pending legal matters concerning dog abandonment in Larimer County" as other reasons for the termination. He demanded that she vacate the house by September 1st and notified Dodie's younger brother Doug, who helped pay the rent, of his demand.

Dodie contacted Colorado Legal Services, a nonprofit organization that offered free legal advice on civil matters to indigents. Her Legal Services attorney arranged for Dodie to pay the back rent and notified the landlord that his client had an enforceable one-year lease good through April 1, 2006. Dodie denied any property damage and accused the landlord of interfering with her "quiet enjoyment of the property" because he'd listed the property for sale and conducted unannounced visits. The renovated home, built in 1926, sat on two acres with prime river frontage just off the main road to Rocky Mountain National Park. It was listed for sale at $957,000.

———

Dodie knew that Judge Schultz would decide whether she could own two dogs. But she had three: Ben and Bernitta, the Labradors, and Huxsby, a Bernese mountain dog puppy. So, she asked Dr. Culver to find a home for Bernitta, and the veterinarian agreed but insisted that she first spay the dog. Dr. Culver was horrified to discover during the spay that Bernitta was about five weeks pregnant. Her receptionist later wondered if the pups should have been left in the womb, whelped, raised, and sold. Dr. Culver related those thoughts to Dodie.

"She can't benefit from something I've done," Dodie snapped back.

The vet then realized why Dodie hadn't tried to place her canines before she walked away from them the previous summer. At the time, she couldn't imagine that Dodie would have abandoned her dogs and thought the Humane Society shouldn't have euthanized the puppies because they were viable. Dr. Culver would have brought up one litter and also believed one Labrador breeder would have raised them all, sold them, and then given some of the sales revenue to Dodie. The vet also knew that Dodie didn't like the breeder.

Now Dr. Culver knew that Dodie hadn't wanted anyone else to "benefit" from "her work," and that explained why Dodie hadn't contacted her or the other breeder.

Dodie said that she wasn't going to breed any more but planned on going into the stud dog business.

"You can't get into the stud dog business; that is still breeding dogs," Dr. Culver retorted. "What is the matter with you? Give up the dogs."

Goldin and her client selected five individuals to speak at the sentencing: Carl, who owned the property where Dodie left her Labradors; Dr. Culver; Barbara Marcus-McKenna and Carol Mayberry-Sanchez, two longtime friends; and Vikki, Dodie's sister-in-law. Dodie also would address the judge. The defense attorney individually prepared the five witnesses and Dodie for the hearing. She encouraged her client to write notes to keep her remarks on track and to the point.

Dodie not only jotted down notes but also invited Carol and Dr. Culver to her Estes Park home to discuss their statements. Dr. Culver noticed that the 1,273-square-foot home was an "expensive little house to rent" and knew that Dodie could have located a cheaper rental. She wondered why Dodie had spent several hundred dollars to buy fifty-plus flowering plants, undoubtedly from a nursery, to decorate her home. Dodie probably wanted to surround herself with some beauty before she was sentenced, the veterinarian surmised, and sensed her client just wasn't thinking.

Goldin understood that Dodie believed the Humane Society had killed fifty-four of her Labradors. The defense attorney decided that she wouldn't argue that point because she lacked "conclusive evidence" that the Humane Society had murdered the dogs. However, she knew Dodie wanted to tell her story to the press before sentencing. In the attorney's opinion, the media had vilified her client.

For the first time in her career and in what many attorneys would consider an unusual move, Goldin agreed to allow her client to meet directly with the media just a week before sentencing. She didn't think Dodie would say anything inflammatory or irritate the judge.

"I knew her story. I had heard it a thousand times. There were times that I would say, 'Dodie I know, we have been through this, I know, it's okay, I know how you feel,' because she would just repeat herself over and over and she was very emotional about it . . . I was pretty comfortable that there weren't going to be any surprises because we had spent enough time together at that point."[2]

Dodie addressed the two or three newspaper reporters gathered in Goldin's office. She'd left a note for her landlord to contact the Humane Society, and it had never crossed her mind to do so herself. Now she was glad that she hadn't called because she didn't feel guilty for contacting those who "murdered" her dogs. Any show of aggression by her Labradors was caused by their fear and unsettlement triggered by the move, she said. Devastated when she learned how many of them had been euthanized, she cried and screamed for weeks and even attempted suicide. She'd rather be on probation for the rest of her life than go to jail, she told the reporters. She had just gotten a job and had started to put her life back together.[3]

Yes, I have indeed heard it all before, Goldin thought as she listened.

———————

Ermani and Field had lived and breathed Dodie's case for months. Their mission was for Judge Schultz to hear the silent voices of the living and dead animals. They wanted him to understand how the Labradors suffered and struggled to live, those that died and those that survived. They wanted him to comprehend the new owners' struggles with the medical and emotional issues of many of the survivors. They wanted him to hold Dodie accountable for her actions by sentencing her to jail and prohibiting her from pet ownership. But they recognized that they faced an uphill battle because Judge Schultz was a reputed lenient sentencer. Field, however, remained confident that the judge wouldn't allow Dodie to own any dogs.

Ermani had faith that the judge would do the right thing but didn't think anyone would take the case as seriously as she and Field. "I could never gauge whether the judge would understand how deeply we feel. Would he think we were just crazy? Well, maybe if enough people are here to support, he would see that we are not crazy, and there should be a consequence for it."

Field and Ermani worked closely with the Humane Society to select photographs of individual Labradors for a PowerPoint presentation to graphically show the condition of the adults and puppies that words alone could not adequately describe. They'd use this powerful visual tool to try to persuade the judge to sentence Dodie to three years of jail time, the maximum allowed under the plea bargain, and to deny Dodie's request to own two pets. Both feared that she'd breed dogs again. Ermani thought she might have hidden canines.

Ermani researched for hours and read about socialization of dogs in general and Labradors in particular. She learned about the importance of puppies' socialization with littermates and humans and the value of proper nutrition. She studied the different development stages of puppies. She discovered that some experts believe the optimal learning period for puppies is between three and twelve weeks, and a fear period runs from eight to ten or twelve weeks.

The two prosecutors decided that Neira would testify first because he was the lead investigator and among the first to arrive at the abandonment scene. They chose three other witnesses: Dr. Spindel, who euthanized fifty-four of the Labradors; Humane Society president and CEO Joe Olsen, who assisted at the abandonment scene; and Christine Samuelian, the Humane Society behaviorist who worked with the surviving dogs. The prosecutors wanted the witnesses to paint a mental picture as they recounted their on-scene experiences and interactions with the canines. They worked closely with them and suggested what their focus should be to avoid any redundancy.

Field didn't enjoy working on the case. He found it difficult because of the "100 souls that did not have a good life" and the owners who coped with the "unhealthy and problematic animals." Both prosecutors wanted the difficult and troubling case behind them.

Before the day of the sentencing, the prosecution and defense received a copy of the Probation Department's presentence report. It disclosed Dodie's account of the abandonment and the Probation Department's position on sentencing.[4]

Typically, a presentence report contains a recommendation for a specific period of incarceration and/or probation. In Dodie's case, the probation officer recommended an unspecified term of probation conditioned on an unspecified amount of jail time. She stated that some time in jail, which "will serve no purpose beyond punishment," was necessary, and rehabilitation efforts were important. The officer recommended mental health treatment, including an evaluation and counseling partially to address anger, grief, and loss; an unspecified amount of public service; and a requirement to work at least thirty-five hours per week at a job that didn't involve animal care. However, she didn't recommend whether Dodie should or shouldn't have personal pets but suggested two of the same sex if the judge allowed any.

The report included a summary of Dodie's criminal history: the 2001 misdemeanor harassment case that involved a process server and the 2003 Weld County felony theft/bad check case that related to her purchase of hay. She'd accumulated a few traffic violations for speeding, expired plates, and lack of car insurance, spanning the 1990s through 2004.

Dodie submitted a written version of her account of the abandonment. She had a high-end "Sporthorse Breeding Facility" from 1996 to 2004. The cost of hay tripled during the 2002 drought, which caused her to spend more than $2,000 each month on hay to feed her horses. She got behind on her mortgage and lost her farm to foreclosure.

She characterized herself as "a professional Potter/Artist—and had a licensed Labrador Breeding Kennel. The farm was totally supported financially by the Labrador Breeding Kennel. I have been a reputable breeder since 1980. I sold one on one my pups by interview only—was not a puppy mill."

Dodie penned that she moved to a new farm (Carl's property) with twenty-seven of her best breeders and eight new litters, but then the farm owner changed his mind. "I had to relinquish my Labs—all of them—for their own benefit so I left a note for Carl to call Larimer Co. Humane Soc. To come rescue my totally Healthy Happy Beautiful-Sweet Labradors."

But, "Instead—Due to their 'Vendetta' against all Breeders they MURDERED over 50 of my sweet labs—within minutes—with no fair evaluation! So they decided to persecute me—to cover up their mass-murder! There was never any neglect abuse or abandonment on my part at all!! Since I did not know that Larimer Ct. Humane Soc. are such cruel & unusual Inhumane people. I would have never relinquished them to Larimer Co—if I had known."

During an interview with a probation officer, Dodie said she spent all her money earned from her dog breeding business, up to $8,000 a month, on her horses and lacked sufficient income to survive. She modified that statement when she reviewed the presentence report. In its margins, she penned that she had at one time earned up to

$8,000 a month, but "not for the last two years—was only making $3,000 a month."

The probation officer also interviewed Neira, who thought that Dodie was "unaware of or unwilling to recognize her wrongdoing, especially relating to her insufficient care" for her dogs. He expressed "serious concerns" about her eventually breeding animals if allowed to have them. The probation officer reported that Neira supported supervised probation, mental health counseling, and a prohibition of any pets but failed to note that he endorsed some jail time.

Was July 2, 2004, just one aberrant day in the life of Dodie, as Goldin intended to portray, or had Dodie neglected and mistreated her Labradors for some time, as Ermani and Field planned to argue?

Judge Schultz would consider those questions at sentencing in a case involving a type of animal cruelty—animal neglect—that accounted for more than 30 percent of all cases reported to the Animal Legal Defense Fund, a nonprofit organization dedicated to enforcing animal protection laws.[5]

CHAPTER 26

Hiking Dog

Dodie proclaimed that she bred to produce quality, good-natured Labradors for pet homes. Our Killkenny Maximilian was proof that she'd done just that. But we discovered our boy possessed some quirks that we learned about only as the years went by.

In July 1998, Dave and I took Max on a week-long camping/hiking trip to belatedly reward him for his loyalty and patience with Molly's puppies. We thought he'd love the individual attention, alone away from his four-footed family. He was our perfect trail dog except when he rolled in cow pies or ate tasty horse poop snacks.

Max happily jumped into our dark blue Toyota T-100 truck and proudly sat on the rear bench seat as we set out for the Flat Top Wilderness in western Colorado. We stopped for lunch at the top of Vail Pass and arrived in the late afternoon at a White River National Forest campground in the western portion of the Flat Tops. Dave and I pitched our tent before the boys ventured off to collect firewood. In the tent, I arranged our sleeping bags and three Therm-a-Rest pads: one for each human and another for Max. Dave and Max returned about thirty minutes later with ample firewood. We built a fire, cooked dinner, and settled in for the night in our three-person tent.

Sometime during the night, I awoke to an unmistakable retching sound. Dave and I struggled to unzip the tent before we pushed Max out. At daybreak, we learned of our partial success. We cleaned the tent and then ate breakfast but didn't feed Max to allow his stomach to settle. Then we headed out to a nearby trailhead and hiked along a fairly level trail for a couple of miles. We stopped for lunch in a meadow and perched on rocks to eat our bagels, cheese, and apples as we enjoyed the view of the surrounding rolling hills. I offered Max a combination of generic and much costlier Milk-Bone dog biscuits. He refused the generic biscuits but chomped down the Milk-Bones.

On our hike back to the trailhead, we met a woman who was leading her horse along the trail. Our conversation soon led to Max's sensitive stomach. She recommended old Doc White, who practiced in Meeker, the nearest town if we decided to take Max to a vet. We thanked her and went our separate ways.

At the trailhead, Dave, Max, and I climbed into our truck and drove east to a cabin that we'd fortuitously rented for the next two nights. Dave and I took cherished showers before I fixed Max a meal of his usual fare, kibble, and canned meat. He walked away from his dish. His stomach must still be off, I thought. But then he wasn't the typical Labrador that inhaled his food; instead, he usually ate methodically.

Max needed strength for our hike the next day. So, after dinner, I offered him some of our hamburger and rice. He licked his dish clean.

Later that night, Dave and I lay in our cozy bed in our even cozier cabin and listened for retching sounds. Max made it through the night without incident.

The next morning, Max again turned up his nose at his kibble. We loaded our packs with a mixture of generic and Milk-Bone dog biscuits and human food before we drove to a trailhead. Near the beginning of our hike, we spied some horse poop, but not before Max had eaten his first snack. Great. Dave and I agreed to watch Max more carefully to discourage him from any like morsels. We reached our destination, a small lake. Max found sufficient strength to swim in the cold mountain water.

Dave and I sat on a boulder that overlooked the lake and ate lunch. Max agreed to give up swimming for dog biscuits but only

Milk-Bones. Afterward, he acted a bit more chipper. That night, Max again refused his dog food and only ate a bit of hamburger and rice that I prepared just for him.

Max needed to see a vet. We planned to hike for five more days.

The next morning, Dave opted out of our planned morning horse-back ride because we couldn't leave Max alone in the cabin for fear that he might throw up. We devised a plan: Dave and Max would visit the Meeker vet while I rode. This was an especially good plan for Dave because he disliked horses and claimed that they always tried to bite him.

I hadn't ridden since an automobile accident in 1992 and looked forward to the outing. The guide saddled two horses because I was the only paying rider. We mounted our steeds and walked past Max and Dave, who gallantly came to the stables to see me off. My nice calm horse spooked and reared. I grabbed the saddle horn and stayed aboard. The guide theorized that my horse reared because it smelled the bear that frequented the area. Terrific. At least I hadn't lost my dignity in front of my blond boys. The guide and I headed up through the green aspen trees and ponderosa pines to a plateau. I enjoyed the solitude of the ride without incident.

When I cruised into our cabin three hours later, I learned that the boys hadn't visited the vet. Old Doc White had an open appointment only for later that afternoon.

Dave, Max, and I drove about twenty miles to Meeker. We arrived well before the appointment and located the town's only grocery store. There we bought a box of Milk-Bones just in case Max continued to eat only the costly biscuits.

We met old Doc White, a gentleman probably in his late seventies, in the veterinary clinic's exam room. His assistant, who might have been eighteen years old, clutched a clipboard and positioned herself next to her boss, whose pure white hair matched his lab coat.

"What happened?" asked old Doc White, who stood about five foot seven and had a slender build.

"Max must have gotten into something during a search for firewood two days before," Dave said.[1]

Old Doc White turned to his assistant and instructed her to write, "Labrador Retriever, yellow, male, age seven."

He took Max's temperature and then opened our boy's mouth, felt his body, and listened to his heart. When he found nothing out of the ordinary, he prescribed a ready-made mixture of Pepto-Bismol and Kaopectate in a long tube that we could insert into Max's mouth.

"You might also want to give him ID to calm his stomach," old Doc White said.

"Oh, Max doesn't like ID," I replied. Max always refused to eat the canned, bland invalid diet whenever I'd offered it to him when his stomach was upset.

Old Doc White looked surprised. He turned to his assistant.

"Add to his chart. 'And spoiled.'"

Max recovered quickly after his vet visit.

We drove the next morning to Buena Vista to spend the final days of our mountain vacation. At night, we stayed in a cabin and during the day climbed fourteeners: Mt. Antero and Huron Peak as well as the state's highest mountain, Mt. Elbert. Max ate little and lived on Milk-Bones.

Once home, we didn't cater to his tastes. He happily consumed every morsel of his regular dog food in front of the always vigilant Molly and Brew as they hovered at his side. Dave and I agreed that from now on, he'd vacation only with at least one of his girls.

Two months later, Max and his thirteen-month-old "niece" Brew accompanied us on another hiking vacation. We hoped that he'd eat his regular dog food and teach proper trail etiquette to Brew. She exhibited alpha dog traits and, unfortunately, inherited her mother's gene for barking at all things, little or big: rocks, garbage cans, people, dogs, etc. We booked our usual cabin in Buena Vista so that we could enjoy the area for the week after Labor Day.

Our goal was for us all to become fit enough to climb Mt. Yale, a 14,196-foot peak. Max was nearly eight years old. Brew hadn't climbed any fourteeners because of her young age. We all conditioned by hiking to alpine lakes up to about 11,000 feet. By week's end, we seemed in decent shape.

After a rest day, we drove to Mt. Yale's trailhead and arrived about 10 a.m. We found only one car parked at the 9,900-foot trailhead and believed its occupants were well up the trail thanks to our late start. Most peak baggers try to summit before noon because of the threat of summer afternoon thunderstorms. September was a perfect month to hike in the mountains because normally the weather was clear without the threat of such storms. Snow, however, was always a possibility. That day, the cloudless and brilliant blue sky buoyed our spirits.

The peak lay about three and a half miles away, with an elevation gain of approximately 4,300 feet. Dave and I found a sustainable pace because we knew breathing would become much more difficult as we gained elevation. With boundless energy, Brew ran up and then back down the trail to find her slower humans. She darted among the lodgepole pine trees and then back onto the trail. Max followed her everywhere. He seemed to have plenty of stamina, probably because he was eating his usual dog kibble under the watchful eye of his niece.

Brew found her voice when she spotted a lone hiker. We introduced the friendly Oklahoman to the dogs and apologized for Brew's behavior. I explained that we were trying to break her from barking and reassured him that she was exceedingly friendly.

The hiker started up again as we took a short break. Then we moved on and quickly overtook him just before timberline as he gasped for air. Dave and I were somewhat acclimated to altitude because we lived at 6,600 feet in Franktown. We hiked on at a steady pace until we reached some giant boulders. There, we lifted the dogs' rear quarters to assist them over the boulders and then hiked to the summit.

We rested, ate some food, and enjoyed the spectacular view. When the Oklahoman summited, we took pictures of one another.

By then it was midafternoon, and our new friend looked a bit tired. Dave and I suggested that we all descend together. The unspoken rule of the high country is that you always hike with someone else so you can help each other if necessary. Our friend agreed to our suggestion, so we ambled down the mountain together. Whenever he slowed his pace and fell behind, Brew ran back to him as if to urge him on. She had found her new best friend.

Both dogs, especially Max, stayed close to us on our descent. We bid adieu to the Oklahoman at the trailhead and wished him a good rest of his trip. The four of us piled into our SUV and headed back to the cabin. After a rest, we took the dogs outside and discovered that Max had really outdone himself. He was very, very stiff. Brew was ready to conquer another mountain. Both dogs had some minor cuts on their pads from the boulders, but we knew that they would heal quickly. Uncle Max never again tried to keep pace with his favorite niece. He was no longer a young dog.

CHAPTER 27

For The People

Nearly fourteen months after she abandoned her Labradors, fifty-six-year-old Dodie stared straight ahead at the empty jury box across the expansive courtroom. She'd pulled her hair back from her face and wore an embroidered flowered vest over a long-sleeved shirt and jeans. Goldin sat next to her at the defense table as they waited for the August 22, 2005 sentencing hearing to begin. Natural light poured into the courtroom from windows high above the jury box.

To their right, Ermani and Field sat at the prosecution table, which also faced the jury box. Humane Society and district attorney staff, interested courthouse employees, and members of the press found seats among the eight rows of light-brown oak benches that lined each side of an aisle in the back half of the courtroom. Townsend, accompanied by Buffington and Stinson, as well as a few new owners of the abandoned dogs and individuals who had bought Dodie puppies, watched from this spectator gallery. Father Barlow and some of Dodie's friends and family did as well.

Judge Schultz, dressed in a traditional black robe, emerged from a door at the front of the courtroom and walked to the bench. He sat and gazed out at the parties and spectators. Stacks of case files were piled within his reach.

He opened the hearing with a four-minute speech: Dodie faced sentencing on fifteen counts of animal neglect and nine (instead of the correct number of five) counts of animal abandonment. The potential penalty for class one misdemeanors ranged from six to eighteen months in jail and a fine of $500 to $5,000.

Judge Schultz acknowledged discussion of a 144-year sentence, but that "option is not, and I repeat, that option is not before the Court today" because of the plea bargain.

"I'll also point out to everybody that today the issue is not whether the Humane Society acted improper or imprudently. That's not a charge. They're not on trial. . . Has nothing to do with the case being presented today."

This "is not a Court of public opinion. This Court has nothing to do with what you, the public, think about the action before the Court today. This is a court of law."

Judge Schultz detailed his options under the plea bargain: impose a maximum jail sentence of up to three years or "if probation is used," a minimum of one year of probation. He'd decide if Dodie could own two pets. She'd swear "that she will not be involved and does not have other animals." He wouldn't impose a fine or public service because he lacked a recommendation for either.

"We're not here to vilify the Defendant. We're not here to make the Defendant a victim and, therefore, not accountable. And we are not here to blame someone else. We are here to talk about what is this sentence to be relative to these specific and only these counts."

Judge Schultz permitted Goldin to telephone Carl, the over-the-road truck driver who was apparently out of town, for a statement. Normally, prosecution witnesses testify first.

Goldin asked Carl questions even though he wasn't sworn in as a witness. He confirmed that he agreed to allow Dodie and some dogs to move onto his property while he was out of town, and learned only upon his return that she had many more dogs than he expected. He'd told her that the dogs couldn't stay after his neighbors complained about barking. Then he left on a trip to Kansas. Upon his return, he couldn't locate Dodie. He telephoned the Humane Society as soon as he discovered her note. Two women helped him feed and water the dogs and cleaned out many of the "cages" before the Humane Society workers arrived.

"Were any of the dogs aggressive towards you?" Goldin asked.

"No. There wasn't any of them aggressive at all. Actually we—I stuck my hand in probably most of the crates and so did my girlfriend and another lady there. And there was never one that actually growled at us or bit."

He'd been led to believe only ten or twelve canines were put down. Judge Schultz cut him off when he explained his shock upon learning many more were euthanized. Prosecutors opted not to question Carl.

Field gathered up his slender, six-foot frame and stood to address the judge. "This Court has been patient and has provided the Defendant every opportunity to exercise her constitutional and statutory rights in this matter."

He highlighted "the depth and degree of harm and sadness felt by not only the owners of the animals but also by the individuals directly involved in the discovery." He promised that the evidence would show "the physical and the psychological damage inflicted on these dogs."

Joe Olsen, the Humane Society's president and CEO, stepped up to the podium. He recalled that many of the dogs appeared friendly, but some were frightened and refused to leave their crates. He'd seen a few bowls of water that had been placed outside the kennels (crates).

"The kennels themselves were foul, disgusting, dirty. Some of them had up to two inches of urine and feces floating in the bottom. If you've ever seen an airline kennel, there is a section about two to three inches where the air cannot get in and if they're sitting flat, they will hold water like a dishpan of some sort. So a lot of the animals had been soaked in their own urine, soaked in their own feces and were in very difficult shape."

Townsend stood up and stormed out of the courtroom. He thought Olsen was less than truthful and couldn't bear to listen further. Buffington, his investigator, followed.

Olsen continued. The stench was beyond anything he had ever smelled, and the condition of a number of puppies was "absolutely heartbreaking."

The soft-spoken former priest related how a brown (chocolate) female came out of her crate and collapsed, unable to stand. "She was dying in front of our very eyes; the puppies were still nursing on her. We had to remove the puppies from the mother and give her a peaceful death."

"It was very difficult," Olsen said as he tried to express the emotional pain he and his staff went through with "this many adult dogs and puppies that were in such dilapidated condition," which "took far more than two or three days to happen. It takes a long time for a full-grown Labrador Retriever to get down to the point where you can count every rib. To get dilapidated to the point where their teeth are falling out from being overbred. To get to the point when their legs can't even hold them up anymore because they've lost so much calcium in being bred over and over.

"This was the saddest case I have ever experienced in my life, and I hope I never have to experience it again."

Neira replaced Olsen at the podium. He spoke rapidly as he recounted that he found most of the dogs in crates exposed to direct sunlight and recalled the foul smell, which "just permeated everything after you touched it for a while. Just being there you could smell it."

He described Labradors with scars and open wounds from fights, and emaciated dogs with protruding hip and rib bones. And, he recalled the chocolate female that collapsed.

One Labrador stuck in his mind: a "puppy that had received some injury at some prior day where his nose had been ripped from his skull in a dog fight or whatever it may have been. We're talking about a maybe three-month-old puppy" that was euthanized because his injury was so traumatic.

"Examining him after that further, I found that his nose had literally been ripped all the way beyond the opening of his nose, and he'd been walking around like that. I can't imagine what—how that could have been missed. It was pure—just pure neglect."

Neira said that Dodie had surrendered more than fifty canines to Weld County Animal Control and, shortly thereafter, still had over eighty dogs. He recounted how Dodie surrendered her "gravely" lame horse (Lord Liberty) to him after he was contacted by individuals with whom Dodie boarded the equine. They'd been unable to get her to care for the horse.

Dodie sighed and whispered to her lawyer.

After dealing with her Labradors and horse, and "from the totality of it, my feeling is that Ms. Cariaso has not shown regard for her stewardship of these animals. She has passed the blame on to anybody but herself. And I think the Court should take that into account," Neira said.

Dr. Spindel, who had practiced veterinary medicine for six years, next addressed Judge Schultz. "The conditions that these dogs existed in were inhumane," she said in a youthful-sounding voice. The mental and physical health of the dogs and the "health" of their environment "indicated that their welfare had been cruelly neglected for some time. Fifty-four dogs were humanely euthanized because of the condition they were in."

The saved canines have "lasting effects of this cruelty. It is my professional opinion that she should be held accountable to the full extent of the law."

Vikki, Dodie's sister-in-law, felt angry as she sat among the spectators. She wanted to stand and yell at the young veterinarian. The Labradors had been stressed from the move and sitting in crates. She knew the dogs. They hadn't needed to die.

"I was there July 3rd, 2004 when the dogs were discovered, and I examined them one by one. I am the person who euthanized fifty-four of her dogs because of severe health and temperament problems. It was one of the hardest things I have had to do in my career. I am also the person who cared for twenty-four of her dogs every day for the next two and a half months as they slowly recuperated," Dr. Spindel said.

The media created a "heartwarming ending as the surviving dogs progressed into loving family members," but for her, "this story will not be over until something is done to ensure that this is not allowed to happen again.

"Those of us who cared for her dogs from the beginning were profoundly affected by the neglect that these animals endured. There are things that I saw that I cannot erase from my mind. For me this is not a heartwarming story of wiggling Labrador puppies going home to happy families. It is a story that is hard to imagine and harder to tell," the young veterinarian told Judge Schultz.

She recounted her on-scene observations: mothers and entire litters that lived in tiny airline crates without space to turn around without walking on each other, filth and feces and urine accumulated to the point of scalding the animals' skin. She hesitated, perhaps trying to compose herself, and then continued. No food or water available; no bedding; malnourished puppies with respiratory infections with ocular and nasal discharge; and several dogs with long-standing, severely infected painful wounds from fighting. Some dogs had "obvious heritable defects, including undescended testicles and abnormal jaw conformation." Laboratory tests disclosed parasites and anemia, "debilitating conditions that often develop when environment and nutrition are inadequate for some period of time."

Dr. Spindel saw many dogs with protruding ribs and "pelvic bones jutted like dairy cows." She recalled the chocolate mother that collapsed was "still so afraid of humans; she used her last energy to try to run from me."

She accused Dodie of abandoning eighty-four dogs "whose health she had obviously been neglecting for some time. She has not yet accepted any responsibility for this situation.

"It is a well-researched and documented phenomena that individuals tend to repeat their actions time and again, and a direct correlation exists between cruelty to animals and progression to sociopathic behavior," Dr. Spindel said.

She concluded with a plea to Judge Schultz. "It is my hope that this story will be finished today with a powerful ending. She should serve maximum prison time for what she has done. A lifetime probationary sentence that will prevent her from owning or breeding animals anywhere is imperative. This should be remembered as a story not only about the Labradors, but also about actions and consequences in the State of Colorado and what happens to people who neglect and mistreat animals."

Christine Samuelian, a Humane Society behaviorist at the time of the abandonment, replaced Dr. Spindel at the podium. The "only way Ms. Cariaso can gain any empathy for what she put her dogs through is to spend time confined to a small area at the mercy of other people's agendas, timelines, and choices," she told the judge.

Fewer than 30 percent of pets live in the same families their entire life in this country, she said. Dodie's canines were truly disturbed and demonstrated "extreme fear of all people. Fear of leaving their kennels, fear of leashes, walking, petting, or even eating."

Samuelian explained that dogs left in kennel situations after about fourteen weeks of age "commonly suffer from kennelosis." She labeled the three- to about twelve-week period as the critical socialization time for puppies to "develop social interactions with people, new environments and sensations." Many people assume that a pup removed from an unhealthy environment at six months old can be rehabilitated and appear normal, she said, but this wasn't true. Dogs with limited social experiences during these developmental periods don't recover, she added.

She described the adult Labradors' behavior at the Humane Society: friendly and approachable in their crates but fearful, falling to the ground if someone tried to pet them outside their crates. The dogs only would eat food in their crates, didn't know what a leash was, and often ducked or cowered in fear when someone tried to attach a lead. Sudden movements or noises caused the adults, many urinating on themselves, to fall to the floor and tremble in fear.

Samuelian implored "the Court to seek justice on behalf of all of the dogs that were left in the cruel July sun without water, limited or no food, no shelter and no cleanliness. Please impose the maximum sentence allowable under the plea agreement for Ms. Cariaso."

Judge Schultz didn't allow Goldin to ask questions of any of the prosecution's witnesses, nor did she request permission to do so.

Ermani stood at the podium and summarized Weld County's investigation into the conditions and number of dogs at Dodie's in late 2003 and early 2004.

She recounted that a state inspector asked Dodie about how many dogs she had on the day before she moved to Carl's. "Her response, Your Honor, is I only have ten dogs remaining. She tells the Department of Agriculture [state inspector] that if she cannot find homes for her ten dogs, that she would abandon them." The inspector warned her that "abandoning her dogs constitutes an act of cruelty" and advised her "to give her dogs to the Weld Humane Society if she cannot find homes for them."

That same day, Ermani said, a bank appraiser saw thirty-eight dogs on Dodie's property, and a different bank representative reported fifteen dogs in crates in the home. Although Dodie surrendered seventy-six dogs between December 2003 and June 2004, the Larimer Humane Society found "so many more puppies in her possession" in early July, Ermani noted.

"What that means, Your Honor," she said in a voice with increasing intensity, "the significance of that is that she was continuing to breed at a time when she knew she could not take care of these animals. She was continuing to bring more puppies into this world at a time that she knew she was moving and unable to care for them."

Field replaced Ermani at the podium. "She [Dodie] has never acknowledged fault to any degree," he began. "She has never once acknowledged that her acts were immoral or illegal. This judicial process has been lost on her."

He directed the judge's attention to Dodie's written answers to questions posed by the Probation Department.

"I never committed any crime here at all. I have been falsely accused and forced into this plea bargain," she wrote regarding her general feeling about the offense (crime).

"Just me and my poor innocent, now dead dogs," she answered concerning who was affected by the offense.

"They are all dead," she penned about how the victim was affected.

"Release me and let me try to repair my life that appears to be now over," she wrote regarding how she could help repair the harm caused.

Field highlighted Dodie's behavior during the case: requesting defense attorneys at the state's expense and then accusing them of coercing her, wanting alternative defense counsel at no expense to her, and refusing to listen to the case against her and walking out of the courtroom. He noted that Dodie told the probation department and the press that she believed she was "innocent, that she is a victim. That the Larimer County Humane Society killed her family."

"You've seen photographs of these animals. If this is how she treats animals that she loves, then God save the animals that she does not believe are her family."

Field requested the judge to sentence Dodie to three years in the county jail and probation for "an extended period of time" with the "first years" to be supervised (by the Probation Department)]. She was eligible for eighty-five years of probation.

He asked that Dodie not be allowed to own, care for, have custody of, or sell any animal while on probation, and if she currently had any animals, that she relinquishes them within twenty-four hours to the Humane Society. He sought restitution "for any medical, behavioral costs for the surviving dogs."

Ermani introduced a PowerPoint presentation that graphically depicted the Labradors as found by the Humane Society. She asked Judge Schultz to pay particular attention to the space in crates that housed multiple dogs, photographs that illustrated behavioral problems, and the waste on the T-shirts of the Humane Society workers after they handled puppies wet from urine and feces. The eight-minute color presentation, which was set to the new age music of Enya, vividly displayed seventy-five slides of the adults and puppies, some alive and others dead. The slides included the fifteen dogs chosen as the neglect victims and most of the other Labradors left behind.

Dodie averted her eyes from the screen at times as she choked back tears. She talked with her lawyer and glared at Ermani during the PowerPoint presentation.

Barbara Marcus-McKenna, one of Dodie's longtime friends, sat stunned as she watched the PowerPoint slides. She'd listened to the prosecution witnesses who portrayed her friend as "a dog abuser—as a total mental case." The PowerPoint presentation hadn't made Dodie "look too good." But that wasn't the situation at all; she'd been overwhelmed and couldn't handle the situation. She loved her dogs, Barbara thought.

CHAPTER 28

In Defense Of Dodie

A somber mood created by the PowerPoint presentation and Enya music hung over the courtroom. Goldin stood to call Dr. Culver as her first witness. She understood the importance of defining the abandonment as a rough spot in the life of her "accomplished and well-meaning client." And she needed to neutralize the Humane Society's portrayal of her client as a puppy mill monster who didn't think that she had done anything wrong.

Dr. Culver was sworn in. She testified how she'd known Dodie on a professional basis since 1980 and first visited her client's property in 1986 when she helped her obtain a county kennel license (permit). Years later, she drove to Dodie's kennel "about once a year" to administer rabies vaccinations because it was "much handier to bring the veterinarian to six or eight dogs than it is to bring six to eight dogs into me."

She hadn't noticed any filthy dogs or odors. The kennels were never spotless, but "anytime you have dogs loose in kennels, you're going to have some feces." Her client "was specifically after a mellow non-aggressive, non-hyperactive dog" with a show-type look. "These dogs made wonderful pets for people." She spoke quickly and paused at times to consider a question.

"To the best of my knowledge, her healthcare was quite good," she testified.

Neira, the Humane Society's lead investigator, couldn't believe what he'd heard. How could the veterinarian attest to good care of dogs that she hadn't seen in almost a year?

Dr. Culver explained that she'd taught Dodie how to vaccinate, remove dewclaws, and treat minor wounds, but "anything she couldn't handle, she brought into me, which is what most of the breeders do."

The veterinarian testified that Dodie provided socialization for her dogs on her property but wasn't taking them out.

"Were her dogs leash trained?"

"No. That's one problem we had is that she didn't leash train the dogs. So these dogs—most of these dogs had never had anything on their necks in their life. They never had a leash on. When she brought them into the hospital, she kind of half carried them in."

In an apparent attempt to deflect criticism that Dodie bred dogs that produced puppies with hip dysplasia, the veterinarian testified that the malady is "extremely common" in large dogs. Hip dysplasia is very difficult to eliminate because it's "not a recessive or dominant" gene but is part genetic and part environmental. "You can take two dogs with excellent hip ratings and still produce an occasional puppy with hip dysplasia." But "certainly if you're breeding non-dysplastic dogs, you're going to get less puppies [with dysplasia] than if you're breeding dysplastic dogs. And we have x-rayed and got certification on a great many of her dogs."

Dr. Culver noted that 12.8 percent of Labradors have hip dysplasia, according to OFA. That figure, she added, wasn't totally accurate as many dogs weren't in the OFA database because "horrible" x-rays weren't even submitted.

Did the PowerPoint images depict how Dodie typically kept her dogs?

"Absolutely not," Dr. Culver shot back. One of the biggest health problems of Dodie's dogs over the years was that they were "a little bit too fat." She characterized Dodie as a very gentle, kind person who conscientiously cared for her animals and noted that breeders commonly had multiple litters at the same time because females cycle together.

What happened to lead up to the situation? Goldin inquired.

"I don't know what happened. I think that she wound up with more dogs than she possibly could handle. On her farm where she had everything set up, you can handle that many dogs. But when she had to move them, then she didn't have the kennels, she didn't have the shelter, she didn't have the shade up and things like that and I think given more time she would have gone back to having a—fairly good operation. But she got caught right in the middle of moving and then . . .

"I've known this lady for 25 years. And for 24 of those years, she did a marvelous job. I think she's a kind person. I think she does love her dogs. I think she got in over her head. But I don't think that's a reason to destroy this person's life. I think she should have some leniency. I don't think anything like this is ever going to happen to her again, and I would like to see her allowed to keep a couple of dogs because dogs are very much a part of this person's life."

Field stood to cross-examine Dr. Culver.

Had she treated the dog that had his nose disconnected from his face?

"No. I haven't seen any of Dodie's dogs for a couple of months before that." Field didn't challenge Dr. Culver even though her records revealed that she hadn't examined any of Dodie's dogs in nearly a year before the abandonment. Judge Schultz could discover that information if he reviewed Dr. Culver's billing records contained in a defense exhibit.

Dr. Culver admitted that she hadn't treated the dog with a hole in its gums, the dogs with bad teeth, or the dogs that were malnourished.

On redirect examination, Goldin asked if any of Dodie's dogs were ever overbred.

"She was breeding dogs once or twice a year. That's standard for what a lot of professional breeders do," Dr. Culver responded.

"Did that cause health problems for the dog?"

"As long as the dogs are well cared for and well fed, no." Goldin had no further questions. Dr. Culver stepped down from the witness stand.

Vikki walked to the podium. She found the dogs clean, fed, and watered when she visited her sister-in-law's farm. They weren't fearful and sought attention. Dodie declined invitations to family gatherings because she couldn't leave the dogs for very long or left early to get back to care for them. She "was not cruel to these dogs. I mean she loved every single one of these dogs and certainly the puppies."

"Your Honor, I think that just what happened in the last few months of her life were things that were out of her control. I don't believe that she deserves to go to jail. I think she should be allowed to have dogs. They are her life. They've always been her life." Vikki asked for leniency and sat down.

Carol Mayberry-Sanchez, who had been friends with Dodie for about twenty-one years, next addressed Judge Schultz. "The Dodie I know has always loved her animals. She has given so much time to the whole endeavor that I was just—shocked to just hear any of this that had happened."

She recalled how Dodie had been "beside herself in her diligence" as she battled parvo brought onto her property. "It's not anyone's fault; it's just something even I going into a veterinarian's office could pick up on the floor of the lobby and go home and give it to my dogs, so it's nothing that you can really avoid." She recounted Dodie's "superhuman" efforts: disinfecting "everything under the sun," putting IVs on puppies, "doing everything possible she could," and crying a lot over the phone as she talked about what she might do next to combat the often-fatal virus.

Carol said that animals were a "huge part" of Dodie as a person and thought her friend would be able to devote more love to only a dog or two.

Barbara Marcus-McKenna spoke next and described her friend of twenty years as a hardworking potter, "extremely professional, and very organized, very efficient."

She recalled how Dodie started to breed more dogs as she phased out her pottery business. "For a while she was doing horse breeding as well. But the horse breeding was not really lucrative in that the cost started to become overwhelming."

Barbara labeled Dodie as "always very responsible. Very strong-willed. Very independent. Very capable. Very even-tempered and just really loving, especially for the dogs."

Dodie couldn't care for her animals when she lost her farm. "That was her livelihood. That was her—her way of bringing in income. And when she became displaced, I think things definitely took a turn for the worse. And I do believe that the pictures and the statements that we saw today on the screen were really only a very small part of who Dodie is and—and what situation she ended up being in."

Barbara didn't believe her friend could survive in jail or that jail was a just sentence. Dodie was a very humane person who expected humane treatment for her animals when she left her note for the Humane Society.

"Justice was not served there. But justice now in terms of her life is very, very, very important." She asked the judge to "be very lenient" and allow Dodie to have pets "because they are her life, and they are her love, and I know that to be true."

Judge Schultz called a recess.

When the proceedings resumed, nearly every eye tracked Dodie as she walked to the podium in the hushed courtroom. In a strong-sounding voice, she thanked Judge Schultz for the opportunity to speak. "I never wanted a plea bargain. I've always felt from day one that I was not guilty of any of these charges. I—I was actually quite shocked," she half chuckled, "when I found out that they had an arrest warrant for me."

In a slow but steady voice, she continued. "At the time of the incident, I really honestly did feel that I was doing the right thing. I certainly could have stayed there and let my dogs rot in the sun and stay in those crates, which they were not used to being in. I realized within three days that—"

She fought back tears. "It," her voice cracked, "was not good. My dogs—some of them twelve years old. I had four old retired females," she sniffled, "at my property for the last twenty-five years [sic], every extra penny I ever made—I never spent it on myself. Look at me. I'm a hag. I mean, I never went to a beauty salon. Never bought jewelry. Never went on a vacation. Never took one day off. I spent every penny on new fencing, gravel, for the yard so that their urine and feces would dry up immediately. Toys. Talking about toys. I had lots of toys. Labradors cannot live without toys as a matter of fact."

Her voice steadied. "What these people have judged me on is, you know, three days and actually these people, right here, fifteen minutes, thirty minutes whatever it took to kill them all," she said, and turned toward the Humane Society employees seated in the first row of spectator benches.

She swung her body back to face the judge and described the "beautiful place" for her dogs and the money she'd poured into the farm. Then she looked down at her prepared notes and asked why she had lost her farm.

"I got into horse breeding. Bad idea for a poor person that doesn't have momma's money to spend. I was into good horses, sport horses, big thoroughbreds that cost a lot of money. That stallion [Lord Liberty] I bought when he was six months old. I paid a lot of money. I hand raised him. He was half paint, half thoroughbred."

She spoke rapidly as she recounted how she searched for a place to live but "was still responsible for those animals. I've always been responsible. I didn't have much money left. I had like $3,500 left in my purse by then and the money," her voice cracked, "I spent on that stallion. I paid vet bills to have him diagnosed . . . I was homeless, penniless, jobless and I was spending every last penny on my horses and my dogs."

Dodie switched to a matter-of-fact tone and related how her horse was diagnosed with Wobblers disease, and she knew she had to put him down. She teared up and struggled to speak. "I didn't have the money to put him down." Nearly shouting, she continued. "It costs money to call a vet, have him come out and put your horse down. Like $500 or something." She regained her composure.

"This guy shows up with this paper and says, here, you know, we'll take him from you, you know, and he's all real nice." Her voice rang with sarcasm. "Weren't you?" She was apparently addressing Neira seated among the spectators. She gave up the horse and knew he wouldn't recover. "It was the end of his life too," she said tearfully.

Dodie pushed on. She'd had a $2,500 monthly farm mortgage and made money. But when hay prices tripled in 2002–3, she landed in financial trouble.

She paused. "But what do you do? You've got eighteen horses in the barn to feed. You pay. You buy hay and feed your animals before you pay your mortgage." She couldn't give her horses away because no one wanted to feed a free horse.

"So how do you catch up? I had nobody else to—I don't have rich people in my family. So I kept thinking, well, I'm a successful businessperson." She'd sell some horses. "The dog business was fine. There was no problem with the dogs. They were fine." But hay cost as much as her mortgage.

For the next seven minutes, Dodie described how she started her "Labrador breeding program" and said Labradors "were the only dog in the world for me."

She finally made money, "bought this little house in Berthoud all by myself," and fixed it up. After a two-year search, she located Diana Richardson, a "top" Labrador breeder.

"I have an eye for quality always, which now I'll get in trouble for it. But from a money point of view. But I always bred for quality. This wasn't just a fly-by-night situation. Oh, yeah, buy this one, this one, and we're just going to breed and have puppies. That was never my intention. My intention was to breed a quality Labrador for pet ownership. In other words, the show breeders at that time weren't even selling puppies to—to pet people. Because show breeders, they only want to sell to other show breeders because it promotes their kennel name, and then they can be famous. And so you couldn't even buy a dog."

But she had. She'd purchased a show quality adult female from Lee Burdick and a show quality puppy from Susan Burke.

Dodie continued. She worked seven days a week and "always have my entire life. Always. I've never taken a day off. Maybe that's why this is so weird."

She shifted gears and described how she sold her home, purchased her farm in 1982, and spent "all my life fixing" up the farm. She switched topics again. The county discovered eight dogs, four over the maximum allowed, when it issued a pottery permit to her, and told her that she needed a kennel permit. She then obtained the permit for sixteen dogs.

Ermani took notes as she listened. Dodie seemed aware of what was going on but appeared disorganized, she thought.

"Well, you're probably wondering well what happened from there," Dodie said.

"Well, what happened was the Humane Society at that time, Weld County was pretty loose, and I said to her how long—how often are you going to come to my property to check me?" she said, referencing her conversation with the Weld County Animal Control officer who had inspected her facilities during the kennel permitting process in 1988. "How often are you going to come out and say well, one, two, three, four, five, six? And she said never. We won't be back unless we get complaints. If your neighbors—if you have a problem. If your dogs run loose, they kill the neighbor's calf, we'll be out.

"And so, guess what? I never saw them. They never came out in all those years. And as slowly it progressed into more of a business than a hobby. In those days, I was having a litter of puppies once a year, at the most two litters. Because I was a potter. So it just evolved. People were calling me, believe it or not, from all over the nation. They wanted a dog from me. I mean, I was considered a reputable breeder."

She quit making pottery in '96 or '97 after she realized that she couldn't maintain three businesses: pottery, dogs, and horses. Her dog business mushroomed. She trained and tried to sell her horses.

Dodie's voice cracked. She didn't put her dogs down when they became infertile at eight or nine years of age but kept them unless she found them new homes. She didn't think putting them down was right.

"My philosophy on life is that God puts us here and that includes our animals and—" She hesitated, spun around, and glared at the Humane Society employees.

"We should be allowed to live until God takes us," she said in a weepy voice, "not some people who decide they don't need to exist anymore. How can you live with yourselves? Unbelievable!"

"You need to address me," Judge Schultz ordered.

"I'm sorry." Dodie regained her composure. "I'm sorry for what happened."

She recounted how she fed and cleaned all her dogs and put brand new bedding in the crates on Thursday and left Friday morning at 9. She knew Carl would return by 3 p.m. later that day, find her note, and call the Humane Society.

"One day without food and water is what I thought was going to happen." She just couldn't handle calling the Humane Society but believed Carl could.

She pivoted to glare at Samuelian before she explained that she wanted her dogs to have a submissive temperament so small children could handle them. Earlier in the hearing, Samuelian described how the rescued Labradors fell to the ground and cowered in fear if someone tried to pet them.

Dodie turned back to face the judge. She admitted some of the females were thin and talked about the stresses in her life. "Why would I give them [the dogs] up?" she asked tearfully. "A puppy mill person probably would have loaded them back in that horse trailer and driven away." Her voice cracked. "But I didn't want to do that. I knew that I wanted my dogs out of the crates and into homes quickly . . . Everything I have ever done was for the health and welfare of my animals because I did love them.

"I'm not qualified. I'm old, fat, and ugly. I can't get a job." Her voice weakened. She said she'd started a new potential career two months ago. "It has nothing to do with animal ownership and believe me I don't think I ever want to breed again . . . I am not going to hide dogs. I don't feel a need to breed. That's okay. Why don't you just give me ninety years of probation, no breeding? That's fine with me. I don't think I ever want to breed again. That's fine," she said in a weepy voice.

Field listened and recognized that Dodie's world had collapsed. She had no understanding that what she had done was wrong.

Dodie wanted two dogs to keep each other company but didn't "have to own dogs that are going to be reproductive machines. That was never my idea from the beginning. I'm not into that. I'm not a puppy mill." She admitted that "the situation got bad" with the dogs crated for two or three days, and that's why she left the note for Carl to call the Humane Society.

"Your Honor, thank you for hearing my story . . . I'm trying to start my life over." Dodie paused. "It's difficult when you're old like me. It's so hard to get a job. It's just—if I go to jail, I'll never get a job again.

And I mean I will come out, and I will be on the streets, and I will be a bag lady. I mean because—no matter," her voice cracked, "if you even sentence me to thirty days, I'll lose my lease, I'll lose the place I'm living that I've worked really hard to get. I'll lose everything. I mean, I'll lose the job I finally got.

"So even if it's thirty days when I get out, I'm going to be homeless, jobless, on the streets and more apt to probably commit crimes. Because, you know, when you're hungry, and you're on the streets and don't have money, unfortunately our society is not pleasant out there."

But she had a degree and could get a job if society left her alone and let her "have the opportunity to become a normal citizen again . . . I'll never own a horse again; that's fine. But let me have my one dog, which really means two dogs because dogs need buddies.

"Anyways, do you have any questions?" Dodie asked in a calm, sweet-sounding, almost little girl voice. The judge didn't. "You can ask me anything you want. Thank you so much." Dodie walked back to the defense table and sat down. She'd spoken for more than twenty-four minutes.

Only closing arguments remained before Judge Schultz handed down his sentence.

Goldin argued that her client met her financial obligations but when faced with feeding animals or paying the mortgage, she chose to feed her animals. Dodie believed through hard work that she'd pull herself out of financial problems but couldn't give up all her dogs to keep her business and sole livelihood going. She faced "an absolutely impossible situation" when she lost her farm and "in a moment of fear and panic" relinquished her dogs to Carl with instructions to turn them over to the Humane Society. Dodie's intent was for the Humane Society to care for them and eventually adopt them out.

The defense attorney maintained that Dodie hadn't abandoned her dogs because she'd called Carl to ascertain that he'd be back on his property on the day she departed; left a hundred pounds of dog food; left her dogs with someone she knew was kind and responsible who cared for them; and left behind specific information as to when the animals had last been fed and watered.

She emphasized that Dodie never lost her state kennel license, and the Weld County animal inspector never accused her of neglecting her dogs, nor had he impounded them. Dodie was a reputable breeder who hit some very hard times and, in the end, faced a "fairly hopeless situation. So after thirty years of hard work, she's reduced to nothing, and she had no resources or energy in which to tap into for that ultimate moment."

Goldin urged Judge Schultz to consider her client's lifetime of hard work and good reputation, not the twenty-four-hour or even seventy-two-hour period when "the conditions for those dogs were not good and things fell apart."

The defense attorney characterized her client as not being "jail material" and asked that Dodie be sentenced to a lengthy term of probation, loaded with restrictions, and be allowed pets. Her client welcomed continued mental health counseling, but a jail sentence would be unduly punitive "given that she has suffered quite a bit already . . . She's not someone that just for the safety of the community needs to be segregated." Goldin sat down after vigorously arguing for more than twenty-five minutes.

Ermani urged the judge to use common sense when he considered Goldin's argument that the dogs had been left alone for only a twenty-four- to seventy-two-hour period. "Teeth do not rot like that within twenty-four hours, Your Honor. Ribs cannot be counted on animals after merely twenty-four hours of not being fed. A nose on an animal does not become disconnected from its face within twenty-four hours."

In a voice ringing with passion, Ermani argued that "She [Dodie] has demonstrated that she is irresponsible in handling animals and she does not deserve to continue handling animals anymore. These dogs were not a companion for her, nor were they a pet. Your Honor, they were what everyone else would call a commodity. She used those animals as if they were a paycheck, and the rules and the laws that are provided in the State of Colorado are to prevent people like Ms. Cariaso from being allowed to keep their animals in these conditions and treating them as a commodity."

The youthful prosecutor implored the judge to consider the photographs and testimony to find that Dodie should serve "some time in jail" and shouldn't own any dogs. "That is what justice requires."

All eyes focused on Judge Schultz as Ermani sat down. He reminded the audience that the plea bargain allowed him to impose a maximum of three years in jail and required a minimum of one year of probation.

"Now if I use three years of jail, there's no probation. You don't do the two. If you use probation, you can use a maximum of sixty days on a misdemeanor as jail and then probation can be used with terms and conditions but it [jail] can't go over sixty days because that's what the law says."

Field couldn't believe what he had just heard. The prosecutor had no idea that the judge thought he could sentence Dodie to only sixty days in jail if he placed her on probation. That wasn't his interpretation of the law.

Judge Schultz continued. If he sentenced Dodie to three years in jail, she'd serve her time and then walk away without any controls, which meant she could resume breeding. But if he sentenced her to probation with terms and conditions, he provided a longer term of control, which was "probably better for society."

The judge sentenced Dodie to sixty days in the county jail and five years of supervised probation with continued mental health counseling and treatment. He ordered her to pay the standard court costs and fees as well as restitution over time. She could own two same-sex pets but couldn't breed animals in Colorado or any other state during her probation.

He cautioned that if her pets didn't receive proper care, he'd revoke her probation, and she'd face a maximum of three years in jail. He ordered her to attest that she had no more than two pets; if she had more, she needed to "dispense with their ownership" and couldn't give them to family members or a straw owner.

Goldin tried to quiet Dodie during the judge's ruling.

Ermani took notes and averted her eyes away from Dodie. She didn't want to make her feel worse or spark an outburst. But she feared that Dodie would breed again.

Judge Schultz continued Dodie's bond and granted Goldin's request to stay the sentence so she could appeal its terms. He authorized Field to submit restitution costs once they were compiled.

The judge asked Goldin if she objected to Field's request that Dodie surrender any animals to the Larimer County Humane Society instead of Weld County because she now lived in Larimer County.

"There are no dogs to surrender, Your Honor," the defense lawyer replied.

"I've given them away," Dodie chimed in.

Judge Schultz stayed his authorization for Dodie to own two pets because he stayed her sentence. Field asked for an additional bond condition to prohibit Dodie from dog ownership.

"I actually don't own them anymore," Dodie spontaneously inserted. But she did: Labrador Ben and Bernese mountain dog puppy Huxsby.

Field told the judge that the prosecution understood that the plea bargain allowed Dodie to be sentenced to probation and up to three years in jail.

Judge Schultz re-read the plea bargain agreement. "I interpreted it as—as I thought it is written," he said, and refused to consider the matter further. Field could file a written argument for later consideration.

The hearing concluded after more than three hours.

Goldin gathered up her legal pad and file. She felt relieved that Dodie hadn't been sentenced to three years in jail.

Field stood up, angry at the lenient sentence. He loved dogs and thought the "evidence was overwhelming" to warrant a longer jail sentence. The whole point of the prosecution had been to rehabilitate Dodie and provide some punishment and security for the county. He thought that Dodie would violate her probation.

"Get away from me," Dodie snapped at the press as she stormed out of the courtroom.

The next day, Judge Schultz lifted the stay of Dodie's sentence. She'd decided that she wanted to start her incarceration after she had a chance to meet with creditors in her bankruptcy case. That gave her just over a month to put her affairs in order before she'd begin to serve time.

CHAPTER 29

Great Uncle Max

Dave and I didn't know how Max would react to his niece's puppies once they became ambulatory. He was going on twelve and had slowed down considerably due to his arthritic spine. Would he tolerate puppies climbing all over him and continue to live up to Dodie's boast of her Killkenny Labradors' mellow, sweetheart personalities? We'd soon find out.

Just after midnight on August 1, 2001, Dave and I awoke to the sound of Brew panting next to our bed. We turned on the light. Max and Molly milled around the room. Then it hit us. Brew was in labor.

We guided Brew into our guest room that we'd again converted into a puppy room and into the newspaper-lined whelping box. Dave and I sat on chairs while Max and Molly lay at our feet. The four of us watched and waited as Brew panted. And waited. We expected nine puppies based on an ultrasound.

Brew whelped a tiny black fur ball at about 2 a.m. Her mother instincts failed to kick in, so Dave cut the newborn's umbilical cord, and I towel-dried the puppy. Dave held out the pup to Brew. The new mother backed into a far corner of the whelping box and stared at her daughter as if the black blob were a rat or some other totally undesirable creature.

Dave and I looked at each other. What should we do? Molly had accepted her maternal duties almost immediately. Brew looked so frightened and miserable that we were uncertain of her intentions.

I found a medium-sized cardboard box and lined it with towels. Dave placed the pup in the box and positioned a lamp over it to generate heat. We stepped back. Molly and Max pushed forward as they vied to sniff the black blob. Brew watched Great Uncle Max and Granny, with tails wagging, inspect the new family addition.

This is a bad situation. The puppy needs to nurse. I picked up the telephone and called Denise, a fellow Lab Club member.

"What should we do?" I asked. "Brew won't let the pup near her, much less allow her to nurse."

"Don't worry. She will get the hang of it once the second puppy arrives," came the sleepy reply. Denise offered to come over later that morning to help. I thanked her and apologized for the 3 a.m. call.

Another hour passed and no second puppy. We telephoned the on-call veterinarian at our vet hospital. He told us not to worry.

We called again when the second puppy hadn't arrived by 5 a.m. and convinced the reluctant young vet to awaken our senior veterinarian. The junior veterinarian called back and told us to drive to the vet hospital to pick up a stimulant to induce labor.

"Your office is twenty miles away. Can't you drive to our house instead?" I asked.

No, he couldn't leave. We must come to him.

I drove in darkness to Castle Rock to pick up the stimulant. Forty-plus minutes later, I arrived back home and learned Brew hadn't whelped any more puppies. Dave injected her with the stimulant. We waited. Nothing. More phone calls. Our senior vet would meet us at his office to perform a C-section as soon as we could arrive.

Dawn was just breaking as I led Brew into the backyard to relieve herself. She squatted in a pooping position and out came a yellow blob. I caught it in a towel and yelled for Dave. He set down his toothbrush and ran outside to cut the pup's umbilical cord. We called our senior vet, who told us to keep him posted.

When Brew hadn't whelped any more puppies by 7:30 a.m., we called again. Dave left to pick up more stimulant. Two pups were born in his absence.

Denise arrived in the late morning to assist. By mid-afternoon, Brew had been in labor more than twelve hours and had whelped nine puppies: two yellow and four black live pups, and three stillborn.

Mother Brew finally took to her pups and turned possessive. She growled at Granny Molly but allowed Great-Uncle Max into the whelping room and permitted him to sniff her pups. Most of the time, he'd lay awake or sleep just outside of the whelping box. His presence seemed to calm Brew as she settled into motherhood.

We named the only yellow male Mini Max. Dave left for Atlanta on a business trip. A day or so later, Brew accidentally lay on him during the few minutes that I was absent from the puppy room. I dissolved into tears when I discovered his warm, lifeless body. Miss Gold, the last puppy to be born alive, developed breathing problems.

Seven days after the pups were born, Patty, my golden retriever friend, drove over to assist with the puppies and to calm my frayed nerves. Dave was still away. Miss Gold's breathing became more labored. I called the veterinarian's office and was instructed to bring all the pups and Brew immediately to the vet hospital.

Max darted outside when we opened the front door to let Brew out and carry her puppies in a cardboard box to Patty's minivan. Brew jumped into the rear seat area as did Max. He settled into a captain's chair and refused to budge. We realized that minutes might count toward keeping Miss Gold alive, so we drove off. Granny Molly remained at home.

A young veterinarian and several technicians hustled out of the vet hospital as we pulled up. They opened the van's rear passenger door. Brew and Max jumped out. I handed the cardboard box full of puppies to a technician and scooted Max and Brew into an exam room.

"Why is Max here?"

"He wanted to come and wouldn't get out of the van," I said. No one asked any other questions about his presence.

Miss Gold couldn't be resuscitated. Her lungs weren't fully developed. Brew suddenly had only four puppies: two black daughters, a black son, and a yellow daughter. Great-Uncle Max stood alongside Brew while our senior vet examined the pups. All were healthy.

Dave and I played with the pups each night once they reached four weeks of age. We blocked off the kitchen with a three-foot-high baby gate to keep out Great-Uncle Max and Granny, and then Brew once the weaning process started a couple of weeks later. Max wanted to be with the puppies, but we thought he wouldn't try to jump the gate because of his decreasing mobility. We gave him prescription anti-inflammatory medication to ease any pain. Our nearly twelve-year-old adoptee sailed over the gate and lay down among the puppies. Two great-nieces snuggled up to him and went to sleep. Great-Uncle Max put his head down and also nodded off. We let him stay with his puppies.

Dave and I agreed that one puppy would join our family. But which one?

I thought we'd keep the black male we called Brutus because of his blocky head or the yellow female, Tubby, so named because she loved to eat. However, she was curious and not as cuddly as the other puppies. Brew favored Brutus and Tubby and permitted them to nurse more than the others.

Ultimately, the adult dogs selected our new family member. Tubby emerged as Brew's only favorite. Molly tolerated both pups. Max grew less patient with Brutus and fancied Tubby, who became our unanimous choice. I finally had the yellow that I wanted after two litters.

We renamed Tubby "Tasmania" after the Tasman Sea off the west coast of New Zealand. Her AKC registered name became Cruising Tasmania of Walden to accommodate my love for New Zealand and her adventuresome spirit.

Max played ever so gently with Tubby. She climbed all over him and grabbed his tail, ears, and mouth. He took her punishment and just rolled onto his back. But when she reached four months of age, she acquired new respect for him. We didn't see Max snap or growl, but he definitely had a "come to Jesus talk" with her.

That winter, Max and Taz accompanied their human servants on a weekend getaway to Buena Vista. We hoped that Max would teach hiking etiquette to Taz: no barking, pulling on a leash, or pooping on trails. Unfortunately, we chose the coldest weekend in ten years to go and snowshoed only a short distance despite our aging adoptee's willingness to go farther in the frigid temperatures. Once again, Max exceeded our expectations of a doting great-uncle and demonstrated that he genuinely was a Killkenny "poster dog."

CHAPTER 30

Consequences

Dodie opened the door to the Larimer County Detention Facility in Fort Collins on September 25, 2005. She'd spend the next fifty-six days there instead of sixty if she stayed out of trouble. The twenty-four-year-old jail was just six miles northeast of the Humane Society, where her abandoned Killkenny Labradors had recuperated.

She'd taken her Labrador Ben and Bernese puppy Huxsby to live with Carol Mayberry-Sanchez during her incarceration and stored property, clothes, and boxes of "important papers" in a locked vehicle on Carol's property. Those papers undoubtedly included Ben's AKC registration, which she obtained by using her Jesse McClure alias. She probably didn't know that the dog registry had requested a certified copy of Judge Schultz's sentencing order to start a process to extend her AKC suspension for another ten years based on her conviction.

But she knew that prosecutors had asked Judge Schultz to reconsider what they believed was her very lenient sentence. They thought that he'd misunderstood the plea agreement and could have sentenced her to three years in jail AND probation. To cover their bases, they also appealed her sentence to the Colorado Court of Appeals.

During the jail booking process, Dodie listed Carol as her next of kin and friend, and Catholic as her religious affiliation. She reported that she was self-employed and identified asthma and arthritis as health issues. And, she denied any current thoughts of "hurting herself or having hurt or attempted to kill herself previously."

No one visited Dodie. Vikki thought Dodie didn't want to see her or James, and Dodie didn't call or write. Dodie telephoned Carol collect several times a week and wrote her. All they did in jail, she said, was watch cable TV movies about love triangles. Carol encouraged her to hang in there when Dodie mentioned a conflict with one inmate. Father Barlow talked to Dodie over the phone and sent her spiritual materials.

To pass the time, Dodie requested colored pencils to draw, so "I don't go insane!" as drawing "is essential to my mental health." She sketched mostly western scenes, often of a horse and rider. Although she lost her inmate worker job after she failed to do the requisite cleaning, she stayed out of trouble. Twice she asked to see a counselor. No current thoughts of self-harm were noted after one of the visits.

Just forty-two days after she reported to jail, Dodie stepped out of the facility a free woman. Authorities listed the reason for her early release on November 10th as jail overcrowding, "female population in excess of 53." Carol picked her up so she could quickly reunite with Ben and Huxsby and return to her Estes Park home.

Dodie embarked on her new life. Several friends and acquaintances noticed that she appeared upbeat and looked forward to moving on with her life. She was headed toward "a genuine spiritual conversion," Father Barlow thought, and acceptance of responsibility for her actions. She told him how much she appreciated her good upbringing and family and vowed never to return to jail.

Goldin perceived an upbeat client when she updated her about the prosecutors' attempt to appeal her sentence. Judge Schultz ruled that he lacked authority to consider any appeal, so the court of appeals would decide whether to overturn Dodie's sentence. The transcript of the court proceedings would be filed with the appellate court on Friday, January 13th, so there was nothing to do but wait until then, Goldin advised.

Although her brother Doug paid most of her monthly house rent, Dodie needed money for other basic living expenses and to pay $75 each month toward the more than $3,150 in probation and various court-ordered fees. She'd received a letter warning her to pay her over-due October bill, or the court might issue a warrant, order a hold placed on her driver's license, assess additional fees, or revoke her probation. No restitution amount was due because prosecutors hadn't asked the judge to impose a specific amount.[1]

James asked Dodie to return a family photo album that she'd borrowed when she came for Thanksgiving dinner. He wanted the album, filled with photos from their childhood, for safekeeping.

When Dodie hadn't arrived as scheduled, Vikki telephoned and reminded her to bring the album.

Dodie showed up just in time for dinner. James greeted his sister at the front door.

"You don't give a shit about me. My blood is on your hands," Dodie yelled. She threw the photo album at him. His twin turned, stormed down the front walk to her car, and drove off.

James watched from the front stoop. He'd heard Dodie's threats before when she was unhappy with him.

By December, Dodie had exhausted her younger brother's goodwill. Doug stopped sending monthly checks and focused on his wife Kathleen as she underwent stem cell transplant surgery for Hodgkin's lymphoma. Kathleen remained in the hospital for a month of extensive therapy.

Dodie turned to Dr. Culver. She dropped by the veterinary hospital to chat on December 5th. She explained that she could buy a business for the cost of its equipment. The Estes Park company where she'd worked before she served her jail sentence picked up meals at high-end restaurants and delivered them to hotel or bed and breakfast guests who preferred to dine in.[2] Could the veterinarian loan her $10,000 to buy a van to use to pick up and deliver meals? Her Nissan 280zx sports car wouldn't suffice.

Dodie, it doesn't take $10,000 to get a car to deliver food; you just need something that will run, Dr. Culver thought.

The veterinarian was "a little surprised" at Dodie's request. The two had known each other for more than twenty years but hadn't socialized except when the veterinarian visited Dodie's farm to administer vaccinations. Afterward, they'd chat over a glass of wine. Long aware of her former client's financial problems and as the recipient of many bounced checks from Dodie over the years, Dr. Culver recognized that she'd never be repaid. Dodie still owed her between $400 and $500 for vet services and hadn't asked the bankruptcy court to discharge that debt. Dr. Culver thought quickly. She told Dodie that she couldn't loan $10,000 but gave a small sum to her to help out because she felt sorry for her longtime client and friend.

On December 7th, the bankruptcy court discharged more than $185,000 of Dodie's debts. On the following day, Dodie talked to a mortgage company, but her terrible credit history once again dashed any hopes of buying a home.

Two days later, Dodie shopped for a van at the Family Auto Center in Loveland. She appeared distraught to a salesman who tried to cheer her up. She laughed and teared up again. Dodie explained that she'd been loaded but now scraped by and had a "kind of antique" business. She returned just two days later and drove off in a 1994 white minivan with a $500 monthly payment. The auto center financed her $10,000 purchase.

Back in Estes Park, Dodie seemed to embrace the holiday season. She strung Christmas lights outside her rental home. Inside, she arranged poinsettias and Christmas figurines around her family room/kitchen area and trimmed a tall evergreen tree with ornaments and lights. Parishioners welcomed her back when she attended church at St. Frances of Assisi. She went Christmas caroling and joined a small Bible study group.

Dodie reached out to friends by writing upbeat messages in Christmas cards. She invited Mary Gates, who'd helped with her horses, to visit and requested her former neighbor Stanlyn Johnston, who lived with her husband in Oklahoma, to let her know if she planned to spend Christmas in Colorado. She penned in her journal how she loved this time of year and was happy to be "finally able to move forward with rebuilding my life in a positive and happy way!"

Just before Christmas, Dodie landed a waitress job in Estes Park but complained to Carol that her knees hurt from being on her feet all the time. She shouldn't be serving people; people should be serving her, she told Vikki.

Mary drove to Estes Park to visit Dodie over lunch even though she wanted to sever ties with her former employer. She thought she was Dodie's only friend.

Stanlyn decided to celebrate the holidays in Colorado and invited Dodie to Christmas dinner at her mother's in Fort Collins. Dressed in jeans and a Christmas sweater, Dodie appeared a bit uncomfortable when she arrived for dinner. She hadn't brought a gift; she thought the gift exchange would be over. But Stanlyn had stowed a wrapped box of candy for her under the tree.

After dinner, the two friends retired to the basement for a quiet chat in the unfinished family room and sat side by side on a couch. Dodie seemed happy and moving forward with her life.

Stanlyn picked up the December 24th edition of the Fort Collin's newspaper, the Coloradoan, to show her friend. A front-page story featured one of Dodie's dogs that had been adopted after its rescue from "an abandoned puppy mill in Berthoud."

When will the press leave Dodie alone? Stanlyn had thought when she first read the article. She couldn't believe her former neighbor had been a puppy mill operator.

Dodie cried as she read the article. She said that she just wanted to put the incident behind her, but people kept bringing it up.

"I'm so sorry. I wish I could help," Stanlyn said. Her heart broke for her.

Dodie explained what had happened: she left her dogs with her landlord and a note asking him to call the Humane Society. They talked on.

Father Barlow was trying to get "something going" so she could leave the state, Dodie said. She thought she'd have a better chance of putting her life back together by starting over where people hadn't formed an opinion of her.

Stanlyn mentioned that she was caring for her grandmother, who needed more home health care than what she and her uncle could provide. Dodie offered a solution: she'd care for Stanlyn's grandmother and stay with Stanlyn and her husband until she found her own place.

It wasn't so much that you want to live in Oklahoma but that you want out of Colorado, Stanlyn thought. She didn't believe that Dodie would enjoy caring for an older person, and her friend couldn't stay with her. Stanlyn's husband and Dodie didn't get along.

Dodie confided that she wanted to start breeding dogs again. She owned Huxsby, the Bernese mountain dog puppy, and Ben, the yellow Labrador, both males.

Wasn't breeding dogs prohibited by the terms of your probation? Stanlyn asked.

Dodie blew up. "The money's too good not to."

Stanlyn saw red flags. She realized that Dodie lacked accountability; her friend didn't think she needed to be accountable because she hadn't mistreated her dogs. Stanlyn didn't want to be an accomplice to Dodie's plan to violate probation. She viewed herself as a staunch supporter of the law; her father had been a Larimer County deputy sheriff and her husband, a sheriff's mounted posse member when they lived in Colorado. She needed to think about Dodie's plan.

Father Barlow noticed that Dodie became easily distraught and frightened after her waitressing hours were reduced. She reverted to her pre-incarceration behavior and thoughts. His parishioner worried about paying her rent and monthly van bill.

She asked that the priest call her younger brother Doug to ask him for financial assistance. He agreed. She handed him notes with tips on what to say to Doug. Then she waited because she expected the priest to call her brother in her presence. He refused but called Doug a couple of days later.

Father Barlow witnessed Dodie's mood swings. At times, she'd talk for two minutes before her voice quivered and tears streamed down her face. Next, she'd compose herself and talk angrily about how the world and her family mistreated her. She'd sob again and say how she missed her father, who was a good man, and hated her mother.[3]

On Saturday, January 7th, Dodie telephoned Stanlyn to ask that she contact Fred, her first ex-husband, to let him know that she was going through bad times. Stanlyn telephoned Fred and left a message.

That same day, an enthusiastic Dodie told Vikki about the possible caregiver's job in Oklahoma. Vikki felt relieved. Dodie had a direction to her life.

Dodie didn't attend mass on Sunday but spoke with Father Barlow the next day.

She also called longtime friend Carol that Monday. She had only $200 of the $500 van payment due that day. Would Carol write Doug to ask him to help her financially? She'd talk to the dealership about the payment she owed. She left a message for Stanlyn and asked her to write a letter to Doug for rent and van money.

On Tuesday, Mary worked her shift at Wendy's on the west side of Loveland, just two-tenths of a mile directly east of the Chase Bank on Eisenhower Boulevard. In the late morning, a fellow employee told her that someone was asking for her at the drive-through window.

Mary walked over to the window. She saw the driver of a van—a woman with a scarf pulled over her head and around her neck. Transparent fabric came down over her forehead, almost to her eyes. She wore sunglasses and looked straight ahead with both hands gripping the steering wheel. Mary realized that she was staring at Dodie.

Did she have time to talk? Dodie asked.

Mary turned and glanced around the busy restaurant. Her general manager stood by her side.

"I'm sorry, I don't. But I can talk when I get a break in about an hour."

"Are you sure you don't have time to talk?"

Mary hesitated. She noticed her friend's solemn demeanor and blank face. Dodie hadn't taken off her sunglasses, which she usually did when she spoke.

"No, I'm sure. We're too busy."

"That's okay," Dodie said, and drove off. She visited her mental health counselor that same day.

Father Barlow telephoned Stanlyn the next day, Wednesday, to say he'd accompany Dodie to Monday's meeting with the probation officer and support her request to transfer her probation to Oklahoma to allow her to care for Stanlyn's grandmother. That's when Stanlyn told him that her cousin, not Dodie, would be caring for her grandmother.

Dodie called Vikki that same day to say that the Oklahoma job opportunity had fallen through. She didn't explain how she learned the news.[4]

"I don't know what I am going to do."

"We'll figure something out, Dodie. You are okay there now," Vikki reassured her.

"No, I won't."

Stanlyn didn't sleep well that night. She anticipated that it would be difficult to tell Dodie that there wasn't a job but couldn't condone her friend's plan to violate probation by resuming a dog breeding business. Earlier that day, she'd mailed her a Bible passage from Job that urged trust in God no matter what, even if pain is experienced in the process, as such testing often deepens one's relationship with God.

She telephoned Dodie at 7:30 the next morning in Oklahoma, 6:30 in Colorado. Dodie picked up on the first ring.

That's unusual, Stanlyn thought. She typically let the phone ring two times, hung up, and then dialed again as a signal to let Dodie know that she was calling.

Stanlyn explained that her cousin was going to care for their grandmother, so there wasn't a job opportunity.

"That's okay, something will work out," Dodie responded in a very quiet and calm voice. She planned to move into a larger place with two bedrooms on February 1st so that she'd have more room and intended to find a roommate. She was used to the good life and would keep her dogs. "I'm not going to go down any farther than where I am," she vowed.

Stanlyn suggested that she care for other people's dogs. Dodie rejected the idea. She needed to be in business for herself.

They'd figure something out, Stanlyn said. My news hadn't been that big a deal, she thought, hanging up. Dodie had already made plans to relocate and find a roommate.

Later that Thursday morning, the twelfth day of January 2006, Dodie telephoned the Family Auto Center in Loveland to say she'd deliver $1,000 in cash that afternoon to make current her van payments.

CHAPTER 31

Desperation

Hours later, Dodie paused and peered into the foyer of the bank. Dressed in a worn blue jacket, jeans, and sneakers, she appeared bundled up for the winter day. A black scarf covered her mouth and nose. Sunglasses hid her eyes. Black gloves encased her hands. A Denver Broncos ball cap concealed most of her gray hair.

She walked up to a teller's counter and hesitated.

"I'm sorry to do this to you." She shoved a manila envelope toward the teller. "This is a robbery. Give me your money" was written in red ink on the envelope.

"Are you serious?" asked the twenty-one-year-old teller.

"I have a gun." Dodie pulled a black crocheted purse from underneath her jacket and handed it to the teller. She kept one hand in her pocket.

"Put all your money in the bag."

The teller stuffed the purse with bundles of bills, including a stack of "bait money" to help identify the robber.

Another bank employee pushed the panic button.

The teller handed the purse back to Dodie.

Dodie turned and strode out of the one-story brick bank building in Loveland. It was 1:30 p.m. on the same day that she promised to make current the loan payments on her van.

Inside, the teller sobbed.

Chase Bank district manager Andrew Degemann heard an employee say, "We were robbed!" and then saw him point to a white van. Its passenger-side door was closing.

Degemann suspected the robber had a driver waiting for her. He watched the van back up, loop around the parking lot, and stop before it turned west onto Eisenhower Boulevard. Something covered the van's license plate. He decided to follow, but not too closely, to give police possible valuable information.

The district manager walked to his small sedan in the parking lot and drove west on Eisenhower Boulevard. After he passed a dump truck a quarter mile later, he spotted a white van traveling the speed limit. He called 911. The Loveland Police Department dispatch answered.

"We just got robbed. Chase Bank, the West Lake Office," Degemann said. He tailed the van as it continued westbound. "I'm not sure if it's the van, but I'm pretty [sure], but I think it is 'cause there's no other white vans."

Degemann stayed behind the van as it headed toward Estes Park, about twenty-six miles away. Then the van slowed and turned south onto a secondary road, away from Estes Park. Degemann couldn't tell if one or two people were in the vehicle. His cell phone cut out. He called 911 again. The Larimer County Sheriff's dispatch answered this time.

"Where's the nearest place you've crossed?"

"We are now south of Carter Lake, so we're headed towards Berthoud."

Cell service cut in and out as Degemann followed the van at the 40 MPH speed limit along the narrow two-lane road between low rolling hills of prairie.

He passed horse ranches with sizable pastures, and farther south, occasional large homes before he temporarily lost sight of the van as the road curved to the east.

The van halted at a stop sign and turned south onto County Road 23. He followed and kept his distance along the straight, open road past good-sized, newer upscale homes on two-acre lots. He thought the robber knew that he was following. Fourteen minutes into his pursuit, he still hadn't seen any law enforcement.

After another mile, Degemann trailed the van around a sharp curve to the east. He saw a Berthoud police cruiser speeding toward them. The van turned right and headed south. The officer also veered south and stayed about forty yards behind the van. Degemann fell in behind the cruiser as the chase sped up to between 45 and 55 MPH.

Investigator Steve Holloway, a twenty-five-year sheriff's office veteran, was about a mile from the bank when he heard dispatch air the robbery. Deputy Sheriff Rafael Sanchez immediately radioed that he'd respond from his location about two miles from the van.

Holloway realized that he was the closest sheriff's unit to Sanchez. He radioed that he'd respond, sped west in his unmarked SUV, and turned on its lights.[1]

At an intersection, Holloway spotted the flashing lights of Sanchez's marked cruiser headed toward him from the north. He didn't see the suspect van in any direction or any dust from the dirt roads to the west, so he turned south.

As the officers neared a sharp curve several miles later, they agreed by radio to drive different directions to search for the suspect. They didn't know that just minutes before Degemann had followed the van around the same curve. Holloway continued east. Sanchez turned south.

About a minute later, Holloway heard Sanchez call out over the radio, "They are over here!" He raced back to the intersection, turned south, and accelerated to speeds of more than 85 MPH whenever he could. He caught sight of a white van pursued by two police cruisers, lights flashing and sirens blaring. A compact car followed behind. Holloway crossed into Boulder County and sped past Degemann, who had pulled over onto the shoulder of the two-lane road.

Eighteen minutes had passed since the white van left the bank's parking lot.

Sanchez pulled alongside the Berthoud cruiser. Oncoming traffic forced him in behind the van. He saw only one person in the vehicle. The van didn't stop. It continued on at the 45 MPH speed limit.

Nearly twenty miles from the bank, the van suddenly slowed and veered right into a dirt driveway. It stopped just fifty feet off the road. Sanchez swerved into an adjacent dirt driveway, separated from the first by ten feet of prairie. He parked about fifteen feet to the south of the driver's side of the motionless van, slightly to its rear. The Berthoud officer pulled in directly behind the van. Holloway stopped just to the right and rear of the Berthoud cruiser. He expected the suspect to run and had heard she was armed.

Sanchez saw the driver's door of the van open. The suspect's legs started to swing out. He jumped out of his cruiser, leaned in and turned off its lights and siren, and stood in full uniform next to his driver's door.

"Show me your hands! Show me your hands!" Sanchez yelled. He aimed his gun at her.

The woman remained seated, scrunched over. Sanchez saw something black near her middle. She pushed her arm forward. He saw a gun barrel pointed directly at him. The deputy dropped behind the door of his cruiser.

"Drop it! Drop it!"

Holloway and the Berthoud officer both heard Sanchez shout, "Drop it!"

Hunkered down behind his cruiser, the Berthoud officer made out the silhouette of a black gun.

Holloway crouched behind his driver's door and watched the van's door open. The driver turned her body, extended one hand, and aimed a black revolver directly at Sanchez.

The woman didn't drop her gun.

Sanchez fired his service revolver. The woman flinched. He thought he'd wounded her.

His gun jammed.

Holloway heard a shot. He thought it odd that the woman's hand dropped and came up before she pointed the gun again at Sanchez. He knew that revolvers usually recoil up when fired, not down.

In his peripheral vision, Holloway saw Sanchez's body drop. Officer down.

Holloway thought he'd be next. He fired his service revolver and blew out the van's rear window. The woman moved in the driver's seat. The investigator stepped into the open to try to get a clear shot and fired again and again.

Crouched down next to his cruiser, Sanchez heard shots coming from his rear. He finally unjammed his gun and yelled, "Drop it!"

The woman took a step and aimed her gun directly at him. He fired.

She fell face-first to the ground, with both hands tucked underneath her body.

And then it was quiet.

Minutes before, Susan Burke Rose had stepped out of her Whispering Pines boarding kennel and headed down the eighth mile driveway toward the mailbox. The Labrador retriever breeder usually didn't take time to collect the mail but wanted some exercise on that warm, sunny day. She walked toward the two-lane road, just a few miles south of the Larimer County border and four miles south of Carl Cushatt's property.

The athletically built, five-foot-four blonde-haired woman heard a siren as she strolled past her training center building about halfway to the mailbox. She looked south down a slope and noticed a police cruiser, with flashing overhead lights, headed north toward the front of her twelve-acre property. In the opposite direction, she detected another siren. Thirty-foot evergreens that lined the driveway's north side obstructed her view. Then it was quiet.

"Get out! Get Out! Drop it! Drop it!" a man yelled.

Rose flashed back to the previous day's conversation with her tenant, whose dog was prone to chasing the neighbors' cows and chickens. The dog has gotten in with the chickens, she thought.

A shot rang out. Rose dropped face-first onto the dirt driveway. Silence.

A battery of eight to ten shots followed.

The shooting ceased. Rose stood up and ran back to the kennel.

"Call 911," she told her daughter. "No, don't do that. The cops are already there."

Investigator Holloway took command of the scene. The woman lay face down in the dirt. He instructed Deputy Sanchez and the Berthoud officer to approach the woman from her feet positioned just outside the driver's side of the white van. He didn't want to risk that they'd be shot. Next, he peered through the van's shattered back window and passenger-side windows. He didn't see anyone.

Sanchez stepped toward the woman. She moved slightly. He bent down and felt a faint pulse before he rolled her over onto her left side and cuffed her.

That's when Holloway caught sight of a black and silver revolver that had been underneath the woman.

It was a TOY gun; the orange barrel tip had been painted over black to make it look real. The toy was about half the size of an authentic antique single-action revolver.

"God damn her, why couldn't she have used a real gun." Holloway knew the shooting hadn't needed to happen.[2]

He picked up the toy gun and placed it on the van's hood. Then he turned his attention to the suspect. Her only chance to survive was to be airlifted. She didn't have much time. He radioed for an Air Life helicopter to be launched.

Sanchez had radioed dispatch at 1:52 p.m. that "shots had been fired and the female was on the ground." He asked for emergency medical help and an ambulance. That transmission was less than thirty seconds after he radioed that the van was stopping in the 14000 block of County Road 23, known as North 83rd Street in Boulder County.

Other deputies who'd arrived on scene and thirty-six-year-old Sanchez, a war veteran, tried to plug the woman's wounds and resuscitate her. Paramedics arrived and took over. An Air Life helicopter circled overhead.

Holloway watched a paramedic wave away the helicopter. He knew that the woman had died. She hadn't spoken a word before or after she was shot.

When Larimer sheriff's investigator Kevin Maul reached the scene, he saw a medical helicopter hovering overhead before it flew off. Near the white van, a woman lay on the ground. Gloves protruded from her bullet wounds to stop the bleeding. He noticed a black revolver on the van's hood. It looked real from about ten feet away.

Maul later recalled his observations of the on-scene officers: Sanchez appeared "matter of fact," the Berthoud officer looked "rattled," and Holloway "was really upset that the gun was fake." Holloway told him that he picked up the gun when the body was moved and only then realized that it was fake.[3]

The Boulder County and Larimer County Sheriffs conferred at the scene. They decided that the Boulder County Shoot Team would investigate the fatality because it occurred in Boulder County. Comprised of investigators from law enforcement agencies within Boulder County, the team investigated cases involving officers who used deadly force.

Officers secured and maintained a perimeter around the scene to preserve evidence while investigators searched the van that displayed a Family Auto placard in place of a rear plate. They located a temporary registration tag inside the vehicle. Stuffed animals adorned the dashboard, and a large stuffed toy dog and a straw purse lay on the passenger seat. Behind the driver's seat, they discovered a black cloth handbag containing $8,595 in bundles of money that included Chase Bank's marked bait bills. They found a scarf matching the description of the one worn by the robber, black gloves, and a second plastic toy handgun wrapped in a black cloth. And they discovered a demand note that matched the description of the one displayed by the Chase Bank bandit.

The dead woman, dressed in blue jeans, sneakers, and a blue and white heavy sweater, matched the Chase Bank robber's description. Officers used her driver's license to identify her as fifty-six-year-old Catherine Cook Cariaso of Estes Park. They concluded that she'd robbed the Loveland bank just an hour before she died.

The Shoot Team photographed Sanchez, Holloway, and the Berthoud officer as well as Dodie's body. They seized the officers' weapons for examination to determine how many shots had been fired and if the bullets that struck Dodie were from those guns. Investigators photographed and diagramed the location of the vehicles and spent casings from the officers' weapons. They collected evidence from the van and the spent casings. When officers ran Dodie's criminal history, they learned that her driver's license was suspended for lack of vehicle insurance.

———

Rose ventured back down her driveway. She spotted a body lying in a ditch near a white van on the far side of the road, about a hundred yards to the north of her driveway's entrance. Police vehicles were everywhere. She met a deputy sheriff on the road.

"I heard everything," Rose said.

"You saw everything?"

"No, I heard everything. I couldn't see anything."

When she listened to the news that night, Rose learned that the body was of a woman suspected of robbing a Loveland bank earlier that day.

———

James hadn't felt well all day. He'd gone home to nap at about 2 p.m. after he'd helped one of his employer's sons install windows in a fix-up home in southeast Denver. A twenty-four-hour bug. He felt horrible. Vikki was home.

She answered a knock on their front door. A Denver police officer and a woman in plainclothes stood on the front step.

"What's up?" Vikki asked. She wondered if one of their children had been hurt.

"Are you Vikki Weeks?"

"Yes, I am. What do you want?"

"We want to talk to you about your sister," the male officer said.

She thought something must have happened to her sibling in Illinois. Then the officer identified her sister as Catherine Cariaso. Vikki rousted James from his nap.

The pair told the couple how sorry they were to inform them about Dodie's death and wanted them to know before they saw news reports. The officer and the Victim Assistance employee explained what support was available to help them cope with the situation.

Although very relieved that the deceased wasn't her sister, Vikki felt saddened that Dodie was dead. She remembered a friend called earlier that afternoon about the Loveland robbery and wondered if Dodie was the robber. Vikki dismissed the possibility because the suspect's car wasn't the type her sister-in-law had. But over the past several years, Dodie had lightheartedly commented that she'd buy a toy gun and rob a bank, insinuating that she'd commit suicide by cop. Vikki hadn't believed her because she made the comments so often and when she wanted money from James and/or her.

James felt numb. His twin was dead. He called his brother Doug.

A shocked Doug recalled that his older sister had said, "I'm fed up" and "I just can't do this anymore," but never threatened suicide to him. He knew she hadn't been "real connected with reality and how life worked . . . she had a hard time integrating and operating within the system called life."

James and Vikki realized that Dodie probably had left Ben and Huxsby in crates in her home. They turned their attention to making sure the canines received care.

Dodie's friends and acquaintances reacted with varying degrees of shock as they recalled their relationships and conversations with her.

Carl chatted with his insurance agent at home at about 2 p.m. on the day of the bank robbery. He wondered later if his former tenant had intended to be killed at his property where so many of her Labradors died a year and a half before. Instead, she drove past his home, with officers in pursuit, perhaps, he thought, because she mistook his insurance agent's large white car parked in his driveway for an unmarked police vehicle. Dodie had discussed religion and faith with him. He was surprised by her death because he thought that she would have believed that she wouldn't go to heaven if she took her own life. He'd perceived her as more of a survivor. She loved her dogs.

A shocked Carol Mayberry-Sanchez wondered if Dodie had been driving to her home when she learned about Dodie's death, which occurred just two miles north of her house. She telephoned Barbara Marcus-McKenna.

When Barbara answered the telephone, she heard Carol say, "Well, she finally did it." A distraught Barbara later recalled how Dodie had stopped by earlier that winter. Although it was a warm day, Dodie's body shook and her voice trembled.

"Let's just go out and sit out back and talk a little bit," Barbara said. She'd never seen her longtime friend so upset.

Barbara listened. Dodie acknowledged that she and her younger brother Doug were different. She resented that he tried to call the shots and didn't feel good about accepting his money. He'd offered to buy a house for her, but she couldn't have any animals.

Dodie talked on. She just wanted Doug to recognize her as "a strong independent woman who was handling a lot." She wished for his congratulations for her accomplishments instead of his focus on what had gone wrong. Although she didn't see a future career as a waitress, she was doing okay even though waitressing was tough on her knees.

Her emotional pendulum swung as she talked; she sobbed and then held back tears. She'd be strong, she said, and life would be okay. Next, she said that she really hated her life.

Dodie composed herself and said that she had a solution. She smiled a little, "as if she had figured out a clever way to go." She'd pretend to rob a bank and be taken out.

Barbara hadn't taken her friend seriously; she knew Dodie had a terrific sense of humor. She handed her a set of metaphysical CDs to lighten her outlook and give new meaning to her life. Barbara assured Dodie that life would get better and thought her friend's mood would pass.

On the afternoon of the shooting, Father Barlow learned about Dodie's death from his parish's retired priest. The bank robbery shocked him; he never thought that Dodie would harm another person. Did she believe that she'd only be wounded, perhaps in the leg, when she pulled the fake gun on the officers? He didn't want to think otherwise.

He drove with his wife to the Loveland Police Department to tell officers what he knew. Dodie threatened suicide on two occasions, but he'd talked her out of it. When they chatted during the recent holiday season, she said she'd pull a knife or fake gun and "let them shoot me" if they came to evict her from her home. He'd passed her comments off as all bluster, made out of frustration about her situation. He counseled her against suicidal thoughts and encouraged her to apply for jobs even though she felt "blacklisted" in Estes Park.[4]

Father Barlow told police that he believed Dodie had suicidal tendencies for some time. He'd referred her to a psychologist friend who refused to accept her as a client because she believed that Dodie was dangerous and suicidal.[5] The psychologist told him that only a true conversion would save Dodie. He disclosed this information so that the officers wouldn't feel bad about the shooting.

Later, he advised police that Dodie said that she wouldn't return to jail even if she ran out of money and had to rob a bank. Father Barlow hadn't taken her comments seriously and believed they were flippant remarks. "It was hard to know when to take her seriously and when not to."[6]

Norm Townsend heard of the death of his former client on the 10 p.m. news. Shocked and saddened, the public defender thought the criminal justice system drove Dodie to her death.

Memories of Dodie's case flooded back to Pam Buffington, the public defender investigator, when she heard the news. A saddened Buffington recalled that Dodie had said more than once that she might have to commit suicide by cop because it was a good way out of her situation. The defense team hadn't taken her seriously. She'd never mentioned robbing a bank.[7]

Stunned by the news, defense attorney Stefani Goldin never thought that her client would ever put someone else in jeopardy. Why did she do this? What was she thinking?

A surprised Susan Ermani, one of the animal abuse case prosecutors, recalled Dodie's words at sentencing, how she'd be more apt to commit a crime if the judge sentenced her to jail.

"She finally got it done," Dr. Culver told her husband as she listened to the television news. She believed that Dodie had considered suicide after she'd been charged with animal abuse but before she was sentenced. Dodie had remarked how easily dogs could be put to sleep, but "there is no way a person can go out easily." She stopped short of asking for help to commit suicide, and the vet flatly refused to give any such assistance.

Rose asked her husband to switch from FOX news to a local station the morning after the shooting. Then she heard the suspect's identity.

"Oh, my God."

"Do you know her?" her husband asked.

Rose nodded. She'd tried to help the deceased nearly twelve years before when Dodie asked her to show a yellow Labrador.

Stanlyn felt devastated when Father Barlow broke the news to her. She recalled that she'd felt two pangs of intense pain in her side the day before about 3 p.m. central time as she worked at the cattle sales. Her friend had died at approximately the same time.

When Dodie called the Saturday before she died, she told Stanlyn that if the police came to evict her for not paying rent, she'd pull a gun, and then they'd have to shoot her.

God's will wasn't to take one's own life, Stanlyn responded. She didn't think that Dodie would take her own life and believed Fred and Doug would provide the support Dodie needed if they knew about her suicidal thoughts.

Stanlyn waited day after day for the mail. She thought that Dodie would have written her to explain why she'd decided to end her life. The letter and explanation never came.

———

After the shooting, investigators contacted the Estes Park Police Department to confirm Dodie's address. That's when they learned that Vikki had told Estes Park officers about fourteen months prior that Dodie had previously threatened to commit "suicide by cop."

Just after 10 p.m., a judge signed a warrant to search Dodie's home. Loveland police and Larimer sheriff investigators arrived at her Estes Park rental house about midnight.

Larimer sheriff's lieutenant Andy Josey, a twenty-five-year law enforcement veteran, knew the search needed to be conducted immediately to look for evidence of Dodie's intent to commit the robbery and end her life. Had she committed prior crimes? Had she planned the robbery? he wondered.[8]

As he drove into the parking lot near the white house with red trim, Josey realized he'd driven by it many times on the way to Rocky Mountain National Park. The ranch-style, rectangular-shaped single-family home shared a common roadway entrance with a "rock museum" store.

Investigators couldn't see the pond just east of the house, which had a front and side deck as well as a chain-link fenced-in side/backyard. A yellow Labrador and a Bernese mountain dog announced their presence in the small yard. Christmas decorations still hung outside the home. Lights were on inside the house.

Officers used a key found on Dodie's body to unlock the front door and stepped inside. Directly in front of them, they noticed a room used for storage. They turned to the right and walked into a tidy but dusty formal living room, furnished with antiques and Victorian-style lamps. A framed photo of Dodie, taken in 1987, sat on one of the tables, and animal sculptures adorned several side tables. Other photographs and paintings hung on the walls.

The investigators moved on into a family room/kitchen area. Everywhere they looked, they saw knickknacks, stuffed animals, curios, photographs, water and oil paintings, tapestries, dried flower arrangements, and live flowering plants. Two dog dishes sat empty under a low step stool between the range and freezer.

The family room area was decorated with Victorian-style lamps with fringed lampshades and hanging stained glass window pieces. Papers were stacked on antique chairs and a table. Christmas decorations remained in place: boughs with holiday lights, ceramic caroler figurines, and wilting poinsettias as well as lights strung along the top of a front window.

Josey first thought everything had been in the home for a long time as he walked through the house. He noticed its dirt and clutter. Various possessions covered all horizontal surfaces. Artwork or photographs hung on walls of all but two rooms. A few horse and pottery books sat on shelves and tables. It looked like Cariaso had moved in but hadn't unpacked, Josey thought. Was all this stuff here when Cariaso began renting, and she just moved in? He didn't know that Dodie had filed for bankruptcy the previous summer and neglected to declare virtually all of the possessions that he now observed.

Investigators stepped into Dodie's small, cluttered bedroom just off the kitchen area. They noticed a neatly made single bed covered with a country quilt and decorative pillows lining a wall abutting the bed. Framed family photographs, including a collage of Dodie and James as toddlers up through about age six, hung on the walls or sat propped against furniture. A small-framed snapshot of Dodie jumping London Fog sat on a bureau. A smiling Dodie, with arms wrapped around Max's grandmother, Charmin' Find, and a springer spaniel, hung on one wall.

Josey walked into an unkempt sunroom and noticed a back door leading to the fenced-in yard and the rambunctious but friendly dogs. A canine owner himself, he realized that the animals were thirsty and hungry. He searched for dog food but didn't find any, even in the sparsely furnished second bedroom, which contained two dog airline crates.

He wondered where he'd find dog food in the middle of the night. Then he recalled that a Larimer sheriff's major, a fellow dog owner, lived in Estes Park. He called him and drove to his house to retrieve some dog food. After he fed the canines, he called Vikki to discuss caring for them and securing the home. She asked that the canines be crated inside the house; she and her husband would come the next morning to care for them. She told Josey that she was sorry and felt bad about what happened. Her sister-in-law had mental health issues and financial troubles, she said, and lived beyond her means.

As they searched the house, investigators looked for evidence that related to the robbery and any medications that Dodie may have taken. They found large bottles of aspirin, ibuprofen, and assorted unmarked pills as well as a brand of amoxicillin, apparently prescribed by a veterinarian, and a large bottle of dog deworming medication. They located license plates for six vehicles: only one had current tags; the rest expired in 2005.

Maul dug through the garbage and pulled out three notes comingled with other trash from the second week of December 2005. The first note was written in black ink on two pieces of white paper: "Robbery! Please put all the $5s, $10s, $20's and $100s on counter like withdrawal Also open the drawer with your key with stacks of $100's."

The second was penned in red ink on a blue piece of paper: "ROBBERY! PUT ALL CASH IN BAG! DON'T LOOK UP! I HAVE A GUN! A third note, written in black ink on white paper, read, "Robbery! PUT ALL CASH IN BAG. BE NICE I have a gun."

Investigators didn't find a suicide note.

———

Shoot Team detectives interviewed Holloway, Sanchez, and the Berthoud officer in the late afternoon and evening hours of January 12th. Over the next several days, team members also interviewed officers and civilian witnesses who heard shots or arrived on the scene shortly afterward. They spoke with friends, relatives, and acquaintances of Dodie, including Father Barlow, Vikki, Carol, and defense attorney Goldin.

They learned from bank employees that Dodie had walked through the bank's foyer about an hour before the robbery. Two employees, at different times, stopped her. She deflected their questions and assured one that she was okay but had a cough, apparently trying to account for the black scarf over her mouth. She asked the other employee for directions to the restroom. A third employee followed her into the basement powder room. Moments before the robbery, a fourth employee questioned Dodie as she entered the bank. This time, Dodie just muttered that it was cold outside to explain the black scarf over her mouth and then walked up to a teller's station.

Officers investigated Dodie's criminal, financial, and personal history. They executed a search warrant for her mental health records, which were sealed and not released to the public.

Dr. Michael Arnall, a pathologist who assisted the Larimer County Coroner's Office, performed an autopsy the day after the shooting. He determined that Dodie had been hit by five bullets, one each in the left bicep, torso, neck, left-back abdominal area, and above the right breast. Another bullet grazed her right back. He couldn't determine the order in which the wounds were inflicted.

He concluded that the cause of death was "the result of multiple gunshot wounds. The manner of death is homicide." However, he noted that there was evidence indicating that the deceased "initiated a police confrontation with the intent of an untoward outcome."[9]

Josey and a Boulder sheriff's detective attended the autopsy. They took custody of the slugs and bullet fragments removed from Dodie's body. These slugs and bullet fragments as well as Holloway's and Sanchez's .45 caliber handguns, were submitted for analysis to the Colorado Bureau of Investigation. Six of the fragments and slugs matched the two weapons. Two came from Holloway's gun and four from Sanchez's. Holloway had fired eleven times; Sanchez, four times. The Berthoud officer hadn't fired his weapon because he didn't have a clear shot.

Toxicology tests on blood taken from Dodie's body revealed that no drugs or alcohol were detected in her system.

———

Boulder County first assistant district attorney Peter Maguire reviewed the Shoot Team's investigation. On February 6th, he cleared Holloway and Sanchez of any wrongdoing in connection with the pursuit of Dodie and her subsequent death.

He found that the officers had probable cause to believe the van's driver had committed an aggravated bank robbery, "believed that she may have been armed and dangerous," and lawfully pursued the van when it crossed into Boulder County.

Maguire concluded that both officers were justified in using deadly force. He found Sanchez acted in self-defense and reasonably believed that he was in imminent danger of being killed. Holloway believed that Sanchez had been shot and saw the weapon pointed at his fellow officer. He fired to defend Sanchez, who he reasonably believed was in imminent danger of being killed or receiving great bodily injury.

The "later determination that the weapon was a toy pistol does nothing to change the fact that the three officers from independent vantage points had reasonable grounds to believe, and did in fact believe, that the object was a deadly weapon and that Deputy Sanchez was in imminent danger of being killed or receiving great bodily injury as a result of Catherine Cariaso's actions," Maguire wrote.

CHAPTER 32

At Peace

More than a dozen friends and family drove to St. Francis of Assisi Anglican Church, perched on top of a mountainside several miles outside of downtown Estes Park, to pay their final respects to Dodie on the evening of January 18, 2006.

They parked their cars in the small dirt lot and walked up the wide wooden stairs to the bright red front doors of the wooden entryway set against the stone face of the church. A short breezeway led to the doors of the small chapel. Inside, they sat on maroon cushions on pews set on either side of the stone floor aisle that led to the altar. Stained-glass windows lined the outer walls. A staircase curved up to the choir loft at the rear of the church. The church's nave measured only about thirty-five feet long and some twenty feet wide.

Many found the setting a fitting location to pay their final respects to Dodie. Father Barlow led the requiem mass in the church named after St. Francis, the patron saint of animals. Buffington thought the church felt old-world, tenth century, a seemingly appropriate setting because she always thought Dodie was pretty old-fashioned. As she sat on one of the ten wooden pews, she understood why Dodie had become involved with this church. She came with Stinson so that Dodie's family would know that they cared about Dodie, who hadn't been just another client. Goldin attended to pay her respects. She didn't know her client's family well, but she liked Dodie.

Mary Gates, who had worked tirelessly to find homes for Dodie's horses, arrived alone and intended to talk to the family. Instead, she spoke only to Dodie's longtime friend, Carol, who attended with her husband. Barbara, another longtime friend, and her husband came as did a few other friends, mostly from Estes Park. Relatives of Stanlyn attended in her place.

"Yeah, I loved her," Fred Cariaso admitted as he drove alone for more than three hours from his remote Wyoming cabin to Estes Park. "It is just too bad that we didn't grow closer to one another, and our values just changed." His former professor-landlord, who had "rented" the Nederland cabin to the newlyweds, had contacted him about the service.

Struck by the wedding vows of "until death do us part," Fred looked around the small chapel and didn't see any mutual friends from their college or married days. He felt sad. James was the only person he recognized and thought the others present were parishioners. James and Vikki chatted with him before he left.

The mass was formal. Carol sang a song that she'd composed in memory of her longtime friend. No one was asked to share their memories of Dodie.

A second mass was conducted on April 22nd for those unable to attend the January service, to pay their respects and lay Dodie's ashes to rest. About twenty friends and family attended the mass again led by Father Barlow in the same chapel as the previous service. Doug and his three sons came as did James, his son, and Vikki, and several of their friends. Kathleen, unable to travel, remained in California. Stinson returned, this time with her boss, Townsend.

After the mass, the group gathered outside to bury the urn that contained Dodie's ashes. Her family had purchased a three-foot statue of St. Francis of Assisi to mark her grave under a large tree near the church's entrance. Always the lawyer, Townsend wondered whether the burial violated any local zoning laws but kept quiet as Dodie's ashes were laid to rest in a hillside overlooking her final hometown nestled high in the Colorado Rockies.

James and Vikki grieved for Dodie but felt terribly for the two officers who had been duped into shooting her. They talked to Doug about writing a letter. James believed that Dodie had seen a way out and took it but never considered what impact her actions would have on the officers once they learned she had a toy gun. Vikki and James sat down to compose a letter to Holloway and Sanchez:

> We are the family of Catherine "Dodie" Cariaso, and have been remiss in getting this letter off to you with the intention of putting your minds and hearts at ease regarding her death.
>
> It is very important to us that you know we hold no ill feelings toward you, nor do we hold you responsible. Rather, we share your pain and anguish, as this was a dreadful way for her to end her life, as well as a dreadful experience for you. We fully understand that you were performing your duty, and had no idea what she carried was a toy. What a grim and painful discovery that must have been for you. We are so sorry for that.
>
> To offer a brief history: over the past few years, Dodie had threatened many times to end her life in this manner, and stated, several times, that she would use that "realistic" toy to initiate the event. Though we tried over this period of time to diligently seek mental help for her, she always refused, and we were never successful in getting her treated. We feel you were victims of this untreated illness, and for that we are very sorry to you.
>
> This was a sad ending to a sad life. As her family, we hope somehow this letter will help free you of any guilt or anguish you might carry, and we would wish you

peace and freedom from those feelings as a result of this experience.

We intend to put this tragedy behind us, and remember the times when Dodie was happy and healthy. We have faith that she is now free of the turmoil in her life, and is safely in the loving arms of God and those who love her. With our heartfelt blessings, we would ask that you do the same.

With warmest regards,

Signed the Wilson Family

James & Douglas Wilson, her brothers and their families

The family of Catherine "Dodie" Cariaso

The Wilsons' March 31st letter helped Holloway. He knew that Dodie's family didn't blame him for the death of their relative. Larimer County Sheriff James Alderden wrote the family to thank them for their letter and found their concern and compassion "heartwarming."

———

Nearly two years after Dodie's death, Susan Burke Rose stood in the driveway of her Whispering Pines boarding kennel. She still remembered the smell of the gunfire.

"The system failed the dogs and Dodie. I complained, and I complained and blew the whistle. The state and the AKC didn't do anything," she said. Rose shook her head.

"And the County?"

"Yes, and the County. She could have been shut down."

Epilogue

I didn't think much about the promise that Dave and I made to Max when I set out to investigate and write this book. From a family of Labrador breeders and enthusiasts, I knew and believed that canine owners bear a significant responsibility. My parents raised my sister Lyn and me with the philosophy that dog ownership required one to not only feed, water, and shelter your charge but also to train and provide the best possible care, attention, and home. As pet owners, we owe proper medical and social care to our faithful companions. Man's best friend is entitled to nothing less.

On July 3, 2003, Dave and I promised nearly thirteen-year-old Max, as he spent the last couple of hours in our living world, that he would climb his tenth fourteener. Max had excelled at his job as our best hiking canine companion because he adored outdoor adventures and loved all dogs and people. We'd hoped that he'd teach proper trail etiquette to Brew, his loyal hiking partner, but she failed to master those manners.

More than four years after we made our final promise to Max, Dave and I set out to keep our word to the only adopted dog that I had ever owned. We both knew that the climb was more for us humans and our way to pay tribute to the loyal blond boy. Our goal was to ascend Quandary Peak, a 14,265-foot mountain in central Colorado. Brew, who was almost ten years old, stayed at home in Buena Vista with her nearly six-year-old yellow daughter, Taz. We didn't think Brew was in condition to enjoy the climb and were uncertain as to whether the terrain would be too rocky for her aging paws. We knew that Taz, given her myriad orthopedic problems, was no match for the mountain.

The day looked perfect for a climb; the cloudless sky was a crystal-clear blue, and the forecast called for only scattered thunder-storms. We reached the trailhead at just before 9 a.m., earlier than our standard start time, to afford us the best chance to reach the mountain's summit perched well above tree line without encounter-ing an errant thunderstorm. The dirt-packed trail began in the woods and quickly turned into a rocky and small stone path as we reached timberline at about 12,000 feet. The clouds rolled in and light graupel fell. By then, I'd really slowed down. Dave and I hadn't climbed a fourteener in seven years, and I'd forgotten what it was like to breathe and walk at that altitude. Conversation was out of the question for me.

Why am I climbing this mountain? Then I remembered: it was to keep our promise and to honor Max. How many people make and then break promises to their dogs? Was Max entitled to this climb? I put one foot in front of the other.

Within feet of Quandary Peak's summit, I glanced at Dave and saw his slightly contorted face. He also was thinking of Max. I trudged a few more feet to the mountain's summit and located the canister that contained sign-in sheets provided by the Colorado Mountain Club. I couldn't muster the strength to open it, but Dave, with his strong hands, twisted the cap and removed the rolled-up sign-in sheets. A fortyish-looking woman from Breckenridge watched as she ate an apple.

I used a pen in the canister to write our entry: "7/30/07: Dave Olmstead and Cary Unkelbach, Buena Vista, CO and Maxwell—in spirit." Under comments, I printed, "Max's 10th 14er." I passed the sign-in rolls to Dave to return to the canister.

"Did you sign in all of us?" he asked without stopping to read my notations.

I nodded as I fought back tears.

Dave crammed the sheets into the canister.

The woman viewed us with curiosity. All?

Dave and I wandered farther to the northwest on the flattish summit to eat lunch. Yes, this climb definitely was more for us humans to honor and say our final farewell to Max. We scattered his ashes far away from the female hiker. Max had climbed Mt. Elbert, Colorado's highest peak; Mt. Sherman; Torreys, Grays, and Huron Peaks; and Mt. Antero as well as Mt. Yale, La Plata Peak, and Mt. Shavano with Brew.

Since 2007, Dave and I have climbed many more fourteeners but selected only three to be graced with Max's and Brew's ashes: Mt. Princeton, which overlooks our home in the valley far below; Mt. Harvard from Frenchman's Creek where Brew and Taz hiked to the base of the mountain; and the Mountain of the Holy Cross, where none of our dogs had ventured. The views from these mountains were magnificent. Max and Brew were entitled to and deserved only the best. And now, so did Taz. Of this, I was certain.

Acknowledgments

Heartbreak Kennel wouldn't have been possible without the patience, indulgence, and willingness of so many individuals to provide their recollections of Dodie Cariaso and her dogs. Nearly one hundred persons assisted me in my journey to research and write *Heartbreak Kennel*. Thank you one and all for your time and assistance.

Very special thanks to Dodie's twin brother James Wilson and his wife Vikki Weeks, who generously opened their home so that I could review Dodie's records, letters, and diaries as well as hundreds of photographs. They spent hours answering my questions about Dodie as I tried to understand this complex and often troubled woman. Dodie's younger brother Doug Wilson and his wife Kathleen also kindly chatted about Dodie and offered insights that only relatives could.

Many thanks to Fred Cariaso, who so graciously provided details of his marriage to Dodie and assisted me in understanding her as a young woman.

Thanks also to Mary Gates, Stanlyn Johnston, Barbara Marcus-McKenna, and Carol Mayberry-Sanchez for their personal recollections of Dodie.

I certainly wouldn't have investigated Dodie's life if Max hadn't joined our family. Thank you so much, John Ulrich, for giving us our beloved companion and recounting his early years.

Prosecutors Jennifer Lee Birken, Susan Ermani Blanco, and Todd Field, and defense team members Norm Townsend, Pam Buffington, Jennifer Stinson, and Stefani Goldin were particularly insightful as they recounted their strategies that allowed me to write a balanced account of the animal abuse case brought against Dodie.

Several current and past members of the Labrador Retriever Club of Greater Denver, Larimer County Sheriff's Office, Larimer Humane Society, Trimble Court, and Weld County government were especially open to questions.

Thanks to Labrador breeders Lisa Butler, Denise Hamel, and Julie Sturman; and Linde Konde, DVM, for reading portions of and/or the entire book and offering valuable technical comments.

Writers Four, my original writing group, painstakingly read my first draft and gave insightful feedback, as did author Susan Tweit. They nudged me forward even years after our group disbanded. Thanks for your unwavering support Maria Weber, Sue Greiner, and Debby Cason.

Many thanks to my other beta readers for your invaluable suggestions: retired Judge Tom Curry, Lani Curry, Evie Haskell Maxwell, Jane Provorse, Ann True, and the late Monica Kern.

I'm also very appreciative of Tom Curry, Mary Downs, Sue Oviatt Harris, Monica Kern, Polly Kruse, and Julie Sturman for their glowing endorsements of *Heartbreak Kennel*.

Thanks to many others who encouraged me over the years, including Patty Brooks, Joan Freeman, Linda Hills, Jola Kieler, Patti Larson, Katy Miller, Susan Oja, Susan Vance, and Sandi Vanni.

Finally, I am very grateful for my husband Dave Olmstead, who suggested that I write this book. He spent countless hours reading book drafts, listened to my investigative and writing travails, edited the photographs, and unconditionally supported and encouraged me along each step of this odyssey. He always believed this book would be published. So did my faithful four-footed editorial assistants: Brew, Taz, Layla, Ranger, and Betty.

Notes

Chapter 1

1. Vikki Weeks, interviews by author, February 22 and April 19, 2010; and March 13 and December 28, 2012. James Wilson, interviews by author, February 22, April 19, and June 9, 2010; November 22, 2011; and December 28, 2012. Information from these interviews and others listed below were used throughout the book.

2. "Pet Statistics: Facts about U.S. Animal Shelters," ASPCA, https://www.aspca.org/animal-homelessness/shelter-intake-and-surrender/pet-statistics (accessed December 12, 2019).

3. Dodie sometimes referred to herself as Cate and, at other times, Kate. For purposes of readability, the author has simplified the punctuation in Dodie's notes, letters, and diaries by omitting some of the ellipses (dots).

4. Rigo Neira, email correspondence to author, September 13, 2012.

5. "Pets by the Numbers," Humane Society of the United States, https://www.humanesociety.org/resources/pets-numbers (accessed November 22, 2019).

6. "Tracking Animal Cruelty," FBI, February 1, 2016, https://www.fbi.gov/news/stories/-tracking-animal-cruelty (accessed December 12, 2019).

7. "84.9 million pet-owning US households in 2018, dogs #1," https://www.petfoodindustry.com/articles/8066-9-million-pet-owning-us-households-in-2018-dogs-1?v=preview (accessed November 22, 2019).

8. "Pet Industry Market Size & Ownership Statistics," APPA, https://www.americanpetproducts.org/press_industrytrends.asp (accessed November 22, 2019).

Chapter 2

1. Fred Cariaso, interview by author, October 20, 2011.

2. James Wilson, Dodie's twin brother, graciously loaned Dodie's diaries to the author. Two covered the period of December 31, 1966 through June 1968, and one from February 1997 to January 13, 2005. These diaries are referenced throughout the book.

3. Bob is a pseudonym for one of Dodie's teenage boyfriends. His first name has been changed, and his last name is unknown.

4. Fred Cariaso interview, October 20, 2011.

5. Ibid.

6. Ibid.

7. Notice of Entry of Decree of Dissolution, Boulder County District Court, Case No. 73-1501, November 12, 1973.

Chapter 4

1. Doug and Kathleen Wilson, interview by author, January 20, 2013.

2. Nancy Zoller, interview by author, February 10, 2011.

3. Phyllis Walbye, "Change Is at Heart of Potter's Work," *Valley Window, Loveland Daily Reporter-Herald*, May 28–29, 1983.

4. Ibid.

Chapter 5

1. Dodie usually spelled her kennel name "Killkenny," and occasionally "Kilkenny." It remains unclear if she did so deliberately or didn't catch the misspelling.

2. Richardson advertised her Labradors in the directory, better known as *Julie Brown's Directory,* from 1971 through 1979.

3. The AKC awards a conformation championship to a purebred canine that defeats a set number of dogs to earn points. To achieve a championship, a canine must win fifteen points: two wins of three to five points under two different judges, and the remaining points under at least one other judge. The Labrador Retriever Club and local Labrador clubs award a working certificate to a dog that retrieves one game bird on land and two ducks in water during an AKC sanctioned test. Samba's sire couldn't be identified. The AKC refused to release litter or individual canine registration records without written permission of the dog's owner. Samba's breeder is deceased.

4. Reputable breeders now test their Labradors for many more maladies than just hip dysplasia and hereditary eye diseases. They test for genetic diseases, including elbow dysplasia, exercise induced collapse, heart defects including tricuspid valve dysplasia, centronuclear myopathy, degenerative myopathy, hereditary nasal parakeratosis, and copper toxicosis. Additionally, they test for dilute genes that aren't possessed by purebred Labradors and, sometimes, long coat genes.

5. George A. Padgett, *Control of Canine Genetic Diseases* (New York: Howell Book House, 1998), 47, 104–5.

6. Many individuals believe that environmental factors such as overweight puppies, excessive exercise, or jumping, can cause hip dysplasia. Padgett notes that while environmental factors may lessen or worsen a dog's hip dysplasia, a canine won't develop " hip dysplasia unless it has the complement of genes necessary to produce that trait." Ibid, 46.

7. Ibid, 104-105. These polygenetic traits must be inherited from both parents.

8. Ibid, 111.

9. In November 2012, OFA and the American College of Veterinary Ophthalmologists (ACVO) established a joint Eye Certification Registry (ERC) and Clinical Database for Ophthalmic Diagnoses. OFA now issues eye clearance numbers to dogs with normal eye exams as well as those canines with observable but passing conditions. Dogs with eye disease "of significance" won't receive eye clearance numbers. OFA only publishes failing results on its website with owner authorization. The results of the tests, conducted by an ACVO member, are valid for a year. CERF closed its doors in June 2014.

10. Dodie's vet may have x-rayed Samba's hips before the dog was bred. If so, those radiographs weren't sent to OFA. James Wilson graciously provided the author with Dodie's canine records from the early 1980s through the early 2000s. These records don't contain any eye exam or CERF documents. OFA's website first began to publish CERF results in 2001, so it remains unknown if either Samba or her mate had any eye tests or CERF certifications.

11. Dr. Millissa Cullver no longer has records of Dodie's canines, so it is unknown if Samba's daughter's hips were x-rayed, if the hips were x-rayed and the radiographs weren't sent to OFA, or if OFA examined the x-rays but didn't award a normal or another pass rating.

12. Dr. Millissa Culver, interview by author, August 29, 2012.

13. Marney McCleary, interviews by author, October 30, 2010, and June 30, 2012.

14. Donna Stacey, "LRCGD Turns 15," *The Retriever Believer* (January 1994).

15. Barbara Marcus-McKenna, interview by author, October 27, 2010.

16. Lee Burdick, interviews by author, March 17 and April 1, 2009.

17. Linda Vaughn, interview by author, March 14, 2009.

18. Ch. refers to conformation champion; CD, Companion Dog (obedience) degree; and AWC, advanced working certificate.

19. Debarking remains controversial. The American Veterinary Medical Association has stopped short of a total ban of the procedure but advises that it should be performed only as an "alternative to euthanasia and after all efforts to stop a dog from excessively barking have been exhausted." Jennifer Fiala, "Veterinarians split on anti-debarking policy," July 6, 2018, The VIN News Service, http://news.vin.com/vinnews.aspx? articleId=49334. The procedure is risky and post-operative pain evident. Humane Society Veterinary Medical Association, Devocalization Fact Sheet, https://www.hsvma.org/assets/pdfs/ devocalization-facts.pdf, and "Welfare Implications of Canine Devocalization," June 2018, American Veterinary Medical Association, https://www.avma.org/KB/Resources/Literature Reviews/Pages/Canine-Devocalization-Backgrounder.aspx All articles were accessed September 18, 2018.

20. Gladys Burke, interview by author, May 9, 2011.

Chapter 6

1. John Ulrich, interviews by author, April 26, and October 3 and 6, 2008.

2. Avenson v. Zegart et al., 577 F. Supp. 958, 960 (D.Minn. 1984). See also: Smith v. The Humane Society of the United States and Missourians for the Protection of Dogs, No. SC 95175 (S. Ct. Mo. 2017).

Chapter 7

1. Carol Mayberry-Sanchez, interview by author, July 29, 2010.

2. Stanlyn Johnston, interviews by author, April 26 and May 29, 2013.

3. Lisa Dickens, interview by author, August 29, 2012. Dickens only occasionally cared for the dogs and horses through the mid-1990s until Dodie no longer traveled to art shows.

Chapter 8

1. Diane Findley, interview by author, December 10, 2010.

2. Barbara Marcus-McKenna, interview by author, October 22, 2010.

3. Bland Nesbit, interview by author, May 19, 2012.

4. Ibid.

5. Susan Burke Rose, interviews by author, October 28, 2007, November 8, 2007, and November 19, 2009.

6. Jennifer Hurley, interview by author, October 23, 2012.

7. "What Is a Puppy Mill?" ASPCA, https://www .aspca.org/ animal-cruelty/puppy-mills (accessed June 7, 2017).

8. Shirley Gonzales, interviews by author, October 30, 2012, and April 25, 2013.

9. These costs were based on the belief that Dodie owned seven adult horses and four foals in 1993. Per horse costs were calculated based on an estimated $3 hay bale, with each horse consuming at least fifteen bales a month; supplemental grain for London Fog and a couple of mares; farrier expenses of $35 to $60 every six to eight weeks per horse; routine vaccines such as rabies, rhino pneumonia, and rotavirus; a Coggins test; routine teeth care; and worming four

times a year. Costs included $25 for a full foal APHA registration, $15 for a breeding stock foal registration, and a minimal sum for an APHA membership. Dodie's propensity for expensive clothing, tack, and other gear was taken into account as well as her participation in horse shows; routine upkeep of her barn, fences, horse trailer, and truck; and replacement of basic equipment such as buckets and water troughs.

Chapter 10

1. Some people erroneously call chunky Labradors "English-type" Labradors. That term is a misnomer. The Labrador standard only recognizes Labradors, not "American" or "English" Labradors.

2. Kristen Everhart, interview by author, May 22, 2012.

3. Ibid.

4. AKC Mission Statement, https://www.akc.org/about/mission/ (accessed December 12, 2019).

5. Barbara Shoemaker, interview by author, May 18, 2012.

Chapter 11

1. Susan Burke Rose interview, November 8, 2007.

2. Gary Schwartz, interview by author, November 20, 2007. During his interview, Weld County Animal Control officer Schwartz said that his office only retained records for five or six years. Thus, any record of Susan Burke's call in 1994 had been destroyed by the time the author interviewed Schwartz.

3. "State Puppy Mill Laws," ASPCA, June 15, 2015, https://www.aspca.org/sites/default/files/state_puppy_mills_guide_w_chart_june2015.pdf (accessed May 15, 2018); "Best & Worst States for Animal Protection Laws, 2016 Report Released," Animal Legal Defense Fund, http://aldf.org/press-room/press-releases/

best-worst-states-for-animal-protection-laws-2016-report-released./ (accessed December 14, 2019).

4. The dog food cost was based on the belief that Dodie fed about 56,600 pounds of canine food in 1996. That was the amount of food that she purchased in 2003, according to records from Sam's Club. The cost of a fifty-pound bag of medium quality kibble was estimated at $15 because a forty-pound bag of higher quality kibble from a veterinarian's office retailed at about $26 in 1996, according to the author's own records.

5. Nancy Zoller, interview by author, February 10, 2012.

6. AKC Care and Conditions Policy, adopted at the July 1990 Board of Directors meeting. See also http://www.akc.org/rules/policy-manual/policy-manual-registration/.

7. Jon McClain, interview by author, August 1, 2012.

8. The state form requested a listing of transfers that included sales. For ease of reading, the author used the term sales.

9. Dodie's copies of Dr. Culver's records for that time frame showed charges for removal of dewclaws from twenty litters.

Chapter 12

1. Mixed breeds may now participate in AKC obedience trials as well as numerous other AKC performance events. Owners of these dogs must register them as Canine Partners before they may enter these competitions.

2. Blanche Saunders, *Training You to Train Your Dog* (New York: Doubleday, 1952), 75; AKC's Event Calendar, https://www.apps.akc.org//apps/event_calendar/.Today, obedience and rally trials are routinely conducted at AKC conformation shows.

3. Two qualifying scores now may be earned under the same judge. AKC also has eliminated the traditional off leash, one-minute group Sit Stay and three-minute Down Stay. It's added a Sit Stay–Get Your Leash exercise, which requires a dog to sit and stay while a handler retrieves a leash from across the ring and returns behind the dog to heel position. Two new group exercises, called Sit and Down Stay, require dogs, on leash, to remain in place in a row of other canines for a minute.

4. Years later, Molly won her class when she earned her Companion Dog Excellent title under the same judge. Max and Molly shared the same favorite judge.

Chapter 13

1. This information was gleaned from Dodie's records as graciously provided by James Wilson.

2. Dodie registered Killkenny's Megan O'Mally with the AKC and listed the dog's sire as Thunder on the registration application. However, on her envelope record, she penned Thunder/Donavan as Megan's sire(s). She used identical photographs to represent Killkenny's Nexus O'Leary, Killkenny's Samba Superior, and their dam, Killkenny's Wisteria Whisperer, in her records, which she undoubtedly showed to puppy customers.

3. Although the AKC declined to discuss and/or disclose details about its investigation of Dodie's kennel, the author learned through interviews that Dodie incorrectly identified Vaughn's dog as the sire of one of the tested litters. The AKC also declined to release the number of Labrador litters or individual dogs registered by Dodie.

4. Regarding the second incorrect litter application, Dodie may have placed puppies from that litter with a surrogate mother but failed to mark the puppies or record her actions, may not have recalled the correct sire, or may have intentionally listed the name

of a stud dog that she knew hadn't sired the litter. Although the AKC inspector may have tested Dodie's litters as a result of a complaint, it is believed that the AKC randomly selected her kennel for DNA tests based on the number of litter applications that she submitted the previous year.

5. One of the litters may have had two sires. In 1998, the AKC changed its policy banning multiple sires. Litters whelped on or after September 1, 1998, may be registered if sired by multiple sires as long as breeders participate in the AKC's DNA Profile Program by submitting DNA samples of the dam, puppies, and multiple sires to the AKC before filing the litter registration application. In 2000, the AKC Board of Directors adopted its Frequently Used Sires Requirement that mandates, effective July 1, 2000, that every sire that produces seven litters in a lifetime or more than three litters in a calendar year has its DNA taken for an AKC DNA profile. The AKC penalties for submitting false litter registrations now are substantially less than in 1998–99.

6. Secretary's Page, The AKC Gazette, December 1999.

7. Dr. Culver charged about $77 for OFA radiographs, and OFA, about $20 for its evaluation in 1996.

8. To calculate these numbers, the author reviewed OFA original and copies of certificates contained in Dodie's records as well as information on OFA's website. Because OFA results are not listed by owner but by kennel and individual dog names, the author couldn't verify if Dodie owned additional Labradors or registered some without her kennel prefix and didn't include them in her personal records. However, the author included in the twenty-six number of dogs owned by Dodie that had passing OFA hip ratings, Dodie's foundation female, Satin Samba of Williston, and two other Labradors that she bought: Burbury's Crystal and Jess-mor's Devon O'Shea. In the author's opinion, it was possible but unlikely that more of Dodie's dogs had normal or other passing hip OFA ratings.

OFA also examined and rated as normal elbow x-rays of Killkenny's Fort Knox, but this dog is not believed to have been owned at the time by Dodie because Dr. Culver's records didn't show that she x-rayed him. Another dog with a Killkenny prefix was excluded from the author's tally because Dr. Culver didn't x-ray the dog, based on Dodie's vet records for October 16, 1995 through December 13, 2004.

9. Dodie's records did not include any originals or copies of OFA elbow clearance certifications for any of her dogs.

10. Sue Pierce Kelling, interview by author, January 13, 2010.

11. Only one of the puppy buyers interviewed for this book recalled that Dodie talked about eye diseases but couldn't remember the precise conversation. No ophthalmologist or CERF documents were located among Dodie's records.

12. Vikki Weeks remembered that Dodie owned one older, blind chocolate female. The dog's identity couldn't be determined or if the cause of the blindness was PRA or another eye disease such as hereditary cataracts.

13. Joan Tilden, interview by author, March 6, 2010.

Chapter 14

1. The author couldn't determine what civil papers were served on Dodie.

2. Mary Gates, interview by author, November 21, 2010.

3. Kelly Henderson, interview by author, January 23, 2010.

4. Pat Cooke, interview by author, January 8, 2010.

5. In late August 2001, the state investigated a complaint alleging that Killkenny Kennels was breeding unhealthy puppies and had sold a puppy at seven and a half weeks.

6. Paula Stack, interview by author, June 22, 2012.

7. Costs per horse were calculated based on an estimated $5 hay bale, with each horse consuming at least fifteen bales a month; supplemental grain for two thoroughbreds and a couple of mares; farrier expenses of $40 to $75 every six to eight weeks per horse; routine vaccines; worming; and teeth cleaning for each horse as well as a regular foal APHA registration fee of $35 plus a $25 APHA member fee. Mary worked for $10 an hour during the week, sometimes four hours a day. Upkeep on Dodie's fences and two barns was probably minimal because of tight finances. Dodie had eliminated stud fees because she only bred her mares to Lord Liberty.

8. Doug and Kathleen Wilson, interview by author, January 20, 2013.

9. The author couldn't determine the exact nature of Dodie's debt to the state because the file had been destroyed, according to the court's retention policy, before the author sought to review it. However, the state collection agency sued individuals who owed debts to a state agency or department. Dodie may have owed CSU's veterinary hospital for care of her horses and/or dogs.

10. CSU declined to specify if the $9,000 bill related solely to the foal or also to dogs.

Chapter 15

1. Gary Schwartz, interviews by author, November 20, 2007, and May 15, 2008.

2. Chris Gathman, interview by author, December 6, 2007.

3. Sara Bensman, interview by author, February 13, 2008.

4. By 2009, Gaia also had undergone surgery for a torn ACL and had been diagnosed with "bad elbows," most likely elbow dysplasia.

5. The author granted this man's request not to be identified by name. He verified information that he submitted to the Denver Dumb Friends League and the state in his February 25, 2010 interview by author. In addition, the author reviewed *The Labrador Quarterly's* Spring 2001 issue.

Chapter 16

1. John never forgot Max. He learned from Max that he wanted his next dog to live free of human expectations. Until he retired to his family's forty-eight-acre midwestern farm, he never was in a situation to allow a canine to "be just a dog." John knew he'd name his new dog Max because he believed that he had unfinished business with the Labrador that had taught him a canine's concept of freedom. Within ninety days of retiring, John traveled to Nebraska to pick up his new Max, a vizsla pup. He left with two puppies, Max and Duke. John taught his new companions only no and sit commands and otherwise let them live however they desired digging holes, chasing squirrels and fallen walnuts, and running all they wanted. They are the happiest dogs that John has ever known.

Chapter 17

1. Erin Furman, interview by author, January 15, 2010.

2. Carl Cushatt, interview by author, October 26, 2012.

Chapter 18

1. It is believed that Dodie fled to Missouri because she thought that she could raise horses more cheaply there than in Colorado.

2. Tim Kloer, interview by author, April 21, 2009.

3. Final Veterinary Statement of Dr. Miranda Spindel, February 25, 2005.

4. Rigo Neira, interview by author, December 12, 2008, and email to author, September 13, 2012.

5. "Pets by the Numbers," Humane Society of the United States, http://www.humanesociety.org/issues/pet_overpopulation/facts/pet_ownership_statistics.html (accessed May 15, 2018).

6. Two other tattooed dogs were euthanized: Killkenny's Rhumba, possibly pregnant, for behavioral and health reasons; and Tandicca of Timber Ridge, for health reasons. Both six-year-old yellows were McDougal daughters.

7. Christine Samuelian, interview by author, December 21, 2008.

8. Lauren Kloer, interviews by author, April 3 and 11, 2009.

Chapter 19

1. Jennifer Lee Birken, interview by author, November 29, 2008.

2. Jon McClain, interview by author, August 1, 2012. Montgomery's walks became increasingly shorter as he aged. He occasionally limped in front. One night, the nearly ten-year-old dog awoke and howled, unable to put weight on his front right leg. Several veterinarians thought he had either a cancerous tumor that had grown and pressed against his elbow joints or had OCD of the elbows. The McClains said goodbye to their beloved Montgomery O'Keefe McClain because they didn't want to put him through more surgery at his age.

3. "Animal Protection Laws of the United States and Canada," Animal Legal Defense Fund, http://aldf.org/resources/advocating-for-animals/animal-protection-laws-of-the-united-states-of-america-and-canada/ (accessed May 15, 2018).

4. Jennifer Lee Birken interview, November 29, 2008.

5. Rigo Neira interview, December 12, 2008, and email to author, September 13, 2012. The Humane Society later put down the horse.

6. Ibid.

7. Susan Blanco Ermani, interview by author, November 13, 2008.

8. Norman Townsend, interviews by author, March 31 and April 23, 2009.

9. Pam Buffington, interviews by author, July 30 and August 4, 2009.

10. Ibid.

11. Kathleen Wilson interview, January 20, 2012.

Chapter 20

1. Since our climb, the trail from the basin to the saddle has been re-routed.

Chapter 22

1. "What Is a Puppy Mill?" ASPCA, https://www.aspca.org/animal-cruelty/puppy-mills (accessed June 7, 2017).

2. Ibid.

Chapter 25

1. Stefani Goldin, interview by author, November 5, 2009.

2. Ibid.

3. Sara Reed, "Dog Breeder Defends Self," *The Coloradoan*, August 16, 2005.

4. James Wilson graciously provided Dodie's copy of the Probation Department's presentence report to the author.

5. "Animal Neglect Facts," Animal Legal Defense Fund,
http://aldf.org/resources/laws-cases/animal-neglect-facts/
(accessed May 15, 2018).

Chapter 26
1. Years later, I learned that Max disappeared for at least fifteen
minutes before Dave discovered him missing on their hunt for
firewood. Dave located his assistant, but only after the goofy
dog undoubtedly had destroyed any incriminating evidence.

Chapter 30

1. The district attorney's office never sought restitution costs
because the Humane Society reportedly didn't submit restitution
figures.

2. Dodie apparently wanted to rename the business Mountain
Express and use the slogan "Fast, Friendly, Fresh" to promote the
dinner delivery service. A proposed expense sheet for her new
venture was located among records graciously provided to the
author by James Wilson.

3. Father James Barlow, interview by Boulder police detective Jane
Harmer, January 12, 2006.

4. Stanlyn Johnston thought that she advised only Father Barlow
that her cousin would care for her grandmother before she apprised
Dodie. It is believed that Father Barlow told Dodie that information
the day before she died and before Stanlyn called her the following
morning.

Chapter 31

1.Steve Holloway, interview by author, October 21, 2011.

2. Ibid.

3. Kevin Maul, interview by author, November 13, 2008.

4. Father James Barlow, interview by Boulder police detective Jane Harmer, January 17, 2006.

5. Father Barlow statement, Boulder County Sheriff's Office detective Steven Ainsworth supplemental report, January 18, 2006.

6. Father Barlow interview, January 17, 2006.

7. Pam Buffington interview, August 4, 2009.

8. Andrew Josey, interview with author, November 13, 2008.

9. The amended death certificate, filed with the state on February 16, 2006, listed the cause of death as "multiple gunshot wounds."

Glossary

AWC: Advanced Working Certificate; a certificate awarded by the LRC or a local Labrador retriever club to a Labrador that retrieves two doubles on land and also in water during an AKC sanctioned test. A double means the birds are shot at the same time, and the dog then retrieves them back to back.

AKC: Established in 1884, the American Kennel Club is the oldest purebred dog registry in the United States and considered by many as the most prestigious in this country.

All breed show: Dog shows that allow all breeds of purebred dogs to compete. The AKC now allows mixed breed canines, registered as Canine Partners with the dog registry, to compete in performance events such as agility, obedience, and rally.

APHA: American Paint Horse Association.

Breed ring or conformation ring: Dog classes at sanctioned shows where dogs are judged for their conformation.

CERF: Canine Eye Research Foundation; a nonprofit organization dedicated to researching canine eye diseases. CERF maintained a database of results of canine eye examinations.

CD: Companion Dog degree; an AKC obedience degree awarded to dogs that earn three qualifying scores of 170 out of 200 points, with at least a 50 percent score in each exercise.

CH: Championship; an AKC conformation championship is awarded when a canine acquires fifteen points, with at least three points earned at one time under two different judges and some of the remaining points awarded by a third judge. Males and females compete separately in each breed for Winners Dog (male) and Winners Bitch (female). The two winners then compete against each other for Best of Winners. Points are awarded to these two winners based on the number of same-sex canines that they defeat or the highest number of canines defeated in either sex if awarded Best of Winners.

Dam: The mother of puppies or foals.

Dressage: A competitive equestrian sport where the horse walks, trots, canters, and performs more specialized maneuvers in response to barely perceptible signals from its rider.

OCD: Osteochondritis dissecans; an inflammatory condition occurring when abnormal cartilage grows on the end of a bone in a joint and then separates from the underlying bone.

Elbow dysplasia: A canine polygenetic (multiple gene) disease.

ERC: Eye Certification Registry and Clinical Database for Ophthalmic Diagnoses established in 2012 by OFA and the American College of Veterinary Ophthalmologists.

Health clearances: Reputable Labrador breeders have added many health tests to their list of required clearances before they breed. They require not only OFA hip and elbow clearances and PRA screenings, including progressive rod cone degeneration (PRCD) but also at least some of the following: EIC (exercise induced collapse), copper toxicosis, dilute gene (D locus), centronuclear myopathy (CNM), cardiac exams and/or echocardiographic exams, hereditary nasal parakeratosis (HNPK), degenerative myopathy (DN), and centron myopathy (CMN).

Hip dysplasia: A canine polygenetic (multiple gene) disease.

Jockey Club: The thoroughbred horse registry.

LRC: Labrador Retriever Club, Inc. is the AKC parent breed club of the Labrador Retriever. Website: www.labradorclub.com

Lab Club: Labrador Retriever Club of Greater Denver. Website: http://www.lrcgd.com/

Obedience legs: Qualifying scores of at least 170 out of 200 points, with at least a 50 percent score in every exercise.

OFA: The Orthopedic Foundation of Animals was founded to evaluate canine hip radiographs to try to manage and combat canine hip dysplasia. OFA now evaluates and/or compiles test results for numerous other health disorders. Its website, https://www.ofa.org/, allows individuals to search by canine name and/or kennel name for various health clearances, including hip and elbow dysplasia, CERF and OFA Eye Certification Registry (CAER) results, and heart evaluations.

OptiGen: A New York-based company that first offered a blood test for PRA genetic testing. Mars Petcare of Brussels, Belgium, bought OptiGen in April 2018.

PRA: Progressive retinal atrophy; a canine autosomal recessive genetic disease that renders blindness.

Pyometra: An infection of the uterus that may require spaying.

Safe Harbor Labrador Rescue: Based in Golden, Colorado, this nonprofit entity rescues and places Labradors in new homes. Website: http://www.safeharborlabrescue.org/

Sire: The father of puppies or foals.

Trimble Court Artisans: An artist cooperative, established in Fort Collins, Colorado, in 1971.

Working Certificate: A certificate awarded by the LRC or a local Labrador retriever club to a Labrador that retrieves one game bird on land and two ducks by swimming in water during an AKC sanctioned test.

About the Author

Cary Unkelbach grew up in a family that bred, raised, trained, and showed their Walden Labrador retrievers for more than forty years. At an early age, she learned from her author parents, Evie and Kurt Unkelbach, the importance of responsible dog ownership and reputable canine breeding practices. She's trained and shown Labradors at AKC competitions ever since age eight, first in the conformation ring and later in obedience, rally, tracking, and working certificate trials. She and her husband have bred Labrador litters, always trying to improve their dogs' quality.

Before her legal career, Cary was a reporter for the *Hartford* (CT) *Times* and the *Hartford* (CT) *Courant* newspapers. She's been a prosecutor in a Denver, CO, metropolitan county and a civil litigator.

Cary's articles have appeared in *Dog World, Labrador Quarterly,* and *Police Chief* magazines, and various dog breed newsletters. She lives with her husband and two spoiled Labradors in the Colorado mountains.

Read her monthly blog and contact her at *www.caryunkelbach.com*